Sailing Home

Gary Geddes

 Sailing Home

a journey through time, place & memory

Harper*Flamingo*Canada
A PHYLLIS BRUCE BOOK

Sailing Home:
a journey through time,
place & memory
Copyright © 2001 by Gary Geddes.
All rights reserved. No part of this book may
be used or reproduced in any manner whatsoever without prior written permission
except in the case of brief quotations embodied
in reviews. For information address
HarperCollins Publishers Ltd,
55 Avenue Road, Suite 2900,
Toronto, Ontario, Canada M5R 3L2

www.harpercanada.com

HarperCollins books may be purchased for
educational, business, or sales promotional
use. For information please write:
Special Markets Department,
HarperCollins Canada,
55 Avenue Road, Suite 2900,
Toronto, Ontario, Canada M5R 3L2

First HarperFlamingo edition

Lines from *Fugitive Pieces* reprinted by
permission of Anne Michaels; lines from
Gwendolyn MacEwen's "The Discovery" by
permission of the author's family; lines from
Stan Rogers' "Northwest Passage" reprinted
by permission of FOGARTY'S COVE
MUSIC; "Seymour Inlet Float Camp: Domes-
tic Scene" reprinted by permission of John
Marshall; lines from Malcolm Lowry's poem
"Joseph Conrad" and his novel *Under the
Volcano* reprinted by permission of Stirling
Lord and the Malcolm Lowry/Marjorie
Bonner Estate.

Canadian Cataloguing in Publication Data

Geddes, Gary, 1940–
Sailing home : a journey through time,
place & memory

"A Phyllis Bruce book".
ISBN 0-00-200007-5

1. Geddes, Gary, 1940–   – Journeys
   – Inside Passage.
2. Groais (Boat).
3. Inside Passage – Description and travel.
I. Title.

FC3845.I5G42 2001 917.11'1 C00-932347-3
F1089.I5G25 2001

01 02 03 04 HC 4 3 2 1

Printed and bound in the United States
Set in Aldus

☀ Preface

In the summer of 1998, I came back to the coast in search of my origins, looking for the mythical home-place, fully aware that it might have vanished in the interim. My marriage had collapsed and I had chucked my tenured teaching job in Montreal to move west. I intended to structure my return around a book, writing my way home, using the day-to-day events of sailing up the coast (weather, reefs, people, errant Chilean submarines and, of course, sirens) as the narrative thread on which to hang my watery reminiscences of growing up out here. Where the story of my life proved too difficult or too incoherent, I hoped the story of my adventure would take up the slack.

Predecessors in the field were legion, including explorers such as James Cook, Juan Francisco de la Bodega y Quadra and George Vancouver, who had colonial business to attend to and produced maps and journals. Every writer who sailed the coast had either acknowledged or ransacked these journals, so I intended to maintain a respectful distance. At least three of the cruising writers I could not ignore were women.

Kathrene Pinkerton, whose *Three's a Crew* (1940) was published the year I was born, recounts her adventures upcoast with her husband Robert and daughter Bobs. I was particularly fond of this book because it casts Kathrene and family as duffers with even less knowledge of the sea than I possessed, although Robert had some mechanical competence and Kathrene was capable of fine writing and acute observation. M. Wylie Blanchet, a widow with several children, cruised the Inside Passage over several summers, condensing her experiences into a minor classic called *The Curve of Time* (1968). The third member of the trio was Beth Hill, whose *Upcoast Summers,* published in 1985, pieces together the 1933–1941 journals of Francis Barrow, who travelled the coast with his wife Amy and two black spaniels and managed to record encounters with 227 coastal residents. If these upbeat, affectionate accounts had a disadvantage, it was in their implicit reminders that sailing is more enjoyably done with company and that the working population of the remote coast—farmers, loggers, fishermen—had almost disappeared.

As inspiring as these books were to me as I gunkholed my way up the Inside Passage, where hazards are innumerable and support can be minimal, I wanted to do something different. I felt I knew and, in some ways, owned the coast already, because I had spent so much time on it as a kid: my grandfather had drowned here; my mother swam alongside her father's boat for miles in Howe Sound as a young woman before dying of cancer at age thirty-four; my father had been part of the rescue team at the collapse of the Second Narrows Bridge in Vancouver; he and I had fished together commercially in Rivers Inlet; I had spent several summers on the waterfront, loading trucks and boxcars at the B.C. Sugar Refinery in Vancouver, working at my uncle's boat rentals in Whytecliffe and, later, driving water-taxi between Westview and Texada Island. For me, a trip up the coast would be not so much a discovery as a *recovery* narrative, a way of getting in touch with people and places and events from my own past.

The lure of the coast is such that people will try to travel it in anything that floats, including bathtubs, canoes, leaky rowboats, ancient hulks with dangerously high superstructures, kayaks, houseboats made of plastic, rotting clinker-built trollers, concrete sailboats, perhaps even bamboo rafts if, as seems likely, Asian and Polynesian navigators actually made it to the West Coast. My own expectations were modest: I wanted a sailboat that was roomy, seaworthy and cheap, but with devastatingly beautiful lines and an exotic track record. My friend Alan Twigg recommended I phone an acquaintance in Victoria who did legal work for the artistic community and might know where to begin. This proved an interesting lead. If I were prepared to give up the idea of sailing, the voice said, and willing to do some basic carpentry work, I might be able to use one of two gillnetters currently serving as props in the Scott Hicks movie of David Guterson's stunning novel, *Snow Falling on Cedars*. The price was right and my earliest experiences in boats on the coast had taken place on my father's gillnetter in Rivers Inlet, so this was a tempting offer. However, I was determined to sail as much as I could and I wanted a boat with a real rather than a fictional history. I also knew better than to try composing my modest memoir in the shadow of such excellence. Eventually, boat and owner came together as if the hand of fate had intervened, but that part of the story will have to wait.

Since the purpose of a preface can only be to tempt potential readers further into the book, I should probably set the record straight. This story is not for professional seamen or the stereotypical beautiful person on a yacht; rather, it's for the rest of mankind, those of us who, with warts and failures and impossible dreams, have tried to go back, with or without a boat, tried to find that intimate space, or state of mind, called home. When I set sail in the last summer of the second millennium, I was joining the ranks of not only intrepid mariners, but also complete novices such as Charles Darwin, who emptied the contents of his stomach over the gunwales during three and a half years at sea on the *Beagle*, and a religious crusader named Jeff Bauchmann, who was rescued off

Tofino on the west coast of Vancouver Island on July 3, 1999, with no charts or maritime experience, only the two hundred bibles he was planning to deliver to Russia. When the Canadian Coast Guard picked him up, he was heading in the wrong direction. Although my missionary zeal was of a different kind, and my library of offerings to the Russians would have had considerably more variety, I certainly knew the feeling of being way off course.

Since so much coastal travel is now done by air, I was, from the outset, a floating anachronism, crawling across the surface of the sea on my belly. That speed, five nautical miles per hour, seemed good to me; I needed to slow down, decompress, take stock, to look long and hard at the places of my desire and, perhaps, see them again for the first time. Somewhere along the way, tidelines would become songlines; life-jackets merge with book jackets; boat and book share something we still refer to, quaintly, as a launch. Books can be excellent travelling companions, as readers have testified. When he looked into Chapman's Homer, the poet John Keats felt he had travelled in the realms of gold; and Emily Dickinson was of the opinion that "There is no frigate like a book / To take us lands away." For a poet, such an extensive voyage into prose is not without risks. However, I'm determined to take you along—queasy stomach, apprehensions, bright orange survival suit and all— on this most ragged, watery misadventure.

The great mystery of wood is not that it burns, but that
it floats.

Anne Michaels, *Fugitive Pieces*

when you see the land naked, look again
(burn your maps, that is not what I mean),
I mean the moment when it seems most plain
is the moment when you must begin again

Gwendolyn MacEwen, "The Discovery"

Very like a whale.

Herman Melville, *Moby Dick*

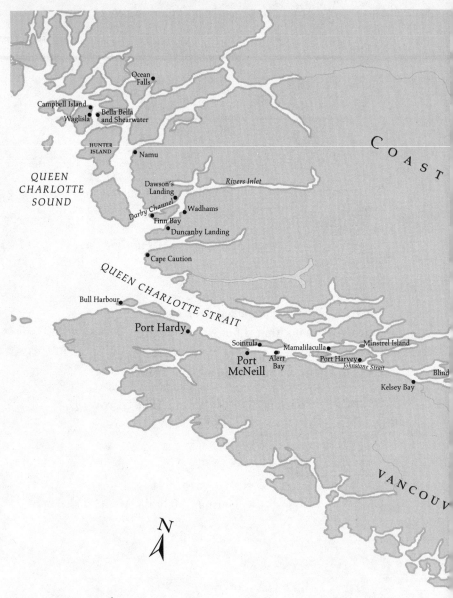

Ocean Falls

Campbell Island
Waglisla
Bella Bella
and Shearwater

HUNTER
ISLAND

Namu

QUEEN
CHARLOTTE
SOUND

Dawson's
Landing

Rivers Inlet

Darby Channel
Wadhams

Finn Bay
Duncanby Landing

C O A S T

Cape Caution

QUEEN CHARLOTTE STRAIT

Bull Harbour

Port Hardy

Sointula
Mamalilaculla
Minstrel Island

Port
McNeill
Alert
Bay
Port Harvey

Johnstone Strait
Blind

Kelsey Bay

V A N C O U V

N

Pacific Ocean

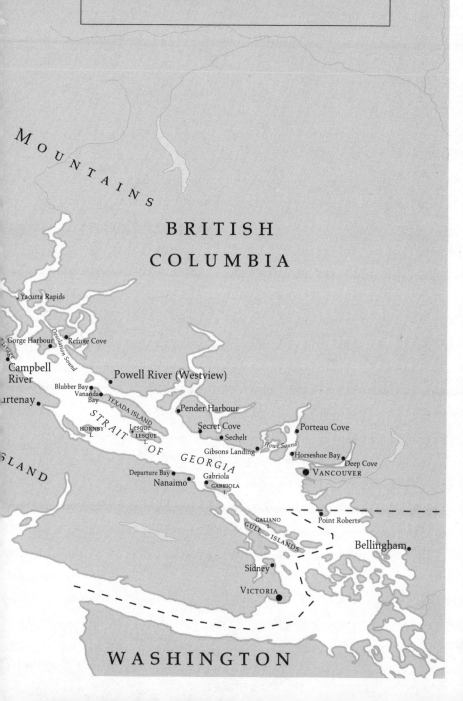

THE INSIDE PASSAGE

MOUNTAINS

BRITISH

COLUMBIA

Yacutta Rapids

Gorge Harbour • Refuge Cove
Desolation Sound

Campbell
River

Blubber Bay • Powell River (Westview)
Vananda Bay
Courtenay

TEXADA ISLAND

Pender Harbour

STRAIT
HORNBY I.
Lesque • LESQUE
Secret Cove • Porteau Cove
Sechelt

OF
GEORGIA
Howe Sound
Gibsons Landing • Horseshoe Bay
Deep Cove

Departure Bay • Gabriola
Nanaimo • GABRIOLA I. • VANCOUVER

ISLAND

CALIANO I.
GULF ISLANDS
Point Roberts

Bellingham

Sidney

VICTORIA

WASHINGTON

✳ One

I watched it spread, as if by magic, from the stern of the boat, a full rainbow, a racing parabola of brilliant colour. No more than a cup or two of diesel had erupted from the nozzle while I topped up my fourth fuel tank, but it had wasted no time spilling into the harbour and rivalling the riotous hues of a Riopelle or Jackson Pollock painting. My mouth was still gaping when the voice of the attendant broke the silence.

"Detergent!" he shouted. "Get your detergent!"

He was running towards me with a plastic squeeze container, flinging its contents into the harbour, stringy worms of liquid that hung suspended in mid-air, then, plummeting, quickly devoured all but the extreme edges of my rainbow, as if sucking each colour back into the spectrum to revert once more to white light. Between the two of us—my having come to my senses and grabbed the container of liquid Sunlight from the galley—we performed our reverse miracle in seconds. I didn't understand the chemistry involved on the surface of the water, but I had no trouble figuring out the chemistry at work in the attendant's look of disapproval as I paid my bill and slunk away in shame.

My sloop, *Groais* (pronounced *gro-iss*), had been moored over the winter at Squalicum Marina in Bellingham, Washington, where I had a temporary teaching position at Western Washington University; it had served as a *pied d'eau*, or floating apartment, for the two or three nights a week I spent there. A thirty-one-foot sloop with a nine-foot beam and made in Plymouth, England, from durable British plywood with a protective skin of fibreglass, *Groais* looked dumpy and overfed next to the Concordia yawl and other sleek beauties moored nearby. Matronly, to be exact, a product of practical British engineering, designed for comfort, not speed. Still, she'd probably out-travelled the entire fleet of yachts in the marina, having sailed with her first owners, Chris and Anni Law, three times across the Atlantic, into the berg-strewn Arctic Ocean, and then to the South Pacific, touching in at Pitcairn Island and the Galapagos as Charles Darwin had once done in the *Beagle*. I'd purchased *Groais* a year earlier in Sidney, on Vancouver Island, a good stone's throw from the Swartz Bay ferry terminal. When the day came to make the initial eight-hour run from there to Bellingham, I set out with my friend Stephen Hume, a poet and journalist for the *Vancouver Sun*, at the helm. I did not mention my malfunctioning reverse gear during that trip. Steve already had good reason to believe he was in danger when, during the choppy crossing through the Gulf and San Juan islands, I looked up from the jumble of charts, my brow as furrowed as the sea.

"Steve, what are all these asterisks for?"

"Gary," he shouted over the beat of the Lister diesel, gripping the tiller a bit too firmly and with a look of shocked disbelief, "those asterisks are rocks!"

I was no newcomer to the world of boats. I'd fished commercially with my father in Rivers Inlet; I'd worked at a boat rental for three summers, taking out fishing tours; I'd learned to sail in a navy whaler in Digby Basin at Halifax during my short-lived and not-very-illustrious career in the "Untidies" (University Naval Training Division); I'd driven water-taxi from Texada Island to Westview between the end of my first teaching job and my subsequent trip to study in England; and I'd also owned a twenty-four-foot sloop in

Victoria before getting beached high and dry with teaching jobs in Edmonton and Montreal. Despite those eclectic, if dubious, nautical credentials, I'd never actually owned or used a chart. I sailed in waters I knew quite well and counted on advice and local wisdom to help me avoid dangerous areas. Steve, who was no doubt wondering what he had got himself into, had retreated for solace deep within the hood of his inadequate raingear. We were both thoroughly soaked from the spray coming over the bow. So was the chart.

When we arrived at Squalicum Marina in Bellingham several hours later, Steve discovered I had no reverse gear. He tried to assume the disinterested pose of the journalist, asking me calmly what the problem was, pointing out the diminishing distance between the boat and the jutting corner of the dock. I had brought *Groais* in slowly, but there was a following wind that threatened us with collision. With a shout, he abandoned inquiry and diplomacy, grabbed the boat hook and leapt onto the dock, fending us off but not quite avoiding a creosote smear on his brand-new trousers. When I suggested we go out to dinner and stay overnight on the boat, he suddenly remembered an assignment he had to complete back in Sidney.

My destination this overcast June morning, nine months later, was Vancouver, sixty miles by water from Bellingham. I was concerned because the reverse gear was still not working. I'd spent several hundred dollars replacing the old clutch-throttle mechanism, which was badly worn. Both the new and old equipment worked fine when the engine had just started; however, after running for a few hours, neither would go into reverse. As I rounded the breakwater and set my course across Bellingham Bay to Hale Passage, a harbour seal surfaced slyly to observe my progress, his bristly whiskers twitching in the cool air. He was definitely not suffering from either locomotion or gear problems; he submerged, then resurfaced nearby to get a closer look at the intruder. He eyed me suspiciously, as if he were in the employ of the U.S. Coast Guard. I had good reason to feel guilty; I'd not only caused a small diesel spill, but also spent the winter in the state of Washington illegally without a proper holding tank on my boat. No doubt this submersible inspector was attributing the pollution from the Georgia Pacific pulp mill and the absence of fish in the harbour entirely to me. I shrugged, increased my speed to a fast crawl, and settled down for the hour's run to Hale Passage, the shortest route to Georgia Strait.

The huge bowl-shaped expanse of Bellingham Bay was perfectly calm, protected year-round from prevailing westerlies by Lummi Island, though quite exposed to southeasters and winds from the north, as I had noticed to my dismay while *Groais* lurched and fidgeted at its berth during the winter storms. As the city of Bellingham, with its multiple hats—fading mill town, upstart college town, former mecca for Canadian shoppers (from the good-dollar days) and growing retirement centre—diminished gradually in my wake, the various greens of new and not-so-new growth on Lummi Island were reflected more sharply on the gunmetal surface ahead. I was glad to be heading out to sea, leaving all that busyness behind, though I was mindful of Lucy's five-cent psychiatric advice to Charlie Brown when, observing a jet plane overhead, he thinks he might escape to a newer, less complicated life: "Charlie, you'll be the same old grump wherever you are." Given my mechanical ineptness and sketchy navigational skills, this was not advice to take lightly, especially on the Inside Passage where, despite the appearance of protection, anything might happen.

My long-range plan was to sail from Bellingham to Rivers Inlet on the north coast of British Columbia where, as an eleven-year-old boy, I'd spent a summer commercial fishing with my father. The return journey, with all its twists, weather-induced detours and alluring side channels, would cover more than a thousand nautical miles and take me back in time to the sites of most of the emotional flash-points of my youth and childhood: my grandfather's death by drowning, a bridge collapse, my mother's untimely death from cancer, my first teaching job on Texada Island, just for starters. It would also, with the vagaries of wind and weather, take me to many unexpected places in the watery world, all of them laced with asterisks.

I was heading to a temporary moorage in Vancouver. I thought I could make it in a single day, but my late start and failure to calculate the effects of wind and tide made it clear I'd never arrive before dark. There was also a surprise in store for me in terms of orientation. Vancouver, I reasoned, is north, above the border, so why am I heading due west on the compass? I kept trying to edge the boat northward. Part of the problem was that what I thought was Point Grey, the western tip of Vancouver, turned out to be Point Roberts, farther south and still in U.S. territory; and the distant high-rises I thought must be in downtown Vancouver were in fact in New Westminster and Surrey. If I'd followed my northering impulse, I'd have sailed overland through the subdivisions of Boundary Bay and White Rock, like Burt Lancaster traversing Hollywood by swimming from pool to pool. Aside from a few backwater detours to avoid the rigours of Johnstone Strait on my voyage up the coast, I would not make a serious turn to the north until I reached Fitz Hugh Sound and Rivers Inlet two months and hundreds of miles later.

I was in good company. Even Francis Drake, who circumnavigated the globe and pushed as far north as forty-eight degrees, was, according to his biographer Ernle Bradford, baffled by what he found as he pounded his way up the west coast of North America: "Drake must have expected to find that the continent now trended away to the east. But even his determination failed when he found that, far from this being the case, the harsh and unfamiliar coastline with its icy weather, fogs, and freezing wind, still hauled out on his port bow. The land seemed to run north and west forever."

I felt a certain small affinity for this famous marauder, if only because *Groais* was of a class of sailboat named after Drake's *Golden Hind*. While looking for a boat, I had been staying with a friend in Vancouver who taught at a community college, sharing the wonders of the semicolon and the comma splice with classes of bored foreign students who'd saunter into class for ten minutes to ask if they'd missed anything the previous day and then disappear again. It was on one of our walks that I picked up a copy of a yachting magazine containing an ad for *Groais*, which referred to it as a Golden Hind sloop. While most boats are advertised with a paragraph of hype and an indifferent photograph, *Groais* was represented only by a generic drawing, obviously provided by the magazine editor for last-minute inclusion. Rather than view this shortcoming as a bad omen, I took it as a sign that the owners felt no mere photograph could do justice to their fine craft. This perception proved to be truer than I had imagined. In fact, the boat was in a thousand pieces and it would have taken all the wizardry of digital technology to reconstruct those shards into a flattering image of the whole. The gleaming white hull, with its aquamarine trim, black antifouling paint and twin bilge keels, dominated the tiny shed in Sidney where it was being restored. Everything else, including the engine, had been removed for replacement or repair and to make it easier to repaint. It was not the boat I wanted, or thought I deserved, but I was intrigued by its history and the way the current owners, Bruce and Karen Bourquin, talked about it. As I left the shed, clutching a published article on its design features and a fading, ghostly fax of *Groais* silhouetted against an iceberg, I knew I would buy it, and without even dickering over the price.

This run to Vancouver was an important leg of my journey up the coast because it was my first solo trip on the boat. Judging from the overcast sky, the prospects were anything but promising. The weather channel on the VHF predicted strong westerlies and gave a small craft warning for the Gulf of Georgia; and the one cruising guide I'd had time to consult warned of turbulence around the North and South Arms of the Fraser, where the powerful surge of cold water pushes out under the incoming tide and opposing wind in relative shallows. I was dressed for the worst, with extra layers of clothing and full raingear, the heavy-duty orange kind used by commercial fishermen, including a hilariously rakish sou'wester with its scooped peak and long drain-pipe tail that sent the water cascading out beyond my back rather than down my neck. My night in dreary Point Roberts had been uneventful and quiet, after a brief excursion in the semi-gloom for groceries, the narrow roads affording little protection from blinding traffic and open drainage ditches. Point Roberts is an ugly if benign lump, an American one at that, on the western buttock of Canada, left there when the apparently neutral Kaiser Wilhelm was asked to draw a line to settle the disputed U.S.–Canada boundary. Like that of Alaska, Point Roberts' peculiar location requires its citizens to enter Canada or go by water or air before they can get to the United States proper. It's been a gummy slough of summer homes for as long as I can remember, as well as a convenient source of the cheap cartons of contraband cigarettes with which my parents used to line the doors of the family car and smuggle back into Canada. A bit more upscale now, since it's become the place of choice in terms of taxes for American athletes playing professional sports in Vancouver.

I was making almost no headway and gaining more perspectives on the Tsawwassen ferry terminal and Roberts Bank coal storage dock than anyone other than a saboteur could possibly want. Though I'd been warned, the degree of turbulence off the South Arm of the Fraser River took me by surprise. The waves were short and steep. *Groais* felt as if it was being pummelled by a professional boxer, a series of short, hard blows to the body. With the rain and the pounding I was taking, I couldn't make out the markers indicated on the charts that located the river entrance and served as reminders that the surrounding water was shallow. As I fumbled with the charts, trying to keep them dry in a large zip-lock plastic envelope, something caught my attention off the port side of the boat. When I glanced seaward, I could see nothing but waves, troublesome, angry-looking waves. Then I saw it again, a flash of black and white against the grey of the sea.

An immature killer whale had surfaced briefly about ten feet off the port quarter and was keeping pace with the boat, its beautiful, streamlined body rhythmically knitting the surface. I'm in the middle of a pod, I thought, and likely to do some damage with my propeller. I'd always cursed the whale-watching boats for not keeping far enough off. But there was no sign of additional clan members, just a solitary juvenile maintaining perfect formation in the muddy, churning water.

Since it's unusual for killer whales not to travel in family units, I began to worry that this one might be lost and in the process of bonding with my white hull and black anti-fouling paint. My orca was no Moby Dick but a mere stripling, a Möbius stripling. And this distant, crossbred fourteenth cousin, an orphan at that, seemed to be having as much trouble reading charts as I was. I'd just dipped into Carl Zimmer's *At the Water's Edge: Fish with Fingers, Whales with Legs*, a brilliant macro-evolutionary treatise that describes how certain forms of life evolved to survive on land, then went back to the sea, so it occurred to me that this inquisitive seagoing mammal might be trying to communicate with a landlubber, for old time's sake, to ask about customs out there or to see how fully evolved legs really worked.

While the huge eye that scanned me each time Möbius broke the surface was doubtless taking in plenty of information about *Groais* and me, I could read nothing there. And I had neither sign language nor sound imitations with which to communicate. I faintly recalled a recording of whale sounds that included Paul Horn's flute responses, which I'd heard many years earlier, high-pitched squeaks and whistles that broaden into something resembling a cat's meow. All I had to offer now was the insistent pounding of the Lister diesel, which might at least pass for a friendly heartbeat.

Möbius kept pace with me for forty-five minutes, from the South to the North Arm of the Fraser, sometimes doubling its distance from the boat but always coming back to renew eye contact. There was something magical in this encounter, an unspoken welcome, a hand reaching out to me from the sea, acknowledging my presence, and distracting me from my fears. Then, while I was fussing again with the charts, it disappeared, dismissing me as a substitute parent or finding other amusement, maybe even lunch. By now the chop had lessened and it seemed pretty smooth sailing around Point Grey, once I'd cleared the shoals and breakwater that stretch out into the gulf, giving shelter to barges and log booms waiting to go up the Fraser River. As I folded up the charts, removed my awkward raingear and stowed it in the starboard locker, I was quietly grateful for the appearance of this guide so early in my travels.

Directly across from Point Grey, I could see the white shaft of the lighthouse at Point Atkinson, the other headland that forms an entrance to the port of Vancouver, where my grandfather, Peter Geddes, had drowned not long after his retirement. His small boat was found rubbing against the rocks below the lighthouse, engine still running, but his body was never recovered. Twenty minutes after emerging from Coal Harbour and passing under the Lions Gate Bridge, he had cut the engine to an idle and dropped his trolling gear over the side. His last act in this world, it seems, was to go fishing, something his people had been doing in the North Sea for at least fourteen centuries, or perhaps from the beginning of human time. During my childhood, and the years I spent studying at the University of British Columbia, I could never look at the lighthouse across the water without thinking of my drowned grandfather. His strange disappearance had given him the mythic stature an ordinary life and death can't supply, at the same time transforming Vancouver harbour—and, by extension, the sea itself—into a place of permanent mystery and menace, the two poles of my nautical consciousness.

As I eased *Groais* into the troubled currents of the harbour entrance, I could feel her skittish dance in the tide and light chop around First Narrows, as if she'd picked up on my own ambivalent feelings about the home-place. Off my starboard bow was phallic Siwash Rock in Stanley Park, beloved of Pauline Johnson, the sweet Mohawk poet and songstress from Ontario who had adopted Vancouver, and the stretch of rocky shore where HMS *Beaver*, with a drunk at the helm, went aground and rotted into history. Vancouver is a stunning city for newcomers, a startling confluence of rugged coastal mountains, tree-studded promontories, and generous beaches where the locals tan year-round, tucked in behind the logs with their reflectors. Even the grouchy Captain George Vancouver, on one of his better days, was driven to eulogize the place:

To describe the beauties of this region, will, on some future occasion, be a very grateful task to the pen of a skilled panegyrist. The serenity of the climate, the innumerable pleasing landscapes, and the abundant fertility that unassisted nature puts forth, require only to be enriched by the industry of man with villages, mansions, cottages, and other buildings to render it the most lovely country that can be imagined.

Although "unassisted nature" has been dealt a cruel body blow by the industry of man, even diehard critics, amidst the grime, pollution, smog, poverty, crime and perpetual rain of Vancouver, have been tempted to agree with poet Daryl Hine, that "a beauty of sorts is always within reach." Hine, of course, managed to resist this beauty by spending his entire adult life in Chicago. For the rest, Vancouver's skilled panegyrists have been somewhat less inclined in the direction of praise.

Off my port bow were the Neptune Bulk Terminal, with its heaps of coal, and Vancouver Wharf, with its familiar inverted cone of industrial sulphur that had decorated the shoreline since I was a kid, a psychedelic pyramid so out of place amongst the evergreens it might have been imagined by Disney. Overhead, defying sanity as well as gravity, loomed the elegant Lions Gate, a suspension bridge built to allow this booming port city to expand and enable a few individuals to get rich selling prime real estate in the exclusive British Properties. I used to cycle over the bridge with my childhood friend Dennis Overstall, who was a couple of years younger and had trouble negotiating the steep grade and high winds. It embarrassed me to have to resort to a companion so young, with his plaid shirt-tails hanging out and, instead of a proper bicycle clip, one pantleg rolled up, but he was all I had. Vancouver's spectacular bridges have inspired both rhapsodies and suicides, including that of Stanley Cooperman, a poet and professor at Simon Fraser University, who leapt to his death, but not before he had described the city as "perched like a neon / thumb / on the edge of nothing."

I cut my speed to an idle as I began my circuit of the inner harbour. The cottages and mansions George Vancouver envisaged, along with high-rises, industry, and economic disparities, were all there in spades, but there was no sign of the Coast Salish village that had once occupied land at Lumbermen's Arch in Stanley Park, not even a commemorative plaque. I could see in the distance what was left of the B.C. Sugar Refinery on the south side, owned by the Rogers family of syrup fame, where my uncle Joe inhaled the deadly sweet dust and operated the machine that stitched twenty-five-pound bags of white sugar until diabetes claimed him. I spent two summers there myself, loading boxcars with hundred-pound sacks of sugar and working, with inadequate protection for my lungs, in a storage shed full of the deadly silicone used in processing. Jack, a long-time employee, who spent coffee breaks on the phone to his bookie, took a special interest in educating me in the ways of the real world of work. First, a lesson in property management: do not touch my personal hand-truck, the one with the nicely tapered hand-grips. Second, a few thoughts on equity in the workplace: if a driver gets pushy, give him "the special," which involved excessive application of wax on the wooden chutes, a procedure that carried hundred-pound paper sacks of sugar down six floors to the loading dock at such lightning speeds they exploded on impact. Burt, the foreman, also known as the Human Trumpet, amused himself by performing lip vibrations of Christian hymns as he rode the steps of the vertical conveyor belt from floor to floor to see if we were working.

I was launched in Vancouver on June 9, 1940, if not in a state of grace, at least in Grace Hospital. I slid into air like an otter into water, though with greater reluctance and not nearly so elegantly. According to legend, my arrival was greeted with considerable fanfare. My father was working at North Vancouver Shipyards when the announcement came over the intercom that he had another son. For fifteen seconds, everyone for miles around the port of Vancouver could have heard the hammers of a hundred shipwrights and riveters celebrate my birth by striking the metal hull of the vessel they were working on.

The tiny clamour surrounding my birth was but a faint echo of the distant rumble of war, growing closer and insinuating itself into people's lives here on the coast, a blast furnace demanding more and more human fuel. Within a year my father would offer himself to the struggle, leaving his job for a position as a hull inspector in the Royal Canadian Navy. My mother would soldier on alone, working as a demonstrator of foodstuffs and cosmetics at Eaton's and the Hudson's Bay Company, smoking up a storm and cultivating the cancer that would soon consume her.

They both survived the war, but the marriage didn't. Having been, all these years, a late arriver and a late developer, I liked to imagine myself conceived on September 1, 1939, the day war was declared, a modest protest against the carnage to come. The air I breathed was thick with stories of war. The continued absence of my father, who made irregular appearances in his uniform and rolled me around the front yard in his duffel bag, was cause enough for such preoccupation, though he appears to have remained safely in Halifax throughout the conflict, except for a brief and unofficial trip to Montreal to do repairs on a private yacht owned by a naval officer. However, there was also my mother's younger brother, Thomas Thompson Turner, alias T.T., whose position as a bombardier in the Royal Air Force was considerably more precarious. An ominous hush would descend on conversations at my grandparents' house whenever Uncle Tom's name was mentioned. Then he'd gone missing.

Beyond the refinery lies Vancouver's East End, the immigrant ghetto I couldn't wait to leave. I grew up in a three-room flat over a store at Fourth and Commercial. Weekends and after school, I delivered newspapers, ran errands for a jeweller, and spent a lot of time scavenging for coal sacks, hubcaps and empty bottles I could sell. The grim apartment, which sported a cyclotron fridge with its coiled tubing mounted on top like an exposed brain, was so small I had to sleep on a fold-down couch with my brother, who was six years older. Commercial Drive was bleak, though dynamic in its own way, with a regular traffic of streetcars and interurban trams rattling past. It was there I watched our local hero, the strongman Doug Hepburn, eat eighty raw eggs on "The Ed Sullivan Show" and lift a platform containing a car and several people. Since we had no television, I stood in front of Manitoba Hardware's window, where there were seven sets switched on. Doug, who parked his silver Cadillac in front of his small gym at the foot of the street, had made it to the big time, though the seven-fold replication of egg yolks dripping down multiple faces and biceps struck me as demeaning. The East End is still just as bleak, though it has become a trendy subculture haven where, for an exorbitant sum, you can own a bungalow covered with dull cut-glass stucco, eat a variety of ethnic foods, watch the colourful human parade, feel artistic, and stay awake all night from the noise of cars, drunks and drug addicts careening through the lanes and backyards. It's still the only place in Vancouver where I could afford to live.

I'm not alone in my ambivalence towards Vancouver. Malcolm Lowry, who did his best writing there and was largely ignored for it, cast a hard eye on the city: "God knows / This place where chancres blossom like a rose, / For on each face is such a hard despair / That nothing like a grief could enter there." It was not only the social and economic inequalities of the place that troubled Lowry, but also the boom-and-bust psychology that still prevails up and down the coast and is so wonderfully satirized in his novel *Under the Volcano*:

It has a sort of Pango Pango quality mingled with sausage and mash and generally a rather Puritan atmosphere. Everyone fast asleep and when you prick them a Union Jack flows out of the hole. But no one in a certain sense lives here. They merely as it were pass through. Mine the country and quit. Blast the land to pieces, knock down the trees and send them rolling down Burrard Inlet.

You can change the flag and the ethnic mix, but the underlying attitudes remain the same.

My slow circumnavigation of the inner harbour, dipping in and out of every indentation, had taken me past the expensive fleet of pleasure craft in the Burrard Yacht Club and, nearby, a coven of black tugboats owned by Seaspan. Freighters from several countries, the *Skauboard*, the *Cosmoway*, and one called *Bunga Oroco Dua* with the words "Misc Malaysia" in large white block letters amidships, were tied up alongside receiving transfusions of chemicals, ore and grain. A man on a smoke-break from the Saskatchewan Wheat Pool elevator gave me the high sign from his folding chair as I passed. North Van is now the business side of the harbour. Although containers, trains, and some fish are still handled on the south shore, the Vancouver side is gradually being given over to hotels, yacht clubs and tourism, as the two Alaska cruise ships I could see flanking the conference and exhibition centre attested.

At last I spotted what I was looking for—Number Five, the old grey shipbuilding shed where my father and his father were working the day I was born, a structure that had been rendered obsolete by the new technology. They no longer used a slip and a complex network of cables for hauling out, only a colossal floating dry dock which sinks to receive a vessel and then is floated again with compressed air, leaving the ship high and dry for repairs or painting. At the turn of the century, when the herring fishery, along with its supporting shipbuilding industry, collapsed from climatic changes and over-fishing in the North Sea, my grandfather, Peter Geddes, joined the most recent of those Scottish migrations that had begun with the Highland Clearances and never quite stopped. He arrived in Vancouver in 1907, a year before his wife and children, and had no trouble finding permanent work on the waterfront, building the fleet of commercial vessels that would carry out the task, over a mere six decades, of stripping yet another coast of trees and wiping out the abundant salmon stocks.

I'd planned to check out moorage possibilities at Mosquito Creek Marina, but the incoming tide was gathering speed as it approached the Second Narrows Bridge and rushed to replace the colossal volume of water that had emptied out of Indian Arm, an eleven-mile taste of the remote north coast tucked away in Vancouver's backyard, a scarcely populated inlet with soaring mountains, marine parks, and the 165-foot-high Granite Falls. Malcolm Lowry had found refuge in Indian Arm, at Dollarton, near Deep Cove, where I'd also spent some precious childhood hours with my mother. I crossed over to the Vancouver side, though it was the bridge that held my attention, a vast steel and concrete span that had cost the lives of many workers when it collapsed June 17, 1958, during construction. Like so many kids, I had watched those two spans daily inching towards each other out across the harbour, a miracle of modern engineering that was under-mined as a result of a simple mathematical miscalculation in the offices of the Dominion Bridge Company which caused the falsework grillage to fail. I remember the event not only because it happened the month I graduated from King Edward High School, but also because my father, trained as a deep-sea diver—complete with canvas suit, lead belt and shoes, and a brass circular helmet with reinforced glass portholes at the front and both sides—was called out to help extract bodies from the wreckage, the current being too strong for scuba divers and their newfangled gear. Its name had been changed to the Ironworkers Memorial Second Narrows Crossing, small consolation to the families who received nothing, or a mere pittance, for their losses.

I'd had enough for one day and was looking forward to a good meal in False Creek, so I pointed *Groais* once more towards the graceful parabola of Lions Gate Bridge, under which the bow of an enormous bulk carrier had just appeared from some distant port of call. Its crew, rather than rummaging amongst old memories, would be gearing up for a night on the town. Freefalling is what this return to origins feels like. There are moments when the past comes crashing in, faces, objects, whole landscapes, threatening to engulf me. Nothing to hang onto, no safe anchorage. White pages, even whiter space.

I'd awakened the previous week from a dream about sailing in a storm. My jib and main had blown away. I couldn't get the Lister diesel to fire. I was only three hundred yards from the rocks and losing way fast. I pulled the cords tight on my Mustang jacket and tucked my pantlegs into my socks, the way my uncle Tom said he'd been taught to do in the RAF when his plane was about to ditch, a means of preserving body heat a little longer. At that moment the boom, which I'd forgotten to secure, swung round and hit me in the small of the back, knocking me overboard. Before I knew what was happening, I was separated by twenty yards from the boat, trying not to swallow water as the waves crashed over me. The boat resembled *Groais,* but I couldn't be sure in the dark. I decided to make for shore farther along the coast, where at least I wouldn't get crushed under seven and a half wayward tons of wood and steel. But as I tried to swim, to strike out for safety, I realized I was still underwater, struggling to reach the surface. My lungs felt as if they would explode. I couldn't do it. I was sinking again. Then everything went dark and this great quiet came over me. The struggle did not seem to matter any more. Great turning arcs of light washed over my body, a pathetic swamped thing, where it shifted back and forth amongst the rocks.

I'd like to say I woke up to someone shining a flashlight in my face, my father in the gillnetter in Rivers Inlet telling me

I'd fallen asleep at watch, letting the boat and net drift onto the rocks. This was something deeper, more primal. A harrowing. I was confronting my own death. Or perhaps reliving the death of my grandfather. Did he have a heart attack or an accident off Point Atkinson, struggling with two fishing rods and a bottle of scotch? I'll never know for sure. But he's out there somewhere still, full fathom five, waiting, pearls for eyes.

When you drop a line over the side of a boat—or onto a page—you have to be prepared for whatever you might catch.

Two

Things were heating up in False Creek. Dragon boats and war canoes criss-crossed the harbour, drums beating time, oarsmen and -women dipping their paddles into the grimy water, preparing for the annual Canada Day races and multicultural celebrations. Some of the paddlers were already in full regalia and, but for their nylon headbands and Nike runners, might have stepped out of the journal pages of George Vancouver or Juan Francisco de la Bodega y Quadra. Instead of trading skins, they were trading insults. The first night there was some sort of ethnic powwow in progress at the Plaza of Nations, which involved music and dances of every persuasion. A tsunami of sound ricocheted from building to building, scattering inebriated revellers into remote crannies of the dock and marina, where they laughed, sang, and otherwise disported themselves. I couldn't sleep and began to yearn for the comparatively benign cacophony of aluminum rigging. At 0300 I sat bolt upright to the sound of a shrill female voice shouting.

"So long, suckers. Too bad I can't keep you awake all night."

This was not the False Creek I remembered—a sleepy, polluted little inlet full of sawmills and small industry, including the Granville Island warehouses of Macintosh Cartage for whom my father drove truck. False Creek got its name for appearing other than what it was, not a source of fresh water but a blunt, stale inlet that extended almost to Clark Drive but was eventually filled in beyond Main Street. My father used to tie up his leaky gillnetter here and I would cycle down weekly to bail it out, fearful it might have sunk in the interim, minnows and bottom-feeders circumnavigating the submerged wheelhouse, the visible tip of the mast pointing an accusing finger. The "Creek" felt doubly false now, rimmed by marinas, swank yachts, a man-made coastal range of high-rise apartments and condos on the Expo '86 lands that had been sold by the Social Credit government of B.C. to Hong Kong tycoon Lee Kaishing for a song. An Asian lullaby. The only industry left intact was a cement company, whose barges came and went amidst the beetling ferries and sleek pleasure craft.

I was feeling a bit of a fraud myself, soaking up the good life of the boater rather than grinding away at my typewriter or grading papers. I had found temporary moorage at the Plaza of Nations Marina, at the poor and as yet undeveloped end of False Creek, in a direct line between B.C. Place Stadium and the geodesic dome of the Science World. The madding crowds of Granville Island, with its hotel, galleries, theatre, craft shops, and bookstores, were at a safe distance; but so, alas, were the restaurants and fresh fish and produce market for which the "island" had become famous. The Plaza of Nations, a remnant of the Expo site, consisted of a casino, a comedy club called Yuk Yuk's and a covered outdoor concert area. The combination made sense. You could try a dose of laughter to console yourself after gambling away all your money; and, if that didn't work, throw yourself into the harbour.

I'd managed to avoid the yacht clubs with their money and pretensions, where no real work was done—the only fish-boats had been converted into pleasure craft—and where even the pimply kid at the fuel dock, where I stopped in search of kerosene, could detect class immediately, in the cut of a boat, in the texture of the sails, and in every short cut taken with the rigging and maintenance. *Groais* and I, with patched, rust-stained sails and no reverse gear, had slunk unnoticed into the nether reaches of False Creek to a half-finished marina, where there were no facilities, not even a washroom. Temporary hoses for running water lay in a jumble amongst electrical extension cords; and the exposed ends of multi-coloured electrical wires protruded from galvanized pipes like the tubular necks of deep-sea flora.

Two small fibreglass sloops, one a live-aboard, were tied up at the Plaza of Nations Marina along with a large dilapidated troller that came and went daily with a few people on board, but most of the dozen or so craft were equipped to take the tourists fishing or on dinner cruises. Jim, the marina manager, would appear late each afternoon in full nautical dress, ready to double as captain and host of a fifty-foot yacht equipped with white linen tablecloths, candles and place settings for twenty-five. At my end of this commercial floating opera, the MV *Strike Force*, a forty-foot aluminum cruiser, was fitted out mainly for gourmet fishing. A party of Mexicans set out the first day, returning at sunset empty-handed but happy and well lathered; they were amused when I addressed them in Spanish on the subject of the disappearing salmon, even more so when I tried to use *mofeta*, the word for "skunk," as a past participle to describe their having caught nothing. The usual contingent consisted of visiting Japanese, shepherded aboard by two female tour guides carrying large baskets of catered food and wine. These well-heeled travellers seemed oblivious not only to the chaos aboard *Groais*—the unstowed anchor, coils of rope and crab trap, bags of unsorted groceries in the cockpit, towels and underwear drying—but also to the sight of me, unshaven, hair uncombed, decked out in runners and grubby shorts, poring over a confusion of lists, cruising guides and charts. The skipper of the *Strike Force*, however, a lean, smiling man in his late forties who introduced himself as Hank, didn't miss a detail.

"Heading north, eh? I know that coast. You'll love it." He nodded towards the last of his retreating clients, who had paused before trying to negotiate what seemed an alarmingly steep ramp to the parking area. "Sure beats the zoo down here."

I'd been having problems with the rigging and was not looking forward to making my way up the thirty-foot mast to free a tangled line. But I was in no hurry; *Groais* and I were at home in this motley crowd, where at least some honest work was being done. I looked around at the mess, trying to assess the boat beneath it all and its potential to carry me safely through the trip ahead. I was pleased, more or less, with my acquisition. While its contours and spaces left something to be desired, I knew it would prove a comfortable womb in which I might wake to hear water lapping and all the familiar harbour sounds: voices, the muted cry of gulls, a distant engine, fragments of recorded music.

I switched on my "Chicken Skin" tape of Ry Cooder singing a laconic version of "Goodnight Irene." The song seemed to have been written for the occasion, as I'd been thinking about my mother. Her name was Irene, though she was known by the nickname Rene (pronounced *ree-nee*). My maternal grandfather, Colin Turner, who had worked most of his adult life for Buckerfield's Seeds in Vancouver, used to moor his boat, the *Windy*, at Fisherman's Cove in Howe Sound; and Rene would often swim leisurely alongside the boat as they trolled for salmon between there and Point Atkinson. I vaguely recall Gramp's boat as grey and nondescript, with a small cabin, but I remember quite vividly those rides in the back of his Plymouth coupe, my brother and I bouncing along unsecured in the trunk with the lid tied up, dizzy from carbon monoxide fumes and from the curves and dips of Marine Drive, which followed the shoreline from West Vancouver to Horseshoe Bay.

I have few clear recollections of my mother. She died at thirty-four, when I was seven years old. However, in remote recesses of my brain, I've kept a sketchy and incomplete archive of images, glimpses really, snapshots of our short life together. I am sitting on the stairs to the basement of our Kitsilano rental, my father in the kitchen doorway behind me, my brother farther down the stairs making a face, and my mother, hands on hips, looking at me fiercely from where she stands on the black-and-white checkered linoleum floor, like the queen on a chessboard. This is a disciplinary tableau, since I have just told my brother to shut up, which is not acceptable behaviour in a four-year-old. I also remember a scene two years later in the cancer clinic in one of the pavilions of the Vancouver General Hospital, where I've accompanied her to her regular radium treatments. My mother is beautifully dressed, in a beige wool suit and high heels, her hair done up at the back. This is a rare occasion, an outing together, and I'm delighted by the attention I get from the nurses and the aura of importance surrounding my mother, as if she were a visiting dignitary. I know we'll stop for chips at the café before taking the bus home, if she's not too tired from being so important. Sitting next to an old man, there's a girl with little white clouds on her dress, which take on the shapes of animals the more I look at them; but she's only three so I don't talk to her. I wonder if they've come because of my mother. I browse through the copies of *Life*, *Cosmopolitan*, and *Saturday Evening Post*, looking at the pictures, then watch my feet, which don't reach the floor, swing back and forth between the shiny chrome legs of the chair.

After her death, when I was still living with the family of

her closest friend, Ann Gill, I used to see my mother's ghost standing at the top of the stairs in the hallway outside my room. I don't recall her wearing anything unusual, just the kind of housedress mothers wear that can accommodate the spillage of food, paint and tears. She had a friendly concerned look on her face, as if she'd just popped up from the kitchen to see if I was still awake. No words were exchanged—or needed—and I would always sleep better after these visits. On one occasion, she wore the white uniform and blue serving apron that were part of her old job as a food demonstrator at Eaton's, though that detail could be pure embellishment. The only thing out of kilter was her hands, which were silently wringing the neck of the dishtowel, a habit I seem to have inherited and apply regularly to paper napkins, much to the dismay of family and friends.

Other recollections of my mother have probably been reconstructed from photographs. All four of us on the beach at English Bay, my scrawny brother Jim, my cousin Tommy Adams, and my rakishly handsome and mustachioed uncle Tom, alias T.T., just returned from the war and a German POW camp, where he'd been incarcerated after he bailed out of his flaming Lancaster bomber over Hamburg. Most moving to me are the photos of my mother when she was still a child, innocent of what life had in store for her. She and her sister Pat, ages nine and seven respectively, hair in ponytails, mauling a plump bulldog on the front lawn at Forty-fourth and Maple, or draped along the running-board of the Star automobile, a model as short-lived as she was. Shooting stars, each of these images and memories, so intense, so briefly glimpsed, reminding us that nothing is permanent, that no effort can keep those we love safely near at hand. And, of course, always the same age.

And then there are the submerged narratives. The photo

taken at English Bay reveals nothing of what is going on in my uncle's mind—or his youthful body, where the tiny fragments of shrapnel from anti-aircraft shells were always shifting, constant reminders of a living hell, Hamburg below him "burning like a Christmas tree," or of burying his parachute in a farmer's field. There's no hint of tragic expression or letter C engraved on my mother's forehead, either, to tell of the losing battle she is waging with wayward cancer cells.

To fill the absence surrounding my mother's death, I had embroidered an elaborate legend about her beauty, her many talents, and her foreign origins, convincing myself she was born in England. I did not realize my mistake until years later, when I had to replace a stolen wallet and birth certificate. I reported her maiden name as Irene Turner and her birthplace as Bournemouth, possibly Southampton. The authorities demanded more information, since their data did not jibe with mine. Fishing amongst relatives, I was startled to learn that her full name was Hazel Irene Lillian Turner and that she had been born in Calgary, the first Canadian offspring of the Turner/Marsh clan, which included a baker and an Anglican minister, all of whom had come here from the south of England before the First World War. I don't know which was more sobering, the thought that her family were bakers or that my first name might have derived from my mother's origins in the city of Calgary.

My mother worked at Kelly Douglas, the large Vancouver food wholesaler that handled products from all over the world—tins of biscuits from England, tea crates from India and Ceylon, Chinese noodles, chests of spices. It was here she met my father, Laurie, who used to sneak her contraband cookies and figs from cases that had split open, accidentally of course. When he was fired for unwittingly offering the boss a cookie on the freight elevator, they tried their luck as florists on West Broadway near Alma, but the Depression was not a time for the flowering of successful businesses, unless, of course, you had the capital and imagination to plan for war. I can see Laurie and Rene—my father embarrassed, my mother laughing hysterically—as they stalled at an intersection in their wretched truck, fumes from the cargo of fresh manure wafting into the windows of indignant cars. After my birth, she went back to work downtown. Maturity and self-confidence had their rewards, including first prize in a beauty contest for working mothers at the Orpheum Theatre where she was crowned Miss Wrigley Spearmint Gum.

My mother remarried briefly before she died, this time to a quiet, reliable, lapsed Mennonite named Jim Friesen, who worked at Eaton's. One of Jim's hobbies was working with the new plastics, cutting delicate figures of animals with his skil-saw from different-coloured sheets of clear plastic, fawns, owls, squirrels, rabbits, some of which he glued to green rectangular plastic mounts so it seemed as if they'd paused to look at you from a patch of grass. My mother was surrounded by an ever-increasing menagerie of two-dimensional creatures, as if by sheer numbers she might be not just distracted, but rescued from her fate.

While the dragon boats made practice runs across False Creek to the beat of a drum or the shout of a coxswain, I fixed the tangle of lines and inched my way down the mast, eyes closed, my heart beating its own wild tattoo. Thank God it didn't need doing at sea, where the unlucky climber would be swinging crazily far out over the water. I don't know the mathematics, but I do know that if a boat is tossed about by waves, the distant tip of the mast and anything attached to it will be travelling back and forth through space at terrifying speeds. Why had I selected this cramped and physically challenging means of salvaging my past—madness, masochism, stupidity, all of the above? Surely it would have been easier to rent a room in Vancouver and spend my days talking to relatives than crawl into this enclosed space, which seemed more likely to prove a coffin than a womb with a view. The French philosopher Gaston Bachelard, whose book *The Poetics of Space* was staring down at me from its comfortable position on the gleaming mahogany shelf of the main cabin, had plenty to say about the psychological significance of such enclosed spaces. He talks about those intimate spaces we recall from childhood—secure attics and nooks, cupboards and caves—into which we retreat and from which we gain new perspective on our troubled and changing lives, where we can recharge our batteries before venturing out again into the fray of the adult world. Bachelard noticed that such intimate spaces figure prominently in literature, and he cited the works of Marcel Proust as a prime example.

Proust fascinated me, but more for what he had to say about memory and its lapses. Something is lost in the English translation of *À la recherche du temps perdu*. It's not just a *Remembrance of Things Past* that Proust is engaged in, but a rigorous attempt to recover, or reconstruct, what has been lost, a process that takes more than memory. I had embarked on a voyage into my own past, but I was severely handicapped by a family that did not always value its stories, that left few legends, no detailed charts for navigation. Because of poverty, a nomadic existence and a lot of emotional turmoil, there were precious few photographs either. Huge gaps appeared in the *mappe-monde* of my family, less in the manner of a Mercator projection, which distorts everything in its margins, and more in keeping with those early maps of exploration, with edges undefined drifting away into speculation, and with their text-filled boxes called *cartouches*, used to cover up the areas about which the cartographer and his sources were ignorant. If I were going to write about the coastal years, I'd have to do more than rack my own memory; I'd have to pester my few surviving relatives, ransack diaries and old letters, dig up material in newspapers and archives. When all of this industry did not suffice, as surely it wouldn't, I would have to imagine the rest.

Before setting sail, I spent more time building up *Groais's* library than I had in learning how to run the boat, a decision I'd come to regret later, when it would dawn on me that although I could consult all the experts, even pull down e-mail messages from the ether, I could not, without radar, detect a ship bearing down on me in the fog. For the moment, however, I was comfortable enough with the thought that my salvage crew included professionals such as Herman Melville, Joseph Conrad, Malcolm Lowry, Charles Darwin, Elizabeth Bishop, and Marilynn Robinson, each of whom knew plenty about water, maps and the processes of imaginative retrieval. Jostling the Big Six, my ship's officers, were midshipmen Walter Benjamin of *Illuminations* and art critic and story-teller-turned-memoirist John Berger in his *And Our Faces, My Heart, Brief as Photos.* Jammed on the same shelf as the first-aid kit, radio, extra pairs of glasses, and toiletries were Peterson's *Field Guide to Western Birds*, books on flora and fauna such as *Pacific Coast*, the poems of Pat Lowther, *Off in a Boat* by Neil M. Gunn and *Coasting* by Jonathan Raban, Louise Glück's *Proofs and Theories: Essays on Poetry*, and Robert Bringhurst's stunning treatise, *A Story as Sharp as a Knife: The Classical Haida Mythtellers and Their World.*

What was the point of this unruly assemblage of authors, clamouring to be read or reread, taking up every inch of shelf space, distracting the skipper, threatening the stability of the boat, and waiting to be chucked helter-skelter in the first good storm? Like Darwin, I was determined to construct my own myth of origins. I wanted to know where home was. If this fifteen thousand miles of ragged coastline, only a fraction of which I would cover, with its deadly reefs, plummeting inlets, and serene coves, its violent storms and surging currents, its unpredictable cycles of dearth and plenty—cataclysmic volcanic eruptions underwater followed by countless millennia of coral growth and sedimentation, glaciers two miles thick superseded by periods of riotous growth; if this place proved, once again, to be home, I wanted to learn everything I could about it, how was it formed, who were its earliest inhabitants, where had they come from, what were we doing to destroy and protect it? To sail home, in a boat and in print, I would need as many wise companions as I could stow on board.

Conrad, always good company in a storm, had spent the first part of his adult life at sea, the remainder writing. He considered fiction a form of history, human history, and liked to refer to his novels as "rescue work, this snatching of vanishing phases of turbulence, disguised in fair words, out of the native obscurity into a light where the struggling forms may be seen, seized upon, endowed with the only possible permanence in this world of relative values—the permanence of memory." I was no novelist, but I knew what he meant; I would have my "rescue work" cut out for me. I had with me several of Conrad's novels, including a copy of The Shadow-Line, which he wrote during the First World War when he was troubled by the chaos that had descended upon Europe, which he believed was in some way related to the pessimism and nihilism poisoning contemporary life. He had explored the fruits of this mature pessimism in Victory. In the shorter, more lyrical The Shadow-Line, however, he stepped back to his own youth, to the exacting experience of first command in the Merchant Service, and found there a metaphor worth exploring on behalf of his son, Boris, serving on the battle-fields of France, and the numberless youth in daily jeopardy for their lives.

The narrator's recollections of suffering from "the green sickness of late youth" somehow mirrored the mid-to-late-life crisis I was experiencing, adrift from family, job, and friends. Sounding a lot like George Vancouver on a grumpy day on the Northwest Coast, the young captain waits to be assigned a ship, consumed with negative feelings, dismissing the world as hollow and absurd. I did not view the world of human relations in precisely these terms, but I could see how the narrator's observations might apply to the worlds of acad-emia and writing to which I had devoted so much of my life, both of them fraught with posturing, self-promotion and other brands of nastiness. And I could identify with the fear of death—that last great shadow-line—underlying the young narrator's existential malaise, his distaste at the thought that "all our hearts would cease to beat like run-down clocks."

Conrad had progressed from sailing to writing, mastering both. I was not unconscious of the irony that, moving in the opposite direction, I might prove myself as clumsy at the helm as at the pen. However, I was determined to mark my return to the coast in some special way. I wasn't coming back to die, at least not yet; I was here to lay claim to the waters that had swallowed the body of one relative and lapped up the ashes of two more, and whose sirens had sung to me, non-stop, during thirty years of wandering in the rest of Canada.

I spent a few hours in the hot morning sun fiddling with the reverse gear, trying the adjust the cable where it attaches to the transmission. The space was cramped and awkward. As usual, it worked fine in reverse at the dock while the engine was still cold; so I decided to check it out by making a short run up False Creek to the fuel dock at one of the marinas. The kid who'd given me the once-over when I lurched into port from Bellingham was still on duty. He sported a furious red welt like a third eye in the middle of his forehead, where he'd massacred a pimple. A bruised look about him. Eighteen-hour days at minimum wage. He leaned in the doorway and watched me top up the four fuel tanks a drop at a time, so I wouldn't have another diesel spill. The square outline of a pack of cigarettes tucked under the sleeve of his T-shirt was so high up it resembled an epaulette. Not exactly an advertisement for fuel safety.

"Good all-weather boat. I seen one like her in an old yachting magazine in the boathouse." He ran my card through the swiper and handed me the control panel of the debit machine. There was a small blue tattoo of a kedge anchor on his forearm. Ex-navy cadets, I thought, Bay of Fundy. "Bilge keels like that, you set her down anywhere for repairs. Don't have to be dependent on nobody." He gave a dismissive nod that took in the whole establishment, the whole country.

I nodded. Why did everyone I meet seem more capable and deserving of *Groais* than I was? He could probably live on the boat permanently, make a living at it and consider himself lucky. I thought of the hazards ahead: Seymour Narrows, Yaculta Rapids, Johnstone Strait, the open Pacific beyond Cape Scott, storms, fog banks, mechanical failure and a plethora of deadly asterisks. The previous night when I dropped into place the two boards that constitute a cabin door, closing myself in for the night, I'd felt quite snug and secure in my floating home. I wasn't keen about marinas, not only because of the privilege they represent, but also because of the noise, the cacophony of taut rigging striking the aluminum masts all night long. My students made appropriate oohs and aahs when they learned I was living on a boat, as if there were nothing more romantic to be doing. I was quite willing to encourage their delusion that mine was a charmed existence, but the truth is that sharing a marina washroom at 0600 with a snoring drunk whose feet are protruding into your cubicle was not my idea of romance. And although the poet in me might wish to describe the not-so-dulcet shrieks of the rigging as wind chimes, their effect was more like that of a hundred asylum inmates turned loose in the hardware section of a Canadian Tire store and having a heyday with the pots and pans.

I wasn't immune to stories about wonderful, even scarifying, voyages during which sailor bonds with boat to form an implacable duo capable of confronting all odds. But cynic and romantic were too well matched in me to let me forget, for more than a moment, that I was navigationally challenged, that my nautical heritage included raw fear, mechanical ineptness, and bouts of seasickness. Even then I could not have imagined that my initial relationship with *Groais* would turn out to be so hostile. In fact, it was mutually abusive, bordering on murderous. I did not handle the boat well and found it awkward and unfamiliar, which caused me to inflict a number of dints and scratches. As for *Groais*, her boom, cradle, companionway hatch and every other protruding piece of wood seemed intent on making intimate contact with my shins, elbows and skull. After only a week aboard, my nails were all broken, my hands a nest of scars, and my body resembled a bruised banana. Judging from this initiation, cruising would prove less a honeymoon than a fight to the death.

As I motored back along False Creek towards the Plaza of Nations, thinking how the marina's tentativeness and ramshackle condition matched that of its namesake, the United

Nations, I saw the converted troller coming towards me under the Cambie Street Bridge. It was moving too fast for the three mile-per-hour speed limit of the inner harbour, a bone of white water in its teeth. Two men were gesticulating excitedly in the wheelhouse, so the boat appeared to be steering itself. In addition to the boxes of supplies on deck, a couple of oxygen tanks and various pieces of diving equipment, I counted five passengers on board, three of them seated on aluminum chairs under a brown tarpaulin crudely erected astern, and two in the bow, one woman propped with her back against the capstan, the other, a man, his rump and lower torso half-submerged in the centre of a huge coil of rope. All five, even the two in the bow, wearing hats and well wrapped against the sun, were reading what appeared to be manuscripts, corners of pages fluttering in the warm breeze as they passed.

Of course, the reverse gear did not work. I came alongside at a crawl, narrowly missing the hull of a new arrival. Hank materialized out of thin air to fend me off and grab the bowline. When the boat was secured, I asked him about the departing troller with its crew of bookworms. He laughed.

"Actors and technicians. They're filming some scenes of a movie in Howe Sound."

"Do you know what it's called?"

"Yah, yah. American. Something to do with cedars and snow."

Guterson's novel, which I was reading at the time, was lying open on my table aboard *Groais*, at the chapter where the waterlogged body of a fisherman is pulled from his net in the frigid waters off the San Juan Islands. They'd filmed the winter scenes in the Queen Charlotte Islands, where you could count on snow, at least for brief periods. Cheap labour, the low Canadian dollar, talented production people and picture-perfect scenery were a winning combination. I thought of Guterson's long fictional sojourn, the meticulous turn of his phrases, of writing as a sort of battle with the elements, with the unknown. Lowry, too, with the twin volcanoes of alcoholism and imaginative failure looming overhead, had struggled to write his opus in nearby Deep Cove. No wonder he had been drawn to the link between writing and seamanship in his sonnet about Conrad, where the poet, with his "truant heart," invites chaos and storm into his study, then uses the "mariner's ferment in his blood" to bring it all under control: "In sleep all night he grapples with a sail! / But words beyond the life of ships dream on."

Before I tucked my head in and sealed up the gangway the previous night, I'd watched the soft reflection of myriad boat and apartment lights spill over the ripples on the black surface of False Creek and thought of my dead mother's concerned face on the hallway stairs so many years before. I had come a long way to find her and this might be as close as I would get. I'd make the run to Point Atkinson, then follow her swimming route up Howe Sound to Fisherman's Cove, catching on my beam a light swell from the Nanaimo ferry that would already be negotiating the entrance to Horseshoe Bay. With Passage Island a mile or so off the port beam, Bowen Island massing ahead, and Point Grey—the site of so many humiliations in my career as student and would-be lover—still visible dead astern in the early morning mist, if I go slowly and pay close attention, I thought, I might catch, in my own brief passage, a glimpse of that lovely swimmer, a ghostly outrigger, just beyond my reach amidships.

✳ Three

"Go ahead, Dad, be a devil, open it. You're allowed. After all, it's last year's Christmas present."

"Do I look like such a hopeless case?"

My daughter Bronwen had just presented me with a belated gift in the car after I picked her up from the Vancouver airport, a T-shirt showing an albino bat silhouetted against a rusty-coloured cave wall, under which was posed the question: WHO WILL REMEMBER ME? I'd never been keen about using my body and clothes for advertising or propaganda, however worthy, but it was an attractive design and I was grateful for the sentiment. Bronwen grinned, but seemed a trifle worried by my reaction. We hadn't seen each other for seven months, since I had visited her in Budapest, where she was working for an agency whose ostensible aim was to make Hungarian business more environmentally conscious. Since her arrival back in Canada coincided with my departure for the north coast, I'd arranged to have my car available for her and her partner James to use over the summer.

"It's a memento of my work, something we produced at the agency," she said, folding the T-shirt and placing it on the back seat. "Part of the endangered species project. I thought you'd appreciate it."

We drove up Granville Street and stopped for lunch at a familiar restaurant on Forty-first Avenue, where they serve delicious pastas and the kind of health food Bronwen loves. She was looking quite grown up and mature at twenty-three, confident, her face more formed than I remembered. She was also vigorously wrapping herself around a quantity of apple strudel.

"The signs are mounting up, Beam. This morning, when he learned I was sailing to the north coast, Hank offered to loan me a survival suit worth four hundred dollars. Now I'm the recipient of a T-shirt for endangered bats. I'm beginning to wonder if I give off the vibes of a soon-to-be-extinct species."

"Feeling a little insecure about the trip, are we?" The spoonful of strudel paused in mid-air long enough for Bronwen to give me one of her penetrating don't-try-to-kid-me looks. "Who's Hank?"

"A Dutchman, my new friend at the Plaza of Nations Marina in False Creek. He runs a guide boat where I'm moored, for tourists who want to go fishing. He calls himself Hank of Holland, obviously a pun on the point of land known as the Hook of Holland."

Hank had been exceptionally generous, also offering to take me to a wholesale distributor where I could get a commercial discount on equipment for the boat. I told Bronwen his story about going to fetch Japanese customers at the expensive hotels in his beat-up station wagon, with sputtering exhaust pipe and duct tape holding the dashboard together. When they saw the car, the tourists were too polite to turn around and run, but he could see them in the rear-view mirror making meaningful expressions and mouthing words, the import of which was: "God, if the car is this bad, what will the boat be like?" Hank would smile and say nothing to assuage their anxiety, merely wait for the overblown expressions of surprise and delight when they saw the boat, a large sea-worthy aluminum craft with all the amenities.

"Ah, nice boat. Smart boat. Good, good. Ha!"

After I dropped Bronwen off and arranged for her to pick up the car two days later when I'd be ready to leave, I headed down to the boat, which had become headquarters, or nerve centre, for my various expeditions amongst relatives. Plaza of Nations Marina, still in the makeshift stages, with its loose planks, gaping water pipes, and nests of exposed wires, was several accidents waiting to happen. Tucked in behind the casino and Yuk Yuk's comedy stage on Pacific Boulevard, it was both a gamble and a bad joke, although Jim Hodgson's dinner cruise, a contemporary version of the infamous booze-cruises which plied the harbour when I was a kid, was doing a thriving business. I considered myself lucky to have found a temporary, if pricey, spot to tie up.

My reconnaissance in Vancouver and environs was being conducted mainly on land. I needed to renew my neurotic affiliations with the family and see what I could learn about my mother and Uncle Tom on the Turner side and about my father and Grandfather Geddes. Because of the long gaps in our contact with one another, several of the meetings felt more like interviews than joyous reunions. Families are not always close, but forty years was definitely pushing the limits.

"Hello, is that the Rink?"

"Yes, who's speaking?"

"This is the Rope, a bit frayed from handling but otherwise intact."

A long pause, then, "No, I don't believe it. Where are you calling from?"

Marcel Tremblay, known as Maurice, alias the Rink, and still a young man when I first met him at Uncle Tom's boat rentals in Whytecliffe, was not exactly a relative. He'd spent his life as a dental technician and was married to Tom's sister-in-law, Cathy Smyth. I thought his nickname came from the link with that other Maurice, the "Rocket" Richard of hockey fame, but no, it had been given to him for no particular reason by a childhood friend and stuck. Having been so easily branded, the Rink was quick to apply nicknames to others. Mine came from his having seen me so many times on the floats at Whytecliffe holding the rope of one of the rental boats while fishermen and joyriders embarked or disembarked. The Rink was now semi-retired and busy sorting out the estate of his brother, a dancer who had taught ballet for many years in Oregon before retiring to the Fraser Valley. The estate consisted mainly of two rooms lined floor to ceiling with long-playing classical records, which Maurice and Cathy were trying to catalogue and sell.

We had lunch together at an Italian restaurant on Denman Street at English Bay, up the street from the dental clinic where Maurice still worked part-time. I was surprised to hear him speak so openly and affectionately of his own family. His grandfather had moved from Quebec to the Peace River area of Alberta before it became a province, then to British Columbia. He told me his grandmother had ridden a horse west from Alberta—giving birth to one son en route—all the way to Victoria, where she and her husband ran the Tremblay Hotel. Maurice was of the opinion that Uncle Tom had been psychologically damaged by the war and described how Tom used to go off the deep end now and then and disappear downtown for short periods to drink himself into oblivion. I knew my uncle was high-strung, but this didn't quite jibe with the memories I had of him, working around the clock and playing with the family.

"Nancy was the strong, stable one," Maurice confided. "She held things together. The business, the family." It seems that Nancy's clan, particularly her sisters, never forgave Tom when he remarried too soon after Nancy died of a brain haemorrhage in her early forties.

I looked at the Rink, tanned and fit. He was ten years my senior, but didn't look it. I was touched by his candour and vulnerability and his obvious pleasure in seeing me again, and I found myself regretting his long absence from my life. He invited me to come over for dinner in North Vancouver, after my trip up the coast, or to visit them at the cottage at Cultus Lake, where he kept a small day-sailer. I promised not to wait another forty years to make contact.

Since I'd talked to the Rink, I'd been thinking about teeth. Dentures, to be exact. The previous week I'd had lunch in Victoria with my cousin Ron Marston, eldest son of my father's sister, Winnie. Ron and his wife Mary were retired. He amused himself constructing a family tree, brewing his own wine, and making occasional forays across the continent in his expensive truck and fifth-wheel trailer. They were gearing up to head east for a wedding in the States. After two hours of plying him with questions about Grandfather Geddes, I was beginning to sound like a broken record, but Ron, it turned out, had a surprise for me.

"He lost his false teeth overboard near Powell River."

"You're kidding. What was he doing up there?"

"Fishing."

This bizarre tidbit of information was almost too good to be true, just the kind of thing I'd been hoping for. I regretted not having known it when I was driving water-taxi from Texada to Westview. I'd have had some delightful moments, as I struggled to keep the *Bluebell* or *Moccasin* on course, thinking of my grandfather's dentures hundreds of feet below me, snug in the mud and murk at the bottom of Malaspina Strait.

I never knew my grandfather fished commercially after he retired from the shipyards. According to Ron, he made regular trips on his small boat, trolling for salmon between Vancouver and Powell River, to keep busy and supplement his meagre pension. When the dentist told him the new set of teeth would take two weeks, he refused to wait and took off again in the boat, gassing up at the fuel dock in Coal Harbour and heading out under the Lions Gate Bridge for his rendezvous with destiny. Somewhere off Point Atkinson he disappeared, toothless, over the side of the boat. Many drowned fishermen are found with their pants around their ankles or with their flies unzipped, having been knocked overboard while trying to urinate over the side of a moving boat. This could never be confirmed in my grandfather's case, since he seems to have headed for deep water. It's not unusual for coastal workers to be unable to swim and he was no exception. North Sea fishermen will tell you that knowing how to swim is a luxury that only prolongs the agony, since the temperature of the water will kill you, swimmer or not, in ten to fifteen minutes.

I knew a little about the North Sea. I'd been to Orkney three times and checked out the ancestral slums along the north coast of Scotland. My grandparents came from the neighbouring towns of Buckie and Port Gordon that lie a short distance east of Inverness and the battlefield of Culloden. Buckie, the larger of the two, has pretty well eclipsed Port Gordon, which was once an important fishing port, with a harbour designed by the father of Robert Louis Stevenson. It's said that at the height of the herring fishery you could walk across the harbour from boat to boat and never get your feet wet. Now it's empty of boats and filled with sand that not even sporadic dredging can eradicate. The sea dominates life in such towns, offers its largesse, takes its toll in lives, and occasionally rises to inundate the houses and shops on the main street. Advice: clench your teeth and hang on—or emigrate.

Cousin Ron's story tickled my perverse imagination for another reason. I'd just returned a few weeks earlier from another trip to Orkney, the first of the three clusters of islands north of Scotland that includes the Shetlands and the Faeroes. Orkney is swept by the North Sea, which carried on its currents the ancient peoples who built rings of standing stones for religious worship and their neolithic successors whose underground villages are gradually being discovered. They were followed by Picts, Irish priests, marauding Vikings, who ruled the islands until late in the fourteenth century, remnants of the Spanish Armada shipwrecked while fleeing their pursuers, and ships of the Hudson's Bay Company which, in order to avoid pirates in the English Channel, sailed up the east coast to take on water, provisions and men in Stromness.

As part of my research, I tried walking along the cliffs to see various ruins and shorebirds, but the winds were so strong I had to get down on my hands and knees and crawl back to the rental car for fear of being hurled into the sea. I was staying at Mrs. Johnson's B&B in Stromness, where I had the pleasure of breakfasting with seven divers from the south of England. A hardy lot, they were in Orkney to explore the remaining wrecks of the German fleet in Scapa Flow, which had been deliberately sunk by its officers and crews after the First World War so the victors could not make use of the ships. Most of the fifty-nine vessels were later salvaged and scrapped, but several had been left to rot and had become a favourite destination for divers. A more recent, though off-limits, underwater site was the hulk of the *Royal Oak*, torpedoed by German submariner Gunther Prien at the beginning of the Second World War, with the loss of almost eight hundred lives. While negotiating a huge breakfast of eggs, bacon, sausage, orange juice, coffee and muesli, I asked the fellow on my right, who had blond hair and a blue scar the shape of a double hook on his chin, what he'd seen down there other than rusting metal.

"Bloody hell. I looked down one of them six-inch gun barrels with my torch and this conger eel came belting out right into my face. Scared the shit out of me."

"Live ammunition, eh?"

"Brilliant! Ricocheted right off my face mask."

He told me the deck on one of the battleships was the size of a football field. They all laughed at my questions about claustrophobia at such depths and offered their theories about how an eel might learn to back up so carefully that its tail would disappear first down the gun barrel, as there would certainly be no room to turn around inside. Since I was a sailor without a working reverse gear on the boat waiting for me back home, this might have been construed as an inquiry of more than casual interest.

Then the only woman in the group of divers mentioned seeing scallops during her descent amongst the wrecks.

"Dozens of them, seventy feet down. They went clicking past my face mask, one by one in the dim light." She was eating a piece of toast and strawberry jam. As she spoke, her tongue darted out and retrieved a morsel of wayward jam on her upper lip.

"Like sets of false teeth."

I'd spent too many hours tracking down information about cellphones and how to make them receive e-mail. The idea of pulling messages out of the blue, with no stationary electrical connections, still staggers me. Radio waves, okay, but all those detailed bits of script? I'd been busy picking up items for the boat, mainly food. My obligatory trip to the dollar store had

netted spices, dishcloths, dehydrated soups, and several dozen
other items, stuff I probably wouldn't use but which seemed
too cheap to pass up. Since there was no refrigeration on the
boat, I purchased two picnic-style styrofoam coolers so I
wouldn't have to eat everything out of cans. Blocks of ice last
about three or four days on a boat. I figured I could count on a
port of call for milk, cheese and fresh vegetables at least once a
week. And, of course, I was planning to supplement my diet by
catching fish and using the crab trap I'd just stowed beside the
auxiliary anchor in one of the lazarettes.

Figuring my mind would prove hungrier than my body on
this lone odyssey, I'd acquired another box of last-minute
additions to my library, including Darwin's *Voyage of the
Beagle*. I'd even grabbed his *Origin of Species* off the library
shelf, as it seemed particularly relevant to my own quest for
roots amongst the living and the dead. More books on geology, navigation and cruising for duffers; vulgate and heretical
versions of the "boater's bible"; and, of course, lest I start
feeling too secure, *Shipwrecks of British Columbia*. There
were also a dozen novels and collections of stories I hoped to
read or reread, some by friends, including *Marine Life* by
Linda Svendsen, Joy Kogawa's *Obasan*, *The Invention of the
World* by Jack Hodgins, Gladys Hindmarch's *The Watery
Part of the World*, George Bowering's *Burning Water*,
Moving Water by Joan Skogan, and Audrey Thomas's *Intertidal Life*. This motley, sopping crew was part of a course
called Coast/Lines I hoped to offer in the fall. I envisaged
myself anchored for days in quiet lagoons, reading, writing,
swimming and cranking out fabulous crab salads. It was clear,
judging from the mountain of stuff piled onto the table and
spare bunk, that I hadn't a clue where to store anything other
than books. Built-in pockets for canned goods and foodstuffs,
as well as a column of small lockers for clothes, were already

crammed to bursting. For some reason, I'd brought along enough T-shirts to outfit a platoon, though my stash of socks and underwear was pitifully small.

At least one of the books had proved useful already, Robert Graves's *Greek Myths*. The night before, when I'd returned with my latest haul of purchases, including rope, second-hand pots and a frying-pan, tools, Tupperware, and four boxes of granola and bran flakes, I found one oar missing from the dinghy, which was full of rainwater. Not so full, I noted, that the oar could have floated away. I thought of the casino patrons, drunk and lamenting their losses on the floats at night. What would they want with a single oar, other than as a weapon or a souvenir? One oar is neither saleable nor very useful for self-propulsion; it forces the user to go in circles. Perhaps there was an Asian koan lurking for me here: the sound of one oar creaking. . . . I'd been reading Graves's version of Odysseus's return to Ithaca after various adventures at sea, including the blinding of the Cyclops, Polyphemus. Odysseus, cursed with bad luck and worse by the dying Cyclops, is advised to go on a long march with a single oar over his shoulder if he wishes to avoid the wrath of Poseidon, father of Polyphemus and God of the Deeps. While I never did catch the significance of the single oar in shaping Odysseus's destiny, which sounded like a comic routine cooked up next door at Yuk Yuk's, I was still inclined to believe, with a superstitious nature I shared with Drake, that everything associated with this voyage had a purpose.

Nevertheless, I'd be out twenty-five bucks and the time it would take me to track down a replacement exactly the right size. Before making a second trip to the Boater's Exchange, I decided to visit my cousin Mel Turner, Tom's and Nancy's son, in Deep Cove where he lived with his wife Pat and their two daughters. He'd spent his life working for local and

provincial parks departments and had been active in setting up
a variety of marine parks, which was how I'd bumped into him
two years earlier, the first time in twenty years. I was staying
with friends on Hornby Island and Mel called after he spotted
a poster advertising my poetry reading. We'd arranged to walk
through the newly designated Helliwell Park at the south end
of the island, whose land he'd acquired for the government.
Now, over a dinner of salmon steaks, he was curious about my
trip and anxious to show me which marine parks to visit on
my way up the coast, but, as neither of us had charts at hand, I
kept steering the conversation back to family history.

Mel had been the one to find his mother, Nancy, on the
kitchen floor when she died of a brain haemorrhage. By then,
the family had sold the boat rentals in Whytecliffe and moved
to West Vancouver so Mel could attend a good high school and
Tom could manage a new marine supply store in Coal
Harbour. With a wartime legacy of memories and ghosts,
Tom was not equipped for the life of a single parent. When I
visited him at his workplace near the Bayshore Inn, he had just
married Doreen, an old friend of his and Nancy's, a divorced
mother with one son, Mike. We didn't talk about his loss.

"D'reen's a winner, Gary, a gem. And Mike's a lovely boy,
a great pal for Mel."

The ranks had been steadily closing. My father, now Mel's.
I took a good hard look at my cousin. I could see Nancy and
my own mother somewhere in his face.

It was time to ship out. Much as I'd enjoyed reconnecting
with family, I was having trouble coping with information
overload and all the emotions called up in me by these
encounters. As I drove back towards town, I was bedevilled by
the memory of my wizened, arthritic Grandmother Turner

begging for aspirin on her rumpled cot and how she'd once told me I was to blame for my mother's cancer, that I was the child she wasn't supposed to have. I could appreciate Ishmael's sentiment in *Moby Dick:* "Whenever I find myself growing grim about the mouth; whenever it is a damp, drizzly November in my soul; whenever I find myself involuntarily pausing before coffin warehouses, and bringing up the rear of every funeral I meet . . . then I account it high time to get to sea as soon as I can." Although it was not November, but a drizzly June night, I decided to call Bronwen and tell her the car would be available in the morning. I'd be leaving at noon.

These belated reunions also made me wonder what kind of creature I was for having been out of touch for so long. I must have appeared a little desperate, even obsessive, in my quest for information. What was I trying to achieve, anyway, in my role as interrogator, all those questions—instruments of torture, to be sure? Was I hoping somehow to justify my existence, fill up the vacuum, blame my own failings on the dead? A man of fifty-nine, compulsively digging up his past was, perhaps, not far removed from the autistic child I'd overheard a few weeks earlier, relentlessly interrogating her mother on the passenger deck of the *Queen of Saanich* as it negotiated Active Pass en route from Sidney to Tsawwassen ferry terminal.

"Did you have to be nice to the camp counsellor, Mom?"

"Yes, dear."

"What brand was your sleeping bag, Mom?"

"I don't remember, dear."

"What colour was it, Mom?"

No response. Aware of my attention and that of several other passengers nearby, the mother flipped aimlessly through her complimentary copy of *B.C. Bookworld*, unable to concentrate, glancing periodically out the window at the disappearing shoreline of Mayne Island, while her beautiful, perfectly normal-looking daughter pressed desperately, heed-lessly, on.

"What colour was your sleeping bag, Mom?"

"Blue."

"Was it a Saturday when you were born in 1954, Mom?"

"Yes, dear. I told you that already."

"Did the camp counsellor sleep with you, Mom?"

"Well, I should hope not!"

"Did the camp counsellor sleep in the same cabin, Mom?"

Information was being processed, or at least accumulated, with a terrifying mechanical efficiency, but all of the usual rules, rituals, courtesies had been abandoned: the give and take, the pause to absorb, reflect, the impulse to give back something of what you receive, to make a joke, lean forward in sympathy, maintain eye contact, nod.

While I was content with whatever I could glean for the sake of the book—an anecdote about false teeth on the ocean floor, a piece of rope in someone's hands, the Rink trading his violin for a pair of ice skates, a few photographs, an epic journey on horseback—I still had a deep need to know more about my family, particularly my mother and father. Three aunts had died within the last year, while I dallied, hesitated, contemplated my return to the coast. I could see that these yearnings were not going to be satisfied in Vancouver, at least not quickly, that I would have to find new ways of gathering, a different methodology, getting to know my relatives again in such a way that the truth—whatever that might be—emerged freely, unsolicited.

On the way back from Mel's and Pat's place in Deep Cove, I paid my respects to the ghost of Malcolm Lowry, whose great literary achievements had finally been recognized with a bronze plaque on the public toilets in nearby Dollarton, an irony he would doubtless have appreciated. I imagined him uncorking a bottle of B.C.'s finest on the forest path to the spring and, with a speech, several loud twangs of his beat-up ukelele, and a few lines of poetry, toasting Bacchus, Pan and all lesser gods. My birthplace had attracted and spawned many writers, but had not exactly nurtured them or developed a cultural climate in which they felt valued and safe. Anti-intellectualism and fear of the imagination were slowly changing, even at Granville Island, where you could find not only a theatre and the Emily Carr Institute of Art & Design, but also the offices of the Vancouver International Writers Festival. As I left the North Shore and headed back over the Ironworkers' bridge, I could see the lights coming on in Port Moody, a few miles to the east, where Lowry had taken such a perverse delight in the illuminated oil refinery sign with the single word S H E L L, which he preferred with the *S* missing. In a more cynical mood, I might have seen it not as "Hell," but as "Sell," in recognition of the motto of B.C. Collateral pawnshop on Hastings Street, which proclaimed, with neither hesitation nor irony, WE BUY AND SELL EVERYTHING.

Before leaving Vancouver, I picked up a matching oar at the Boater's Exchange at Mosquito Creek and made my last sally to the supermarket for extra containers of juice, though Neptune only knew where I'd find a place to store them. The city seemed less foreign and hostile than it had when I arrived, all those ghosts clamouring for attention, painful memories and humiliations lapping at my ankles. Less crass, too, thanks to the dozen or so connections I'd made with family and friends and the long rides I'd taken on my folding bicycle along the paths around False Creek and out to Spanish Banks. A couple of superb meals with Bronwen at Capers and

Salah Thai didn't hurt either. An unexpected zone of comfort, even support, had opened up for me. While I knew it was time to go, I moved with more reluctance down the ramp at the Plaza of Nations Marina than I had anticipated.

"Well, I'm ready to leave. I'll pick you up in ten minutes." I was calling from the shopping centre in North Van, where I'd dropped another hundred dollars. It was beginning to look as if I were stocking a fallout shelter rather than a boat. Bronwen sounded half asleep when I called. "The price of having the car for two months," I said, "is that you stand on the dock, witness my departure, and make all the appropriate noises."

"It's not too late to change your mind."

"I have to go now. I couldn't possibly manage for two months without a car."

The sun was shining on False Creek, relieving it of some of its air of deceit. War canoes were still practicing for the next day's races. One of them swept past the marina at a fast clip, its twelve-woman crew in bright red T-shirts and headbands digging their paddles deep into the glistening water. In the distance, three kayaks in close formation picked their way cautiously along the south shore, changing direction suddenly to avoid a dinghy from one of the sailboats anchored illegally in midstream. An ancient tug named *Haida Chief* was nudging a barge of crushed limestone towards the cement-works' loading dock. I could feel it again, something changed in my perception of the city. The rhythm of work perhaps—or, more appropriately, the rhythm of work and play. I gathered up the plastic bags of groceries I'd deposited at the bottom of the ramp and made my way along the line of floats, whose loose planks and exposed wires had miraculously been attended to.

Back at the boat, Hank had stowed the survival suit in the rear locker, along with a smoke-bomb distress signal and two heavy-duty flares.

☀ Four

When I set out from False Creek under the Cambie, Granville and Burrard bridges, I phoned my aunt Doreen in West Vancouver. I could see her apartment in the distance and wanted to thank her for lunch and the items she'd given me a few days earlier, which included a diminutive set of camper's utensils—a spatula, a coiled eggbeater, and serving spoons—that looked as if they'd been made for children, plus a hand-held compass. I didn't need these relics, but they had belonged to Uncle Tom and held a special significance for me. It was one of those glorious Vancouver days, a dazzling performance, when the all-too-rare sunlight was showing off, outdoing itself by reflecting off the waters of English Bay and a million windows on shore, the kind of orgasmic moment that makes you forget all the small grievances you've ever harboured against a place. The kaleidoscopic colours—honey brick, plaster pastels, even the more brazen tones of recent townhouses and condos with their metal roofs—were somehow muted but radiant, as if emanating rather than merely reflecting light. Even the ugly human incursions—industry, tasteless subdivisions pushing the forest farther uphill, and countless box-shaped residences perched incongruously and precariously on cliff faces—seemed not just forgivable, but positively necessary, a vast collective tribute to the natural splendour of this amazing intersection of earth, air and water.

I described my position as carefully as I could and sat there waving stupidly for five minutes after I'd hung up, in order to give D'reen time to locate her binoculars. My squat little aquabus was pleasantly stuffed, bursting at the seams with supplies—books, crab trap, laptop computer, auxiliary anchor, cellphone—all the detritus of civilization, ready to take on the world, or least Howe Sound. Two freighters, the blue *Alaska Rainbow* of the Tokai Line and the *Lepta Mercury* of Panamanian registry, lay at anchor, high out of the water, awaiting permission to pick up cargo; the *Ever Gloria*, a Lauritzen bulker, swung on its chain, fully loaded and low in the stern, in line to discharge its bulk cargo. A hundred other craft of every description, beetling or careening this way and that, were busy plying the local waters, knitting a crazy fabric in the bay.

The original Atkinson Lighthouse, off my starboard bow, had been built in 1874 on a rocky headland jutting into the sea. It was replaced in 1914 with a taller structure, its great Cyclopean eye now 120 feet above water level. As with James, the young lad in Virginia Woolf's novel, my trip to the lighthouse had been delayed too long; it no longer had the same impact on me that it might have had when I was a boy, pointing out the exact spot where my grandfather's empty boat had been found nudging the rocks. I could see from Point Atkinson's odd shape and location, though, how turbulence would be inevitable here, the surge of water from Georgia Strait pulled in two directions, towards Burrard Inlet and Indian Arm or into the deep trench that forms Howe Sound.

The Point itself resembled an enormous foot disappearing into the water. Two lovers were seated high on the arch of this foot and, as the tide was out, two young boys were fishing down by the big toe. While I toyed with the idea of warning them about my grandfather's toothless body, still there waiting to be snagged, a harbour seal, whiskers and eyes just above the surface, was taking note of my slow passage. Another of Neptune's private eyes, his domed skull as curious and unexpected as a periscope, watching, always watching. Could my grandfather have been one of those selkies of legend who'd finally grown weary of the earth and of the awkwardness and humiliations of a human body, gladly exchanging it for his comfortable old sealskin? If so, these sleek creatures would be my relatives, second or third cousins. I waved at the seal just in case. The boys returned my greeting. The watcher, offended by such presumption and lack of decorum, dropped out of sight.

Perhaps my waxing rhapsodic about Vancouver had as much to do with leaving it, watching it recede into the distance. Although the city and its tentacles reach around the shoreline, filling every bay and precipice, the presence and scale of the coastal mountains—something so ancient, so elemental—tended to put these intrusions into perspective. Or so it seemed at 1300 hours.

I turned in to Howe Sound and cut the engine to a crawl so I could absorb every detail: bits of driftwood, a white styrofoam take-out container, two gulls buzzing *Groais* to look for discarded bait, a single cormorant flexing its muscles on the drying rocks, islands whose names were familiar to me— Passage, Bowen, Anvil, Gambier—the towering mountains of the eastern shore, along the base of which a rail line and narrow highway had been scratched, even new housing pasted onto nearby cliff faces. The eastern slope of Howe Sound is so steep it's subject to regular landslides and avalanches on the road leading to Whistler and the pulp mill at Woodfibre; beyond it lies an impassable jumble of mountains. The short stretch of road upcoast on the Sechelt Peninsula is accessible only by a ferry that runs from Horseshoe Bay to Gibsons Landing.

This was the area of the south coast I knew most intimately, having spent several summers there at Whytecliffe Park from age twelve to fifteen working at the boat rentals run by Uncle Tom. It was there, too, I learned to operate and maintain the small boats so much in demand by sport fishermen and joyriders, to troll for salmon, jig for cod, and to water-ski. Grandfather Turner and I once pulled up a ninety-pound ling cod off the reef at Whytecliffe, almost swamping the small rowboat as we tried to haul it over the stern. For me, those summers constituted an apprenticeship in paradise. I was so keen and loved the job so much, even at the starting salary of fifteen cents an hour plus room and board, I put in an eighty-hour week. Though clearly pleased with my industry and enthusiasm, my uncle put on a good show of being shocked when he had to cough up twelve dollars after my first week on the job.

I parked my gangly and shamelessly unpredictable body in the boathouse, which consisted of two small storage rooms where we kept tools, paint, rods, lures, engine parts, coils of rope and a bunk for me. The space, crowded and dark, was attached to changerooms for the park's occasional and intrepid swimmers. I spent a couple of futile, unpaid hours each week with one eye glued to a knot-hole in the wall adjoining the ladies' changeroom, hoping to glimpse the mysteries of the female form. My devotion and overtime efforts were rewarded by little more than slivers, a sore neck and temporarily impaired vision, leaving me as unstable as a drunk after I emerged into the sunlight and resumed my duties on the uneasy network of floats. In these last vestiges of innocence, and thanks to the constant winds that battered the small cove, or at least stirred it to a frenzy, I was, in the words of Walt Whitman, out of the cradle, endlessly rocking.

Presiding over this non-union sweatshop and hell-hole of

adolescent yearnings was T.T., my uncle and hero, Flying Officer Thomas Thompson Turner, terror of the skies, survivor of twenty-seven raids on enemy targets during the war, who'd parachuted from a flaming aircraft over Hamburg and resisted interrogation by repeating, like a mantra, only his name and serial number.

"My name is Thomas Turner, number J36305."

Smash.

"My name is . . ."

I worshipped my young uncle, with his wiry body, dashing mustache and quick wit, and secretly longed for his beautiful wife, Nancy, who managed Tom's accounts and the food concession in the park. While she can't have been thrilled to have an extra mouth to feed and an extra presence to clutter her busy life—an awkward, pimply-faced relative, to boot, rather than a local who would go home after work—Nancy was a good sport. I can see now, with my uncle's nervous problems and occasional disappearances, why she held a tighter rein than seemed necessary at the time. Running two businesses and a household, you didn't want sloppy work habits and costly mistakes. If she was a bit fierce, a bit remote, it was all the more rewarding when she smiled.

Tom taught me the ropes, literally and figuratively. The clove hitch, useful for mooring a boat to a dock, also for securing a rope to a spar or guard rail. I learned to splice rope, soaking up the sexually provocative terminology: whip each rope, unlay the strands, marry the two sections. Then the eye-splice, so essential for securing a bowline. Years later, when I spent a summer in the navy, my second-hand copy of the *Manual of Seamanship*, whose previous owner was someone named Marcel Cloutier, included the italicized warning: *"All splices reduce the strength of the rope by one-eighth."* Perhaps for my edification, Marcel had left a small Catholic greeting card inside the front cover, with a picture of Christ radiating light on the front and the words "Jesus I Have Faith in You" in French. Inside was a Christmas message dated 1957, and an invitation to participate in a series of religious services culminating in a midnight mass at a place called Montmartre Canadien, signed by André Godbout, A.A., Dir. The eye-splice, it seemed, like the eye of the needle, had its uses along with its limitations.

Under Tom's watchful eye, I cut bait, trimming the ragged herring filets so they resembled Cubist replicas of smaller fish, then scraped and painted hulls, applying copper anti-fouling paint to the bottom, the rental's trademark sky-blue to the sides and forest-green trim to the rest. Before long, I was allowed to take out the smaller clinker-built boats with their three-and-a-half horsepower Briggs and Stratton engines, and even to camp overnight in Tunstall Bay at the far end of Bowen Island with my fellow workers, Derek and Danny, whom Tom had dubbed Crane and Boone. Eventually, I graduated to the sleeker outboards until I was allowed to drive the eighteen-foot Sangster Craft known as the Drool, which had a cabin, a steeply flared bow and an engine strong enough to pull a water-skier. He even gave me driving lessons in an old army jeep, which could be seen careening down the incline to the boathouse in a cloud of dust, Tom at the wheel and Toughy, the mottled brown boxer with black markings that was his constant companion, seated with unwavering self-importance in the passenger seat, chin up, like a presiding general.

Honest and hard-working, when the rental season was over Tom would do a variety of odd jobs, including coal delivery in Vancouver or cutting Christmas trees in Washington and Oregon. Although he inspired my respect, there was a ruthlessness in him as well that had to do with the ethos of the coast and his wartime experiences, two worlds dominated by men and guns. He did not hesitate to shoot seals, viewed at that time mainly as predators on the diminishing salmon stocks. He once shot and mounted a bald eagle, which thereafter sat on top of the television in silent disapproval, not only of the low quality of programming in the 1950s, but also of all human proceedings. I still recall the fierceness of its eyes, its beak dramatically hooked for ripping flesh, and the size of the talons clutching the wooden spar so cleverly installed by the taxidermist. I don't suppose it occurred to Tom that in destroying this magnificent specimen, he was re-enacting his own fate in the sky over Hamburg. I shared his worldview, for a time, and was quite capable of filling a frozen herring full of nails, tossing it out to the scavenging gulls, and watching to see how long the prizewinner could stay aloft.

A few months before he succumbed to a second bout with lung cancer, I wrote a poem about Tom that addressed this culture of violence we had shared. I had no idea that he was now terminally ill. I had been recalling with shame a scene in 1954 of the two of us bouncing across Howe Sound in pursuit of a solitary killer whale that had been sighted earlier, me at the helm, waves breaking across the bow of *The Drool*, 30-30 shell casings clicking off the deck and into the chuck as Tom fired a dozen rounds at the retreating animal. When I arrived at Tom and D'reen's place near Schooner Cove just north of Nanaimo on Vancouver Island, I was not prepared for the news that the cancer had returned.

I could hardly bear to see how his body had changed, his epic stature eroded by time and disease. I was startled, too, to see how closely his physical shape and facial hair resembled that of my brother, Jim.

"I can't complain. I've had a good one." He looked up at me apologetically.

I have a photograph of Tom in full flying gear—helmet, gloves, sheepskin jacket, and parachute—standing in front of the nose of a Lancaster bomber. He's grinning, a kid pleased to pose with a favourite toy, fearless. And yet he spent his entire life after the war carrying in his body pieces of shifting shrapnel as reminders of that time, not to mention the recurring nightmares that would eventually cripple him: "Elevation: 11,900 feet. John, mid-upper gunner hit. Pilot to navigator, pilot to navigator, there's one closing in at five o'clock, guns blazing, zipping the flight jacket to hold in John's guts, Vic bailing out without a chute, Mel riding the goddamn Lanc to the end, sixteen thousand-pounders and half a tank of fuel." These notes are from the brief "history" he gave me years earlier at a time when the memories wouldn't stop. What troubled him most were not the air raids, but having killed a young German soldier during an attempted escape.

As the war ground to a halt, Tom's group of POWs were moved to another location. During this forced march, he and Howie, the only other surviving member of his flight crew, slipped out of line and disappeared into a heavily wooded area. They picked their way cautiously through the bushes at some distance from each other, but Howie's movements were spotted by a young soldier, who stopped him at gunpoint and rattled away at him in German. Tom crept up behind the soldier, covered his mouth with one hand, and pulled him back onto a home-made blade, holding him until his punctured lung had filled with blood. It was all very well to say, Hell, you had orders to try to escape and that's what happens in wartime. Tom knew that, but he also knew that he and Howie, realizing they had no hope of escaping, had slipped back in amongst the straggling marchers and that their little "adventure" had been pointless.

I read the poem as T.T. and D'reen sat on the couch listening.

It was all I could do to stumble over the words. My uncle had changed. Wisdom and tact had made short shrift of the stuffed eagle. As Tom drew closer to his own death, even fishing for salmon lost its appeal. He shook his head at the image I'd called up in my poem and shifted uneasily in his seat, as if those shell casings fired at the killer whale had finally merged with the flak forever moving in his back and shoulders.

I cut the engine and drifted past Garrow Bay and Whytecliffe, thinking of Uncle Tom and our mutual legacy. Of the clichés that endure, I thought, the ones regarding civilization's thin veneer are hardest to shake off, for their persistence is in direct proportion to the residue of truth they contain. Call it the primitive self, the impulses that drive us to destroy nature and each other have not diminished, despite education, science, health care, computers and all the niceties. I was as much a part of this process as anyone else—the logging companies, Britannia Bay Copper, Shell Oil, and all the ever-increasing gang at exterminate-dot-com. I carried the guilt-bundle with me wherever I went.

While I was waiting for Bruce and Karen to finish their restoration work on *Groais*, I had made a three-week trip to Germany, where I was scheduled to read my poems and talk about Canadian literature in cities of the former Hanseatic League, including Bremen, Rostock, and Greifswald. My friend Gustav Klaus, principal host and organizer, lived in Bremen but taught in Rostock, in the former East Germany, making the three-hour trip twice weekly. My uncle was very much with me during this trip, as his stories of bombing German targets had made an indelible impression on me as a child. Tom was not loquacious or boastful, but the stories extracted from him were disturbingly graphic, especially the firebombing of Hamburg. Gustav, my age, a lefty who hated the Nazi legacy, was seated by the window as we wound our way by train through a rebuilt Hamburg, the tracks banked for safety and comfort. I felt a terrible urge to confess to this gentle scholar, a specialist in Scottish and British literature, especially works of fiction that related to labour, that my uncle had bombed and been shot down over Hamburg.

I was staying with Gustav, his French wife Lidia, and their two gorgeous children. Rafi, seven at the time, spoke little English, so we communicated mostly in French. Before his father and I caught the train, Rafi had presented me with a paper mock-up of a computer game that involved pockets and graduated paper slips you could slide in and out, varying in mood and design from a benign sun and happy-face to a tragic mask below the rough approximation of a rain cloud. I could see the corner of it in my shoulder bag protruding from a copy of Vladimir Nabokov's autobiography, *Speak, Memory*, the account of a privileged and exceptional Russian existence, remote from Gustav's social realism but imbued with brilliant, intricately woven insights into life and lepidoptera. As we came in full view of the river, on the dazzling waters of which were playing the early morning shadows of post-war commercial buildings, neither my uncle nor Nabokov seemed quite suitable subjects for conversation. Suddenly, Gustav sat bolt upright as if he had been reading my mind.

"I can never forgive the Allies for what they did to Hamburg." He gesticulated wildly, waving his arms and pointing out the window at the river, where two motorized barges were passing in the distance beneath a second bridge. "The firebombing was deliberate. People leapt into the river to save themselves, but the surface of the water was aflame with burning petrol. It was hell." Then, embarrassed, he fell silent and busied himself adding milk and sugar to tea in a styrofoam cup.

It was as if I'd pulled the wrong slip of paper in Rafi's game and come up with the tragic muse and the rain cloud. I wished there were something I could say to ease the situation. Gustav and Lidia had graciously taken me the night before to a public reading by Günter Grass, just prior to his being awarded the Nobel Prize in literature. It was a sold-out affair at the concert hall in Bremen. Gustav tried to translate for me, but I shook my head. I sat next to my friends, listening to the music of the German language, all those gutturals falling on the English-speaking ear like a familiar organ base. I didn't understand a word, but I kept track of several poems Grass read and looked them up later in *novemberland*, in a translation by Michael Hamburger. Poem after harrowing poem, with a few breaks for comic relief, warns against forgetting and complacency, against undue pride in a reunited Germany. "Gale Warning," a sonnet, reminds us of how easily the "general madness" of fascism could erupt again as a result of something as simple as a sustained change in the climate of Europe, where, fuelled by fears of race, drugs, AIDS and the unknown, Germany's self-hatred might once again turn outward.

It was an experience I'd like to have shared with Uncle Tom.

I made myself a peanut butter sandwich and looked with astonishment at Whytecliffe as *Groais* and I drifted past. There had once been a Union Steamships dock here, when my mother was alive, with regular passenger service to Bowen Island; and, atop the rock, a large dine-and-dance hall called Cliffhouse, where I'd stood outside in the dark as a teenager, like Heathcliff peering in the windows of Thrushcross Grange, listening to music and laughter, watching the couples' elegant bodies move in perfect synchronicity. Cliff-house had been lost to fire a few years later. I knew the rental business had folded too, but I had not expected to find the cove deserted, stripped of buildings, not even a creosoted piling in sight: the pier, the boathouse with its herring strips and naked ghosts in bath towels, all gone, as if the sea level had risen to cover a lost world, or a tsunami had swept it all into the sea.

Something about Howe Sound seems to defy human effort. The very scale of the place made Uncle Tom and his fledgling enterprise seem almost heroic. Now both were gone and in their place was a dedicated park, with plastic-covered lecture boards describing local flora and fauna, as well as official benches. Howe Sound, on the other hand, remained not only a place to swallow dreams, a vast fjord ringed by high moun-tains with water a thousand feet deep in places, but also the graveyard of countless ships. I was passing over the very spot where Union Steamships' *Lady Cynthia* collided with the *Dola*, a large wooden steam tug, 109 feet long, on October 29, 1953, only six weeks after I had returned to school in Vancou-ver. The *Dola* was towing a barge of railway cars north to Squamish and had just passed Atkinson Light in the fog. She could hear the *Cynthia*'s horn, but had little manoeuvrability and had obviously misjudged distance, speed and direction. *Lady Cynthia*, more ruthless than her name might suggest, had a bad sea record; she had rammed and sunk the *Cowichan*, a large steel ship 157 feet long, off Sechelt Light in 1925. And three years before the Whytecliffe incident, she had struck and sunk the *A. L. Bryant*, a forestry vessel, off Snug Cove, with the loss of three lives. Perhaps the captains of the *Lady Cynthia* felt themselves immortal, or invincible, in their fast, sleek ship with its knife-like bow. Thanks to a quick, last-minute spin of the wheel by First Mate Montgomery on board the *Dola*, the *Cynthia*'s bow struck just aft of the boiler room. The ships remained engaged long enough for the crew to scramble aboard the *Cynthia* before the doomed tug slipped free and sank in six hundred feet of water, but not before crew members on the barge had detached the towline.

Vancouver poet Pat Lowther found this stark terrain less awesome than I do, even "companionable," and was able, in her poetry, to describe the jagged peaks, blunt proclivities, and plunging slopes of the Coast Range as if they were nothing more than the eccentricities of an old friend: "they sputter with / billygoat-bearded creeks / bumsliding down / to splat into the sea." The music and sound and imaging in those few lines demonstrate a loving attention to coastal detail that has never been surpassed. For Lowther, the mountains were intractable, undeniably *there*, beyond metaphor and beyond art. And she was not alone in her vision of the land. Maggie Kyle, in Jack Hodgins' novel *The Invention of the World*, observes the Vancouver Island mountains from a small plane on her return from Ireland and is stunned to notice how thin is the strip of human habitation. The pilot, a new Canadian, claims to see the "real island" pushing through. Maggie imagines this is how it looked to Cook, to which the pilot replies: "Cook did not see it from a plane, but yes, yes, you are right, it hasn't changed. That's what real is, that's what true is, it can be hid but it can't be changed."

Both theories are subjective assertions of the sort we manufacture to help us understand a seemingly hostile or indifferent world, but they certainly don't stand up to careful scrutiny. Even since Cook's first visit in 1763, shorelines have altered and the Mendenal Glacier in Juneau has retreated six miles. The Coast Range and Vancouver Island mountains are constantly changing as a result of continental drift, glaciers, or climatic erosion; and the whole shebang is underscored by a seething pot of molten lava looking for the least excuse to relieve some pressure. What was happening in this vast waterway—incremental, hardly noticeable, but long-range, and perhaps irreversible—was neither benign nor stationary.

Although Howe Sound gives the impression of being pristine and largely uninhabited, a convenient chunk of wilderness except for half a dozen small communities and sporadic summer homes, human encroachment has been steady and significant to the point where salmon fishing is banned in the summer months and shellfish are prohibited year-round, as a result of emissions from the pulp mill and chemical contamination leaking from the abandoned Britannia Copper Mine. According to my daughter Bronwen, my chief source on matters environmental, a developer has proposed making the mine a major dumping ground for toxic wastes, as that would generate the revenue needed by government to make the site truly safe, a logic that rivals the story of the American officer in the Vietnam War who said it was necessary to destroy the village in order to save it.

Whether chummy or red in tooth and claw, as the afternoon drew to a close, nature seemed analogous to the human condition, where violence is capable of erupting at any moment. It's as dangerous to think of nature as indestructible or eternally self-renewing as it is to create a simulacrum of innocence around human behaviour. When Bill McKibben, whose book *The End of Nature* appeared ten years ago, was asked recently if he hadn't exaggerated the situation, he said, "We are no longer able to think of ourselves as a species tossed about by larger forces—now we are those larger forces."

It would have been the understatement of the week to say I was feeling vulnerable and confused. The past, its landmarks, and so many of those I loved had been erased. What had happened to the glorious day I'd started out with? It had turned turtle. Like the fog-bound skippers of the *Dola* and *Lady Cynthia*, I should have seen it coming; you can't process painful moments from your private or collective past without stirring up the pot. There is no short cut home, no Northwest Passage. You can, I suppose, if you're a certain type of person, ignore it all or decide to dance in the grave-yard, keeping in mind Earle Birney's words: "There is no fog but in the will, / the iceberg is elective." For me, and for my troubled uncle, however, the issues were more complex, the fog not so easily dispelled.

I rounded the point into Horseshoe Bay and brought *Groais* alongside the floats at Sewell's Marina, the one business surviving from my childhood, thanks to the growth of the Whistler ski area and the continued patronage of B.C. Ferries. I phoned my cousin Mike and wangled an invitation to dinner; he warned me not to expect too much since they had a three-week-old baby and a thirteen-month-old daughter to keep them on their toes. When I arrived, D'reen was there as well, having driven out from West Vancouver after I spoke to her on my cellphone from the boat. She was seated on the couch, all smiles, laden with new life, basking in her role as grandmother. When I mentioned my shock at seeing Whyte-cliffe stripped of all familiar sights, she told me there was a metal plaque bearing Uncle Tom's name on one of the park benches. I looked at D'reen, her own vulnerabilities, includ-ing those difficult final years with Tom, so close to the surface. His restlessness and insecurity had prompted at least four moves in a single decade, one of them to a trailer camp. Although she realized, as well as I did, that a plaque on a park bench was not much of a memento for so busy, complex, and tumultuous a life, she was doing her best to cheer me up.

"Nothing fancy, just his name." She used a Kleenex to wipe some drool from the baby's chin and replaced the soother that had fallen onto her lap. "By the way, I saw you sail past this morning after you called."

"Did you see me waving?"

"No, but I saw your bright red sails, just beyond the super-tanker. I was very impressed."

I smiled. My sails were dirty white and I didn't have the heart to tell her I'd motored all the way to Horseshoe Bay.

✳ Five

When my friend Lewis and I motored out of Porteau Cove Marine Park, between Horseshoe Bay and Squamish, Howe Sound was socked in with low-lying fog, rendering the world intimate and claustrophobic. The blunt top of Anvil Island was barely visible on our right above the cloud-bank, but a light drizzle was threatening to wash it all away before noon. In our huge slickers and rubber boots, we looked like ads for Captain High Liner cod filets or Fisherman's Friend cough lozenges. I'd been hesitating for an hour since breakfast, thinking about the *Lady Cynthia* and all the other fog-induced disasters I'd read about in *Shipwrecks of British Columbia*. Lewis was all for venturing forth.

"Fog is not a killer item," Lewis said. He was quoting a pilot, David Hoover, one of his sources for the new book he'd written called *Plane Talk*, a compilation of aviation vocabulary, slang and lore, of which he'd just given me an inscribed copy. Lewis, a retired colleague from Concordia University, is a lexicographer, a gatherer of words. He began his secondary career with the *South Shore Phrase Book*, a collection of Nova Scotia idioms and expressions. This was followed by *Hockey Talk* and *Car Talk*. Lewis was a genuine packrat when it came to language, but his colleagues had never warmed to his efforts, which they viewed as quirky and far too popular for the groves of academe.

"If fog isn't a killer item, what is?" I had one eye on the strip chart for Howe Sound and the Sunshine Coast and the other on the few landmarks still poking through this gauze curtain of mist.

"A mountain is a killer item."

Mountains didn't scare me out here, unless they were the stunted, underwater kind; it was other boats. I was sipping my second cup of cowboy coffee, brewed in a saucepan because I'd forgotten to buy a percolator. "Fog *is* a killer, Lewis, and I've got just the book to prove it. Page after page of exempla."

Lewis was standing on the stern pulpit, a rectangular teak grid mounted on a stainless-steel frame behind the cockpit, and puffing on a cigarette. In all that raingear, he looked like a medieval monk, eyes lost in the shadow of his cowl. I could see only nose, mustache, and cigarette, but I could detect amusement in his voice. In addition to guarding the word-hoard, he was a teacher of Victorian literature. Tennyson, never far from mind, was suddenly served up to three surf scoters having a tête-à-tête on the dull, grey waters off Britannia Beach:

Sunset and evening star,
  And one clear call for me!
And may there be no moaning at the bar,
  When I put out to sea...

Twilight and evening bell,
  And after that the dark!
And may there be no sadness of farewell,
  When I embark.

The scoters, also known as skunk ducks, were demanding critics. They turned away unimpressed, shaking their orange-lined bills and white head-patches in disapproval. As they were headed in the direction of Keats Island, I assumed their tastes ran to the Romantic poets rather than the earnest and pompous Victorians.

I told Lewis about Möbius, my private orca guide, pacing me between the South Arm and North Arm of the Fraser. He nodded his head, but I knew he didn't believe me. I turned off the engine and coasted in the fog so I could listen for other boats, then let off a couple of short blasts of my new portable compressed-air foghorn. I waited for a reply, but none came, except for a couple of crows no doubt fighting over the right to our remains.

"If this pea-soup gets any thicker, we'll be needing a sky pilot."

Lewis and I were raised in the church and had both contemplated the ministry; I'd even done a stint in the navy that could have led to a commission as chaplain, a regimental "sky pilot," so-called for their skills in spiritual navigation. I couldn't master celestial navigation, never mind the other kind. Besides, I had no use for the mindless regimentation and hierarchical mentality of the military, although I could understand their uses in wartime. In my ill-fitting naval uniform and silly hat, I looked more like Charlie Chaplin than a repository of spiritual wisdom. Lewis had rebelled somewhat earlier, though it was taking him a lifetime to shed the toxic residues of fundamentalism. His father was a Methodist missionary who took his family to Africa, but did not get on well with his associates—too much enthusiasm, perhaps—and was sent back to the U.S. This stern and narrow legacy is what Lewis had been fighting. It was something I could identify with, as my own teenage years had been devoted to the frenzied rituals and narrow-mindedness of a Baptist church in Vancouver.

"The fog is lifting."

"Of course." Having completed his homily to the birds and

chucked his cigarette in the drink, Lewis descended from pulpit to cockpit. A final cloud of smoke emerged from within his cowl like a speech bubble. "I've been keeping a close watch, so we wouldn't go Tango Uniform."

"What's that?"

"A phonic code alternative used by air crew in the face of disaster, so that passengers won't understand. It actually means 'tits up.'"

My aim was to cover the seventy-five-mile distance from Howe Sound to Westview during the three remaining days with Lewis. The leisurely pace enabled us to spend a night at Gibsons Landing, where I shopped for essentials, including clothespins, an AM-FM radio and a can of WD-40 oil to coat the folding bicycle I had foolishly brought along and which was slowly rusting away fifty feet astern, where it reclined in the dinghy like a drunken minor dignitary in a parade to which no one had come. The chores done, we'd had a huge dinner at Molly's Reach, site of "The Beachcombers," a long-running television series that, along with the federal government's Local Initiatives Program, had done much to foster the view that the good life could still be had in beautiful British Columbia. All you needed was an old boat, a good eye for lost boom logs, and a heart of gold. Young and old, with ponytails, liver spots or both, flocked west; and draft dodgers had fled north across the border from the ethos and recruiting arm of the Vietnam War. This summer, three decades later, at century's end, the myth of the good life remained undispelled, not by the recession in B.C., not even by the collapse of the Asian economies. Every day a new horde of barbarians from the rest of Canada descended from the mountains in convoys of SUVs, Winnebagos and moving vans, credit cards at the ready, while weekly, on remote beaches of the north coast, Chinese illegals were being unceremoniously dumped by the boatload.

What brings them all here? Words. Not just the single word "freedom," but a whole bevy of words, including "beauty," "opportunity," "climate" (meaning mild weather), and "wilderness." As surely as it was destroying what they signified, British Columbia was frantically using the signifiers to advertise its attractions to populations of the world who once thought the Lake District, the Scottish Highlands or the Black Forest the epitome of rugged, unspoiled nature. I quizzed Lewis about the power of names as we alternated between fishing and sailing up the coast past Sechelt in the bright sunlight. The area extending from Gibsons Landing to Pender Harbour was an interesting case in point. Thanks to the population explosion in Vancouver and to a very clever ad campaign, this expanse of remote cabins, summer cottages, and damp, inaccessible hamlets, affectionately known as the Raincoast, had been transformed into a bustling and expensive resort and retirement area with regular ferry service. The key factor had been the changing of its name to the Sunshine Coast. Some locals swore the name change had actually improved the weather, producing more sunny days; others argued that the new perspective helped residents accentuate the positive, to think of their climatic glass as half full rather than half empty. Nursing a second beer, Lewis gazed past me at the explosion of cottages and marinas this magic act had spawned. A veritable sea change—and all linked to ceremonial renaming.

"In the beginning was the Word." Lewis gestured towards the approaching shoreline with its naked arbutus extending out over the rocks. "Look at this place. It's amazing, even without words."

We were easing our way into Smuggler Cove, a protected

basin with anchorage for a dozen boats. At the narrow entrance, there was a ten-foot clearance on each side of the boat. An officially designated marine park, picture-postcard stuff. With sternlines to shore to prevent rubbing, the seven boats at anchor were so close they might as well have been rafting or pulled up in the marina for painting. Three women were sunbathing between the masts of a ketch, their pale yellow bikinis so thin and transparent it seemed as if nature had once again triumphed over art. The one in the middle sat up to examine the intruders, adjusting an imaginary shoulder strap.

"And the Word became flesh and dwelt amongst us." Always the dedicated naturalist, Lewis disappeared into the cabin for his camera.

"Hang on, Lewis. Secret Cove's just around the bend."

"The cove I'm yearning for is no secret."

While Lewis contemplated the sublime, I was taking note of the submerged reef, adorned with purple starfish and fronds of kelp, looming like a leviathan a few feet from the hull.

Secret Cove produced at least three surprises: an amazing display of jagged reefs, the Jolly Roger Restaurant and a stunning waitress with a gap-toothed smile. There was nothing piratical about the place, not even the prices, although Lewis and I, unkempt and unshaven for three days, looked as if we'd been press-ganged and keelhauled. Beauty the Waitress seemed unperturbed; a hook in lieu of an arm or a knife between our teeth would not have fazed her.

"Hi, guys. Made up your minds yet?" Minds? After two days on the water, we were as blank-brained as the clams we ordered.

I was glad to be eating out again. With Lewis on board, I'd tried my hand at preparing a complete meal at anchor in

Porteau Cove, a modest spaghetti sauce and salad. The entire sleeping, cooking and lounge area of *Groais* was so small it made a bachelor apartment seem like the Taj Mahal, so even this simple task proved to be a challenge. I cooked on a small two-burner stove, about the same size as a Coleman camper's special, which burned methyl-hydrate, a safe and nearly odourless fuel. This involved lifting the hinged lid off to light two small fuel tanks, each slightly wider than a shepherd's pie and with a three-inch diameter hole covered with a rubbery, non-combustible patch when not in use, to keep the fuel from evaporating. Because of pressure from the spring-latch that held the contraption down, sometimes one of the patches would stick to the bottom of the stove lid and I wouldn't notice I'd doused the flame until it became obvious that the only thing coming to a boil was my temper.

The surface in which the stove was recessed consisted of a small counter space two feet deep and four feet wide, with two removable square lids providing access to compact storage lockers underneath for dishes and such cooking items as vinegar, olive oil and anything you didn't want knocked over or flying across the cabin during a storm. The lockers were useful but a nuisance, always covered with food and supplies when you needed something from below. The alternative— preparing food on the engine cover—presented its own hazards and drawbacks, one of which was that you could only enter or exit the cabin by gripping the hatch cover, tucking up the lower body and executing a Tarzan swing over the disputed culinary territory, a manoeuvre that was likely to result in an ass in the salad.

While Lewis talked to me about retirement life in Montreal, I had sautéed onions and garlic for the spaghetti sauce and begun the makings of a salad, with fresh tomatoes and red peppers from the market in Horseshoe Bay and, as a splurge, an expensive can of hearts of palm. Every available surface was jammed, including the engine cover, where the cutting board balanced on top of a small pot. There was sufficient headroom in the cabin, but not where the ceiling tapered over the galley, so I had to keep a small corner of one step clear as a seat, to use when my back got sore from bending over. In the background, Barbara Budd was interviewing an immigration lawyer on CBC radio in connection with the most recent boatload of illegals from China. The water had come to a rapid boil, so I dropped the spaghetti in and watched it surrender its stiffness in response to the moisture, heat and enthusiasm of the water. The table was set with a new yellow cloth; the spaghetti sauce was bubbling happily; and the salad, with its greens, reds and myriad white buttons of palm, looked like a work of art.

I reached for the bottle of Merlot to top up our glasses. As this was by now a familiar gesture, I scarcely glanced up or noticed the arc of my hand as, misguided by the reading portion of my bifocals, it swung around and struck the neck of the bottle, setting off a series of reactions that tipped the cutting board off its perch and onto the side of the stainless steel salad bowl, which responded gracefully by depositing its colourful contents on the lower step and floor of the cabin.

"And would you call that a wise move," Barbara Budd interrupted her radio guest to ask, "especially under the circumstances?" No, I thought, but at least I understand now why the dining area on board is called a mess.

Everything was shipshape at the Jolly Roger, including dinner and Beauty the Waitress, pouring the last of the wine.

"And the boat?" Lewis asked, after ordering another bottle and laying waste to his main course of salmon, green beans and artichoke hearts. His appetite had shifted once again to words. "How did *Groais* acquire its unusual name?"

The first owners, Chris and Anni Law, I explained, were a

Cape Breton dentist and doctor who had bought the boat from Terry Erskine's shipyard in Plymouth, England, and sailed it to Canada, with the intention of naming it after their first landfall, which turned out to be the Grey Islands off the east coast of Newfoundland, referred to on certain charts as *les Groais Isles*, a Norman or Breton variation of the French word *gris*. It's not an easy word to wrap your mouth around, but should probably be pronounced in the French manner with emphasis on the second syllable, and with a little Canadianized question at the end: *Gro-éh?* It's more likely to elicit "Gross," even "Grow-Ass." I follow the previous owner's habit of saying "Gro-iss." Lewis asked if I'd ever considered changing the name. I said I was usually far too busy cursing the boat or thinking of pulling the plug and letting it sink to the bottom of Malaspina Strait to join my grandfather's false teeth.

I said I couldn't rename *Groais* because I was superstitious, that changing a boat's name brings bad luck. The Orkney pirate John Gow changed the name of a ship he'd stolen; it was recognized and he was hanged from the gallows in Wapping. I'd read that during the Second World War, the American vessel *Yorkton* was given to the Canadian navy, refitted in Victoria and renamed the HMCS *Orkney*, which uses as many of the original letters as possible. As far as I know, this proved a lucky name change, as the ship survived the war; and the people of Yorkton, Saskatchewan (with a little town called Orkney nearby), adopted the ship and supplied it with parcels of socks, record players and sundry items for the comfortable exercise of vigilance upon the sea, if, as I was beginning to wonder, comfort at sea is possible. I knew the story because the father of my friend Colin Browne had been *Orkney*'s first commander.

Since Sir Francis Drake, with an eye to posterity and

fame—and perhaps a nod to piratical booty—had changed the name of the *Pelican* to the *Golden Hind* during his circumnavigation of the globe, I supposed I could change the name of my own Golden Hind sloop. But I liked the boat's history and had grown fond of its unusual name; besides, a friend, John Steffler, an adoptive Newfie, had spent a summer on the Grey Islands, writing a book of poems of that title that blends his own camping experiences with an imaginary history of the islands' early inhabitants. The name had definitely earned its place in legend; far be it from me to tamper with history or fate.

I read Lewis my most recent e-mail message from Chris Law, one in which he extolled the virtues of *Groais*. He described how the boat had "dutifully looked after three very seasick, apprehensive neophytes as she barrelled across the Bay of Biscay in a whole gale on her maiden voyage wid very likkle help from us. Took six days to 'find' Spain but she did it!!!! Carried me across the North Atlantic solo when I wuz still larnin' the ropes . . . thru a knockdown . . . a frightening tropical storm . . . and thru tickker fog in the shipping lanes for 6 days on my return to Kanada. I cut my cruising teeth on *Groais I*." Chris was writing, of course, on a laptop in the cabin of *Groais II*, which he and Anni were sailing again to the north coast of Labrador, a region he referred to as "Iceberg Alley," only weeks after he'd lost a thumb on board.

"Jolly, to be sure," Lewis slurred as we staggered out of the restaurant, bestowing imaginary kisses and too large a tip on Beauty, "but a bit thin on the rogering." Beer, wine and two scotches on the rocks had restored our faith in humanity, even in language, though you wouldn't have suspected this from the quality of our articulation. We had solved the world's problems. Our only task now, navigating the dinghy in the dark, was staying *off* the rocks.

Lewis was in good form on the first portion of our trip from Secret Cove to Pender Harbour, another windless, sunny day. He noted on the strip charts the full range of our literary landscapes ahead, from Atwood Point to Agamemnon Channel, and lamented that tomorrow, pressed for time, we'd reluctantly bypass the entrance to Jervis Inlet. He'd been feeling adrift and out of sorts since retiring. Adding to the problems of navigation and staying afloat, his girlfriend had suddenly changed the romantic rules of the road and he didn't know what to make of it. He'd put on a brave enough face, but the beer had given it away. Now he was toying with the idea of writing his own memoir: the African years. It had a nice ring to it. He'd also made a list of the names of boats we'd encountered and appeared to be working on his own philosophy of naming.

"Listen to these," he said, reciting a dozen names. "*Dream Boat, Betty J., Integrity, Native Chief, Naughty-Yachty*. And here's my favourite: *French Kiss*, with a tender named *Smooch*. What is naming but the expression of a desire, an assertion of power, the evocation of a loved one or a place? Or simply the wish to appear clever or sophisticated in the eyes of the minuscule portion of mankind that pays attention to boats? In naming a boat, you isolate something life itself has in short supply, but which the time at sea may restore." Lewis was on a roll. I could see another book in the offing: *Boat Talk*, or *Floaters I Have Known*.

Names. The previous summer I'd gone to Saint John, New Brunswick, to give a keynote address at a conference organized around the idea of region and nation. I'd been thinking about Canada, its short, neurotic history, and what constituted a good, or appropriate, name for such a vast and varied place. After examining what Senator Keith Spicer would have found if he'd taken his own advice and consulted the poets before writing his controversial and largely ignored report on current constitutional negotiations in Canada, I concluded my talk with a quotation from Brazilian philosopher and social activist Paolo Freire: "To exist, humanly, is to name the world, to change it. Once named, the world in its turn reappears to the namers as a problem and requires of them a *new naming*. . . . There is no true word that is not at the same time a praxis. Thus, to speak a true word is to transform the world." Canada, I suggested, requires a new naming; the whole shebang might be renamed Quebec, which would solve one problem. We might also start by imagining a new flag, with half a maple leaf and half a fleur-de-lis joined in the middle section and each of the two red end-panels containing a single eagle feather, so it appeared that Canada, as we know it, is contained within the parentheses (and by the permission) of the First Nations.

British Columbia seemed even more in need of a new name. The earliest mapmakers, whose imaginations were usually more reliable than their sources, depicted present-day British Columbia in the oddest of ways—as a hanging appendage much like a blown-up version of the Alaska panhandle; as a vast blob or goitre protruding from the side of the continent; or as a protean, shape-shifting impediment to Asia that would best be ignored if only it would reveal the exact location of its mythical Strait of Anian, otherwise known as the Northwest Passage. Drake had called the region from California north New Albion. On one map it's called, simply, Russian Possessions. The Spanish, who named every nook and cranny just as fastidiously and ruthlessly as the English did, refer to it on one map simply as La Costa de Norte America. Would my grandfather have drowned, I wondered, if the name Punta de

Bodega had survived, rather than Point Atkinson? The Americans called the region, variously, Greater Oregon, then Oregon and Columbia. Even the great satirist Jonathan Swift had a go at it, choosing this as the site of Brobdingnag, the land of friendly giants in *Gulliver's Travels*. The inhabitants of this land, on hearing of the warlike propensities of Europeans, had pronounced them "the most pernicious race of little odious vermin" on earth, a fictional insight that was to prove prophetic.

The prevailing view of Canada's westernmost province, which has been described as gloomy, sublime, racist, sterile, utopian, hostile, polarized, even fun, is still very much a blend of fact and fiction, a sort of California North, a lotus-land of hot tubs and hotheads, a resource exploiter's paradise or a last great wilderness getaway which is unfortunately plagued by socialists, idealists, and other pesky natives.

Somewhere between Secret Cove and Pender Harbour, Lewis had run out of words. He remained silent when I challenged him to come up with a new name for the province.

"What should we call it, Lewis? You're the keeper of the word-hoard. I have in mind something elegantly post-colonial."

He was trying to use the boom cradle to frame a photograph. A portion of Georgia Strait was still visible to the southwest, bounded by the mountains of Vancouver Island and capable of swallowing any number of names. A full barge of sawdust was being hauled north to the pulp mill in Powell River. The tugboat, out of sight behind Lasqueti Island, appeared to have abandoned its charge, whose square lines and conical peak of sawdust seemed as isolated and incongruous as a solitary railway station in the middle of the Prairies. I rephrased my question.

"How about Brutish Columbia?"

Lewis was in pain again. Navigating the unfamiliar territory of late—and post-feminist—middle age was taking its toll. His response surprised me.

"I like the British designation," he said, stretching out across the cabin to frame the image he wanted. "It's the last vestige of empire and therefore rather camp. The term 'British' is hardly used any more and 'United Kingdom' is unravelling as we sail. Keep it, it's quaint."

Several hours had passed since I put Lewis on the early bus from Westview/Powell River to Vancouver. I was sorry to see him go, but anxious to get on with the trip ahead. Down in the harbour, several large powerboats were heading out, as well as a motor launch named *Mission Control*. A young boy, not much older than my grandson Jeremy, was standing at attention in the bow in a red tracksuit, ready to hoist the jib and main, his father in a matching outfit at the helm. I was hoping to get my own mission under control, but first I had all these ghosts to attend to on Texada Island. We'd had the reverse gear fixed before leaving Secret Cove, then stopped at Pender Harbour long enough for a visit to Uncle Tom's cousin Bill Turner and his wife Doris. While Lewis stayed on board and finished off the beer, Bill went through his albums, yarding out old photographs he knew would mean nothing to his own kids, including several priceless shots of my mother.

Having a lexicographer on board, I'd been preoccupied with how we use words, as well as paintings and photographs, to construct our view of nature, including our place in it, configuring it with various codes: tame or wild, empty or inhabited, cultivated or raw, commodity or sacred place, heaven or hell. The messages were mixed, as Bruce Hutchison suggested in

1953: "The history of Canada for about three hundred years has been a struggle to escape from the wilderness, and for the last half-century has been a desperate attempt to escape into it." My own definition of wilderness had always had less to do with wild nature, or rugged landscapes, than with those barren reaches of the country where you couldn't pick up the stations of CBC radio, the intrepid Barbara Budd notwithstanding. Lewis and I had talked about our shared interest in the works of Howard O'Hagan, especially his novel *Tay John*, which O'Hagan had struggled to write during a summer on Bowen Island, in a cabin owned by Senator Eugene Forsey and his wife. After several days of staring at the waters of Howe Sound, his mind as blank as the page, O'Hagan had turned his writing desk to face the wall. Then not just words, but the *idea* of words, began to come. It was very much a novel about language, about ways in which words and stories shape and impinge on our lives.

The narrator, a remittance man named Jack Denham, tries to describe what was happening in the Rockies during the great period of railway building, when the word "progress" was very much in the air and Canadians, Americans and Europeans were pouring into the region in the wake of the railway, stunned by the scale of the mountains and equally mesmerized by the commercial opportunities that seemed to lie before them. If a Northwest Passage had failed to materialize, it would surely be forged overland on tracks of steel. In the Rockies, man's rush to discover and colonize had left him unprepared for wilderness; he seemed to have outrun not only his own shadow, but also language itself, plunging into a region without boundaries and without names:

A country where no man has stepped before is new in the real sense of the word, as though it had just been made, and when you turn your back upon it you feel that it may drop back again into the dusk that gave it being. It is only your vision that holds it in the known and created world. It is physically exhausting to look on unnamed country. A name is the magic to keep it within the horizons. Put a name to it, put it on a map, and you've got it. The unnamed—it is the darkness unveiled.

The Rockies weren't "unnamed country," any more than the West Coast was unnamed prior to the arrival of Europeans. The mountains and inlets didn't need the foreign labels, the imperial naming, to make them exist; the Native peoples had their own names for these places: Valley of the Great Breath, the Entering Place, Stepping Off Into the Sky, Soul-Snatcher Narrows. I let the old names roll over me: Squamish, Nanaimo, Namu, Waglisla, Nootka, Haida Gwai. Naming takes its toll. By the time the sea otter's name had become universally known, the creature had virtually disappeared. Soon salmon, cod and Douglas fir will exist only in the shadow of their names. O'Hagan was not unaware of the power of, and the dangers inherent in, words. Red Rorty, the lying and fornicating priest in *Tay John*, is ritually killed by the Shuswap, tied to a pine tree in a kneeling position and set on fire, a stone thrust between his jaws. Later, when his charred skull is found amongst the roots of the tree, the stone still intact, Yaada, his executioner, says, "See, he was a great liar, and the word has choked him."

When my mother died, the plan was for her closest friend Ann Gill to adopt my brother and me. However, my father showed up from Saskatchewan with the intention of taking us to live with him and his second wife, Marge. I'd been encouraged, as a necessary distraction, to take piano lessons. I remember sitting at the piano in Ann's living room, my father behind me on the couch smoking a cigarette. I tried a few tentative bars of "Swans on the River." I was terribly nervous, thinking, I suppose, that if I did not play well he might not want to take me to live with him. As I recounted the incident many years later, in the company of a psychiatric counsellor, I suddenly burst into tears, deep uncontrollable sobs that kept rolling over me like groundswells. I was encountering, somewhat belatedly, my own "deep name." However misconstrued, for surely my father would have taken me with him no matter how badly I played the piano, the name written upon me in that instance had been He Who Sings (or Plays) for His Own Life. It contained a useful, if sobering, lesson about the origins and nature of my own creativity.

The Arabs believe that an hour spent sailing is not subtracted from the sum total of your life, but the walking zombies on the floats at Westview suggested just the opposite. Perhaps they'd been shanghaied or were reluctant recruits who got seasick, hated confined spaces and would rather be back in Portland or Toronto watching the telly. Such terminal landlubbers—or barrack stanchions as they're called in the navy—had obviously waited too long for this nautical medication to have any effect. Not so, yours truly. Two hours after seeing Lewis off, I had motored across Malaspina Strait to Marble Bay on Texada Island and was securing the bow- and sternlines in preparation for my next adventure.

"Nice boat. Does it have a name?"

Sid Butler introduced himself and invited me for coffee on board his fibreglass sloop, which he was sailing with his wife, Nita. It was called *Karavia*, a name easier to pronounce but just as odd as *Groais*, since it's the Greek word for boats. Who would have thought of naming a boat *Boats*? A word-man, of course. Sid was a retired elementary school teacher who'd spent his final working years teaching language arts in the Education Faculty at U.B.C. As it turned out, he came from Plymouth, where *Groais* had been built.

What's in a name? Not even a professor of language arts can answer that one. *Groais* is odd and awkward on the tongue, somewhat like being married to an Ethel or an Algernon. The name grates a little at first, then gradually endears itself to you. At that moment, however, the name of my boat was still associated primarily with bruises, expense, fear, a frustrating wait and a crazy gamble with the unknown. Maybe, as Chris Law suggested, I'd learn to bond with *Groais* and be able to say, with my nautical predecessor with the missing digit out there in Iceberg Alley: Thumb up!

When I poked my head out of the cabin, the sun had licked up the last of the mid-morning shadows in Marble Bay. Sid and Nita had left on the *Karavia* to catch the ebb tide to Pender Harbour. And the chap I'd spoken to on the classic wooden boat the night before, about grey whales in Smith Sound, was casting off his lines and heading back to Victoria. He never offered his name; in fact, he'd been so tight-lipped and reticent, I suspected him of being a writer.

Texada Island, a massive, scarcely habitable ledge of rock thrusting up several thousand feet at its highest point, lies on the eastern side of Georgia Strait, extending thirty miles north from the entrance of Jervis Strait to Westview. It was first charted in 1791 by Francisco Eliza and Dionisio Alcalá-Galiano, then later by George Vancouver, but appears to have tempted neither group ashore. As the modest middens—deposits of shell and bone that indicate human habitation—at Shelter Point suggest, even the Coast Salish population seems to have found the pickings slim on Texada. After a brief scandal over mineral rights in 1873, efforts were made to extract iron, copper, gold and limestone. During its boom years from 1880 to 1910, the bevy of mines and camps clustered around Texada City and Vananda boasted a hospital, jail, saloons, hotel, regular steamship service, a weekly newspaper called the *Coast Miner*, and the usual cast of prospectors, settlers and drifters with names such as Lucky Swede, Hobo Tom and Black Jack McLeod. After three major fires in 1910, 1912 and

1917 destroyed its finest buildings, a loss which was coincident with the petering out of the gold and copper, Vananda never quite recovered. When I first arrived in late August 1962, it was a depressed backwater, a two-industry town with a scattering of older cottages and small businesses that had never quite coalesced into a community. It still resembled a hastily constructed mining camp. Iron was on the decline but there was still enough limestone for a century or two; all the best trees had already been logged, the fish had fled, and the topsoil, such as it was, proved inadequate for farming. There was also nothing for the high school kids to do but make out or drive at excessive speeds along the deadly five-mile strip of paved highway that linked Vananda and Gillies Bay.

Of course, I considered it Shangri-La. After escaping the slums of Commercial Drive and the soulless urban redundancies that passed for housing at Twentieth and Main in Vancouver, I found Texada exhilarating. I loved its exposure to the sea on all sides, its view of the Coast Range and the mountains of Vancouver Island. I was engaged to be married; I was finally earning a real salary, the grand sum of $4,000 per year, including isolation allowance; I had my own apartment; and, besides, I was blessed with a captive audience of students for everything I had to say. I thought I'd arrived in heaven. The buildings that comprised Texada Elementary-Senior High School were less than a year old when I stepped ashore, both of us spanking new.

"I used to teach here. Do you mind if I have a look around?"

The man I was addressing was standing on a stepladder, doing something to the wires. His head and shoulders had disappeared into the hole left by the removal of one of the foam ceiling-squares. The part of him that remained for public consumption was decked out in workboots and striped overalls. His reply came back muffled, but distinct.

"Sure, go ahead. But I may have to conduct a body search before you leave."

"Of course."

The wit hooked me, but also the verb "conduct." An electrician with a sense of humour. It was shocking. I muttered something about my old classroom having been turned into a computer lab. The young woman steadying the ladder, a daughter or apprentice, sported earphones and couldn't have cared less about my sentimental journey; her body was tuned to a different drummer, less silly and lugubrious. I opened a few doors: Freda's home ec lab, with a view of Malaspina Strait spectacular enough to get a rise out of the lamest cake or loaf of bread; Patrick's corner room, from which so much laughter emanated; and the gymnasium, where the high school boys drafted their lanky but inept new coach and phys ed instructor to play centre for them in the annual basketball game against the local miners. Normie Kwong, quarterback for the Edmonton Eskimos, was playing centre for the miners; he was eight inches shorter than I was and built like a tank, so it seemed an easy toss for me to snag. In those days professional athletes did not earn big salaries and many of them had to take regular jobs during the off-season, which was why the China Clipper, as Normie was fondly known, was selling suits and sundries up and down the coast for Tip Top Tailors.

The referee's hand released the ball into the air and, while my brain was busy contacting the relevant muscles to request action, a blur crossed my field of vision. I was off the ground, but something rocket-propelled was hurtling past at four times my speed. I felt like some minor planet being lapped in its own sedentary orbit. I could hear the crowd explode with laughter as I touched down heavily on the varnished hardwood floor and turned to see Normie pass the ball into the corner and cut across the key to receive it again for a perfect lay-up.

Although I had to turn sideways to squeeze past the ladder, the apprentice, and the cardboard boxes, I managed to slip briefly into the general office, absurdly conscious that I might be suspected of trying to remove some equipment or confidential document. The counsellor's office and its contents—the blunt blond desk, the grey filing cabinet, and a perky pre-Diana picture of the Queen, all the paraphernalia of ignominy—hadn't changed in four decades. This was the lair in which Jimmy Bunn's education had been dramatically accelerated by an unexpected encounter with a reptilian brain—mine.

I was not a good teacher, just another of those faceless English and philosophy graduates, churned out by the thousands each year, who, trained for nothing in particular, find themselves drawn by default to the only profession that seems determined—nay, doomed—to attract incompetence: teaching. Many are called, few are chosen, and the odd one, like myself, is hired out of desperation. I'd cast my net widely, sending letters to school boards all over the province, a daunting barrage of what seemed likely to prove a futile exercise in self-promotion. To my own and my family's greater surprise, a school board up the coast at Powell River was in dire enough straits—Malaspina Straits, to be exact—to offer me a one-year renewable contract to teach. I packed my bags in an old VW bug and took three ferries up the coast. The last of these was an ancient relic called the *Atrevida* which, with a little jockeying, could handle five cars and forty passengers, but seemed more likely to deliver its cargo to the far shore of Lethe than to Texada. In due course, I was deposited along with my meagre belongings on the dock at Blubber Bay, a former whaling station turned quarry, which was just as painstakingly rendering the island into fine particles of limestone dust and sending it by the barge-load to the Lower Mainland for the ever-proliferating sidewalks, basements, and high-rises of Vancouver.

With little more than enthusiasm to offer the denizens of this leprous leviathan called Texada, my love of literature and iota of showmanship would have to do the trick. I was expected to teach English, though I had sloughed my way through university by talking about the moral conflicts in *Esther Waters* and never fully engaged myself with the texts. I hadn't quite noticed the words. I had to teach something called HPD (Health and Personal Development) to sexually active teenagers, though I was still a virgin myself, albeit a reluctant one. In addition to Canadian history, a subject I had never studied formally, I was assigned all the high school French. My Vancouver accent had been praised by Dr. White, but never tested on the street in Montreal or Paris. The students were polite and generous; they knew I was in over my head, but they'd had replacement teachers almost every year and seemed prepared to give me the benefit of considerable doubt. That is, with the exception of Jimmy Bunn.

Jimmy was a huge farm boy who sat at the back of the class and did his utmost not to conceal his utter boredom and his contempt for my fledgling pedagogical efforts. His wondrous circus act included spitballs, burps, yawns, paper airplanes, and farting noises simulated by pumping locked air from his armpits. If he'd put half as much energy into his studies, he could have graduated in a year and had my job to boot. I'm ashamed to report that this power struggle was settled in the old-fashioned, though now politically incorrect, way.

"Down to the office!"

Not a sound could be heard in the school. I was surprised by the outburst. I saw Jimmy Bunn rise from his seat, hesitate. He's going to kill me, I thought; I'll be like one of those cartoon characters driven through the wall by the charge of a raging bull. Instead, he walked quietly up the aisle and turned aside just before reaching me to pass out the open door. I followed him, like a skiff in the *Titanic*'s wake, down the corridor to that ill-fated encounter where our relationship would move quickly from mundane reality into myth. Years later I published a poem called "The Strap" about this incident, which had been my sole attempt to use physical violence as a teaching tool. That day, however, the damage done, I simply nodded for him to return to the classroom and sank into the chair, thinking I'd failed, that I could never face a class of students again.

"You okay in there?" It was my headless interlocutor, Ichabod Crane, still lost in the wiring.

"Too many ghosts."

"Ya, me too. Every time I install a smoke detector in one of those rooms it brings something back. And not always happy." The verb "install." Why not just the good old Anglo-Saxon verb "put"? Probably studied Latin with Spragge. His apprentice was moving her lips and nodding her head, but not in agreement. This was not her space. Her eyes were vacant; she was wired to some separate reality, most likely located in Westview or Powell River, since high school students had been ferried to the mainland daily for the last fifteen years. I wasn't a good lip-reader. The closest I could come to figuring out the words she was mouthing was "Far out," but that was archaic sixties thinking. More likely "Fuck off."

Having extracted my bicycle from the dinghy and replaced

the tire and inner tube, I was able to make several rounds of the town in a short time. Bob Gordon was dropping chunks of raw hamburger off the Vananda wharf to attract crabs. He'd come from Kenora, Ontario, twenty-two years earlier to plant trees and decided to stay; he ended up on Texada and bought the oil franchise. The decision had been easy.

"I look out at the sea every day during the winter and it's still not frozen. I'd never go back."

Bob's reaction was shared by Bill Fraser, a Scot I'd met earlier down at the breakwater in Marble Bay. He'd moved to Texada after an industrial accident in Victoria because living costs were cheaper. Did he miss Scotland? I asked. No, he'd seen more of Scotland since he came to Canada than when he lived south of Aberdeen, where the only transportation he'd owned was a bicycle, and where he had only one week off each year but couldn't afford to go anywhere.

Bob and I were standing on the dock where the Union Steamships vessel *Cheslake* sank, an event commemorated on the town's former cenotaph. The *Cheslake* left the dock at Vananda on January 7, 1913, but the cargo shifted immediately in the rough seas and the boat listed, causing water to enter the open portholes amidships. Captain John Cockle brought the *Cheslake* back to the wharf and put ninety people ashore, but the ship sank, drowning a cook, twenty-one sleeping loggers trapped below decks, a mother and child, and two maiden schoolteachers who refused to leave their cabin improperly dressed. The ship was salvaged, stretched, and went on to serve the coast as the SS *Cheakamus* and, later, as a troop transport during the Second World War.

I could feel myself immersed in layers of history: geographical, biological, psychological. Was I on Texada, in Pope's words, merely to haunt another of the places where my honour had died? I thought of Cornelius de Jode's colourful 1593 map of North America, whose western edges were purely imaginary. He filled the space with dragons, a mythical seahorse, and two galleons, one of them firing a cannon, and used cartouches to cover up vast areas of the continent about which there was no reliable information. There was plenty of mapping to be done here, if I was up to the task, since Texada had been the site of various emotional cataclysms, minor to be sure, but with enough seismic force to have long-lasting effects.

In the spring of 1963, civil defence rallies were mounted throughout the country by agents of the federal government to warn locals about the dangers of nuclear fallout. The one planned for Texada was scheduled to be held at the community hall. The faculty room at the school was abuzz. We'd been through the Bay of Pigs invasion months earlier and were acquainted with the infamous Diefenbunker, a fallout shelter for those holding power in Ottawa and nicknamed for the current prime minister. Patrick MacFadden, a sociable lefty from Belfast who said he'd been in such a hurry to get out of Northern Ireland that he missed Canada by five miles, was doing his best to instruct me in the intricacies of global politics. All our talk was of books, issues, ideology and music: Judy Collins, Pete Seeger, Stokely Carmichael, Ralph Ellison, Tariq Ali, Bertrand Russell, even Linus Pauling, who was determined to soften the evils of capitalism with megadoses of Vitamin C. It was heady stuff, but not always appreciated by the principal, an apoplectic, heavy-drinking ex-army type, affectionately known as the Menace, who would have preferred to think he was in charge of a boot camp rather than a nest of guerrillas.

"But, Gary, look at the facts." Patrick's red hair, freckled face and infectious smile would be partially obscured by smoke from one of the Gauloises he loved to smoke. He was a good teacher, patient, ready to reward effort, however piddling. "You're right, Castro's regime is a bit stiff. What can you expect in the face of such opposition? The U.S. embargo has pushed the Cubans to the wall, but they still have the lowest child mortality and the highest literacy rates amongst Latin Americans today."

Of course, everyone showed up for the civil defence rally. After lengthy introductions, a well-dressed man in his late forties or early fifites, whose complexion seemed a bit mottled, accepted the microphone. He was a bastion of confidence and goodwill, thanking the organizing committee for the invitation and making a few jokes tailored for the local audience.

"A nuclear explosion is not unlike the kind of explosion you hear regularly at the quarry, just a little stronger." If he thought he was addressing an audience of yokels, he was in for a surprise.

"What about strontium-90?" Roger Gibbard, an elementary school teacher from Gillies Bay and a regular at the MacFadden household, was on his feet. Roger was a Kiwi who'd served in the Royal Air Force and a dead ringer for Uncle Tom. When he wasn't regaling us with stories, he'd amuse us by gripping the arms of his chair, slowly raising himself up into a full handstand position, which he would hold for sixty seconds. He was not only fit, he'd done his homework.

"Dynamite is not radioactive, whereas strontium-90 has a half-life of fifty thousand years." A pause. There was some uncomfortable shuffling in the audience, a few muttered comments about Communists.

"I was only trying to find a way to connect what I want to say with something familiar to you here on the island. A little analogy." This was followed by some remarks about how to organize safe zones in the event of a nuclear bomb hitting the Lower Mainland, seventy-five miles away.

"At least you're not a prime target. That's one advantage of being on the periphery, of living on an island." He must have been thinking about the long haul up here by car and boat and the white water waiting for him in Malaspina Strait. His little joke backfired.

"England's an island. And continents are islands that didn't know their place and kept on growing." Patrick was in his element. "We're all islands, for that matter, but interconnected and mutually dependent. It seems clear to me that you're misinforming this audience about the dangers of an all-out nuclear war. In the event of such a war, we will all die, either from radiation poisoning or from the ensuing nuclear winter. Making fallout shelters or pretending there are ways to survive a nuclear holocaust is not only dishonest, but also counter-productive. What you need to do is tell people they are all going to die unless they stop their governments from acquiescing in this mad race to destroy the world." By now the audience was beginning to hum, like a disturbed nest of hornets.

"That's rude. Let our guest have his say."

"If you don't like the way we do things here, go back to Ireland."

"Ladies and gentlemen, let's try to bring this meeting back to some kind of order. These are important matters. The Canadian government . . ." The speaker coughed nervously into his sleeve, then squared himself up with the podium, taking a deep breath. His face glistened from perspiration. "The government is concerned about the safety of its citizens."

"Don't you realize you're being duped by the government? You know these safety measures are useless. We need to promote understanding, not fear and paranoia." The one speaking was yours truly. On my feet and shaking like a leaf, I wouldn't let go. "You're being used. The Russians are just as frightened and badly informed as we are. I'm sure they'd welcome peaceful overtures rather than warmongering." I could see several people getting ready to leave, or come out slugging. Then there was a beat of silence as Captain Harrison rose to his feet.

"All men are animals, aggressive animals." The captain was a large, imposing man, a Falstaff without a sense of humour, and commanded a degree of respect in the community, though no one could explain quite why. "The only way to deal with this aggression is to be well equipped, armed. These teachers—rude, loud-mouthed idealists who are being paid with taxpayers' money to warp the minds of our children— are the ones who are dupes. I suggest they leave and let us get on with this meeting."

"Hear! Hear!"

"You may be an animal, sir, but some of us are trying to operate at a higher level. We believe the human mind capable of change, of improving conditions." All my old religious fervour, like the contagion in Pandora's box, had been released to the wind, fuelled by memories of hiding under a school desk during air-raid drill in grade six at Grandview Elementary School in Vancouver. I was spouting more nonsense than the good captain and was completely oblivious to how badly and absurdly both of us were demeaning our fellow creatures in the animal kingdom.

Boos, scattered applause.

"Sit down and shut up!" A woman ran from the room, slamming the door behind her.

Just as the place seemed about to explode, the civil defence expert tapped the microphone with his pen for silence. He looked like a man stricken. The blotches on his face pulsed, as if radiating heat. He rolled up one of his shirtsleeves to the elbow and held the bare arm out for inspection.

"Wait! It's true. I'm sorry, it's all true. I have been conned by the government and this is not the first time. During the war, I painted airplane dials with phosphorescent paint. They told us the stuff was harmless. We painted our bed frames in the bunkhouse with it, so we could see where we were going when we sneaked in drunk late at night. It wasn't harmless. And now I've got skin cancer on my face and arms and all over my body." He sank into a chair beside the podium, his head in his hands.

For an extended moment, the only sound was a vast collective in-taking of breath; it seemed as if the room might implode. Then everyone was getting up to leave. We headed back to our separate places; this was not the time to celebrate a hollow victory, but to ponder what had just transpired. I've often wondered, horrified by my own pleasure in that cruel interrogation, what happened to the speaker after that event. My moral education was far from complete.

I left my bicycle leaning against a metal railing outside the post office. The Vananda general store had relocated across the street. The space it vacated was being occupied by several tentative concerns, including the makings of a café, hardware store, and travel centre. The mainstay, however, seemed to be the sale of Lotto tickets, fishing licences and a meagre assortment of lures. My cellphone, laptop and I were happily recharging our batteries in the café, me with a steaming cinnamon roll and the promise of tea, for which Phyllis, the waitress and mistress of ceremonies, was boiling water. So far, I'd met no one who remembered me. Mary Gusman, who hobbled the length of five floats to collect the moorage fees, thought maybe one of her sons had been in my class, but she didn't expect to be in touch for a week or more. I rhymed off a few names of former students—Jill Brennan, Jimmy Bunn, Cory Barker, Robert Yip, and Gary Paton, who'd quit school early to work at the iron mine in Gillies Bay but was killed when he tried to free a stuck door on the vertical mine shaft by jumping on it. Phyllis told me she'd only been on the island twelve years, since she married Eino Akre, pointing to the big man seated at the next table. Eino, whom she'd met at a dance in Powell River, was holding court, surrounded by five women. In addition to the tattoos on both arms, he had upper teeth on only one side of his mouth, giving him a lopsided, almost manic expression when he smiled, which he was doing now.

"So who owned the water-taxi back then—Ben Nicholas?" I'd mentioned to Phyllis that I drove the *Bluebell* and *Moccasin* between Vananda and Westview during the summer when school was out, to earn additional money for my studies in England.

"I don't remember Ben. Did he have a younger partner?" Eino decided I must have been hired by Ben's son Nick who helped with the business. Eino had worked forty years in the quarries, but had also done logging and several other jobs on the island. He was only four when his parents brought him to Texada, but he'd gone to school later in Vancouver, living in the three-hundred-block on Cordova Street, an area even drearier than Commercial Drive.

"The biggest bootlegger in town was located right across from the police station."

Eino looked up from his Lotto card to the video screen on which a series of balls was depositing numbers, apparently at random, on a grid. The high-tech video game called Keno

Club was interrupted regularly by flashing graphics announcing the latest Lotto 6/49 jackpot of five million dollars. Herbie, whose real name was Urbain Robillard, turned towards us from the self-serve coffee thermos.

"I went by the cop shop in Vananda this morning and noticed a number of new planters outside. You seen them?" He sat at a third table and stirred milk into his coffee. "We should drop a few pot seeds amongst those petunias, see how long it takes the cops to notice."

Since I seemed to have been included in this exchange, I couldn't resist throwing out to the group a question that I'd been dying to have answered about the family who used to run the quarry and had named their children Rocky, Pebbles, Sandy and Dusty. Before I could complete the question, Eino's harem erupted with laughter.

"That's us," the woman on his left announced. "I'm Rocky and this here's my sister, Pebby."

"Were there any more siblings born? You can't grind stone much finer than dust."

"Yes, a fifth. Smokey, the one who owns this place." Rocky made a gesture that included the store, but which might also have encompassed the entire province.

Eino informed the group that Phyllis's ice-cream machine was now working, but the news seemed to be mainly for Herbie's benefit. Herbie couldn't eat that stuff any more because of diabetes. He and Eino compared blood-pressure and blood-sugar levels. Eino was having trouble with his veins, but boasted that he ate sweets whenever he got the urge. This led to a discussion of the cinnamon buns, one of which I'd just demolished, smothered in butter. Herbie quickly changed the subject.

"By the way, Eino, your boat is covered with weed."

Eino laughed. "Not possible, I had it out of the water for cleaning a month ago."

"Look for yourself. You can see the stuff from the float. It's inches long."

"That stuff will drop off as soon as I start the motor and get underway. You know why?" He looked pleased and inscrutable in his Buddha pose. The nude tattooed on his right forearm was moving her hips to cheer him on. Herbie took the bait.

"Why?"

"Because I put Penaten on it. It stops the weed." His half row of upper teeth was displayed in a triumphant grin.

I said I'd heard of some strange uses of products in my time, including men using WD-40 for arthritis and women using the hemorrhoid formula Preparation H for temporary relief from facial wrinkles, but I'd never heard of using baby-rash ointment for stopping growth on boats.

"Well, it works on babies' bottoms, why wouldn't it work on the bottoms of boats? It's the zinc." Everyone laughed and it gradually dawned on me that I'd been set up.

Herbie was doubled over. "You might as well use shortening," he said. "It's cheaper."

Eino pushed his chair back from the table and stood up. He had an appointment at the medical clinic in Gillies Bay. He placed a hand gently on Herbie's shoulder.

"Ya, shortening is cheaper but also more dangerous, *mon ami*. You have to be careful what you get it on."

Seven

Before taking leave of Texada Island, I spent an evening on board *Groais*, reading Jack Leslie's unpublished memoir, *Fanny Adams*, about being farmed out as an orphan to foster care and then shunted into the merchant service and Royal Navy. Mine was the only transient boat using the facility. The locals had given up tinkering with their engines hours earlier and retired to the hotel beer parlour. Since Mary Gusman was lame, I'd gone to her house to settle my moorage account and have a final stroll through the town of Vananda where I'd spent the first year of my life as a full-time worker. In the lengthening shadows it seemed cozier, less shabby. Here and there lights were coming on, spilling their soft glow over the cluttered yards, decaying machinery, woodpiles and serpentine streets, bestowing a unity lacking in the harsh glare of midday. Back at Marble Bay, a sepulchral quiet had settled over the harbour and marina, the kind that makes you catch your breath, and the silhouettes of cabins and wheelhouses leaned towards each other like tombstones in the reflected moonlight. I negotiated my way along the unstable line of floats, the sound of my sandals echoing on the grey cedar boards.

Scrock! Scrock!

A noise like the ripping of a sheet of styrofoam rent the silence. I leapt back in alarm and had to grab the shrouds on a sailboat to keep my balance. There was a beating of air and then a solitary blue heron lifted off into the semi-gloom between two boats, propelling itself across the surface of the bay with those slow-motion sweeps of wing that call up images of prehistoric flight, the great marauding pterodactyls that were its ancestors. The blue heron had packed it in for the night and was not pleased with my intrusion.

I stepped aboard, still pumped with adrenaline, expecting to find *Groais* half-submerged or overrun with rats. When I flicked on the shore-power, there was no scurry of movement in the cabin and not a single cushion afloat. Jack's manuscript lay open on the table where I'd left it and the rest of my literary crew were standing at attention or sleeping in the upright position on the bookshelves. I poured myself half a glass of Lamb's Navy Rum, which I'd bought for its symbolism rather than taste, and began to read. Jack had no use for religion, which he dismissed as superstition and "pious humbug," or for any other kind of authority, all of which he viewed as organized bullying.

"That's religion's role, Gary," he had said to me once, sweeping up wood shavings from the fully rigged model schooner he was building and dumping them into the small stove throbbing in the corner of his workshop at the tip of Clam Bay. Spray from huge waves pounding the rocks and carried by a brisk westerly was striking the windowpanes in intermittent gusts. The fact that we'd just met did not deter Jack from educating the teacher. "Its task is to invoke a higher power to sanction and justify the actions of the ruling group." As evidence of the collusion of religion and state in maintaining the status quo, Jack loved to quote the lines drummed into the heads of Victoria children:

> The rich man in his castle,
> The poor man at his gate;
> God made them high and lowly
> And ordered their estate.

I'd underlined something he'd written about Britain's conduct during the Boer War, a few lines on internment camps in which Boer women and children died like flies, as incisive in its writing and thinking as Noam Chomsky's later critiques of America's habit of demonizing its enemies in Vietnam, Cuba, Nicaragua and Iraq: "Reverses suffered by British troops were being used to fan the war fever and obscure the real issues. A successful attack on the part of the Boers would be called a 'cruel massacre' by the press; if the British were successful, it was hailed as a 'glorious victory.'"

Nora Barnett, an elementary school teacher at Blubber Bay, had taken me to meet Jack shortly after I arrived on Texada, making it clear from the start that this was a special favour. He lived in a one-room cabin he'd built himself from wood scrounged off the beach and had constructed a second cabin, smaller, where he stored tools and made scale models of the great ships of discovery, some of which he sold to supplement his meagre pension. Orphaned at an early age and inspired by the novels of Captain Marryat, Jack dreamed of escape and adventure and could not endure the confined life with his publicly appointed guardian or the severely circumscribed future awaiting him. Through the good offices of a wealthy neighbour, he was offered the chance to sign on to a merchant marine training vessel moored in the Thames, where he learned to identify and handle every moving part of a sailing ship. Even in his eighties, when I knew him, he would boast that only the running blocks on his models were larger than scale, since anything smaller would have been too delicate to drill or too difficult to manipulate with his arthritic hands.

Jack's career in the merchant marine was short-lived. He was transferred to the Royal Navy, which he describes in his memoir as a "pompous parade of armed might," and which he found as vulgar as it was brutal, malicious and incompetent.

He jumped ship with his mate at the first opportunity in Halifax at the turn of the twentieth century, making his way west by working in logging camps. He thought nothing of rowing a small boat from Vancouver to a job seventy miles up the coast. More than once he was blacklisted for trying to organize unions and was still convinced, in the 1960s, that his mail was being monitored by the RCMP. Given the Cold War atmosphere of the time, with McCarthyism still rampant and file clerk Gouzenko defecting in Ottawa, Jack's suspicions were more than justified. Of course, I found the checkered career of this self-educated iconoclast terribly exciting and spent as much time as I could afford drinking his home-made dandelion wine and listening to his equally intoxicating tales, while the waters of Malaspina and Georgia straits contended outside his cabin.

Jack's status on the island intrigued me. He was described by the locals as a hermit, yet he was extremely sociable, welcoming me and a host of other teachers with whom he kept up an active correspondence. He was busily engaged in reading and thinking about the world, active in pursuing his hobbies and friendships. He was a squatter; other than books and tools, he owned nothing, not even the cabins he lived and worked in. He had no electricity or running water. And yet he seemed completely happy and self-contained. Having taken a full-time teaching job that required every spare moment for preparation and marking, and that left me feeling exhausted, inadequate and humiliated, I was quite conscious of the differences in our two lives.

As I turned the pages of *Fanny Adams* late into the night on board *Groais* in Marble Bay, I came to a passage I'd scarcely noticed before—Jack's description of leaving Plymouth on a voyage from which he would never return home:

Standing with my mates watching the familiar places slowy fading
into the hazy background of the Devon landscape, we little realized
that many of us would never see it again. As a schoolboy, I had
pictured it as a fabulous place, the home of great men and great
deeds. I had found it dirty and cheap and one of its present "great"
personages, a noble Lord who seemed to own half the countryside,
small-souled enough to charge those who he would expect to defend
his property a half-penny to cross one of his bridges—this done out
of sheer spite. And the misery and brutality I had endured at the
hands of the successors of its sea heroes led me to conclude that they
had been as cruel and ruthless in their day. The glamour of
Plymouth and its heroes for me had gone, and I was glad to be gone
too. I left it with no regrets.

I was startled not so much by the quality of the writing, but
by Jack's unique view of this famous seaport, which I'd visited
the previous summer while doing some research on the
origins of *Groais*.

I'd found Plymouth down at heel but quaint, with its colourful waterfront area, the Barbican, still bearing the name by
which it was known to one of Chaucer's pilgrims. I'd walked
along back alleys and seawalls, thinking of Cook, Vancouver, Darwin on his *Beagle*, Scott, and the host of other
famous mariners who'd set forth from this quay; even the
Pilgrim Fathers had departed, finally, from Plymouth,
having been driven there by a storm after leaving Southampton. I'd even paused to copy in my notebook part of a
long list of drowned fishermen posted in the window of the
Seamen's Benevolent Association:

Thomas B. Taylor, 55
William J. Taylor, 44
Cecil R. Thomas, 30
Samuel Lamont, 27
John J. Callard, 42
Charles F. Brown, 56
Harry L. Thomas, 56
John E. B. Cole, 29
George F. Vaughan, 30
Ronald A. Pearn, 25
Victor Hicks, 16

While I was busy romanticizing the place, identifying with both the famous mariners and the lost fishermen, I talked with an old codger named Stan Prickett, seated on a bench on the esplanade.

"I was a train engineer all my life, but I love it down here. I live alone, the last of fourteen children."

"My God!"

"You think that's a lot? The town crier had twenty."

"No wonder he developed a loud voice."

Phil Johnson, a Cockney who drove the water-taxi that took me up Portlett Creek to where *Groais* had been built in Terry Erskine's now-defunct shipyard, was full of stories about the power of the sea around Plymouth and its strange attraction for him.

"In the winter I work as a tugboat skipper, dumping hundred-ton blocks of concrete overboard to shore up the breakwater. The sea tosses them about like kindling sticks."

When we reached the estuary where *Groais* had been launched in 1973, Phil told me that the *Royale* had been deliberately sunk there; it was the multihulled yacht of Alain Colas, who'd drowned during a race when his boat capsized. His widow refused to sell the sailboat, which was quite valuable, but had it scuppered instead as a tribute to her husband.

Back at the Loma Loma B&B, I found the walls of the subterranean breakfast room covered with paintings of boats under sail, the most startling of which depicted a fishing craft on a perilous tack between the rocks and a buoy that appeared as useless as a spinning top. The boat was drawing with only one sail and didn't look as if it was going to make it. The other boats had no sails up and were clearly adrift, awaiting their fate, but the crew of this one were gathered in the bow, expectant, leaning hard into the possibility of a safe landing. The dramatic perspective of the painting drew you in, made you pause, because it could only have been the fleeting glance of someone already in the water or on another doomed craft. On the way up the stairs, I could see a window box brimming with purple petunias and hear the voices of a couple in their late teens, obviously students, who'd booked into separate rooms on the second and third floors for propriety's sake. They hadn't noticed me. Unlike their imperilled ancestors in the fishboat, they had fed on honeydew and drunk the milk of paradise.

"Shall I come up?"

"Yes, brilliant. And bring the condoms with you."

When I turned *Groais* to port at the mouth of Marble Bay the next morning and headed west towards Blubber Bay, I was still thinking about Jack and the kind of choices I'd made in my life. "Classic workaholic" was the phrase my two ex-wives might have used on the subject, if they were feeling generous. Tucked inside my photocopy of *Fanny Adams* I'd found a letter from Jack Leslie to my first wife, Norma, in which he refers to an exchange he and I had had on the subject of Joseph Conrad, a point of disagreement about the novel *The Nigger of the 'Narcissus,'* which features a spectacular storm and what might now be called "dramas of the workplace." Jack took exception to Conrad's portrayal of Jenkins, perceived by his captain as a troublemaker. Jack was too polite to voice his criticism directly, but took some delight in pointing out my folly to Norma, who was living separately with our daughter Jenny and with the model schooner Jack had been building for me, which he'd named the *Norma Joan*:

I received a reply from Gary recently on my comment to his essay on Conrad's novels and the characters he portrays. I admire the way Gary sticks to his guns though our views differ. I pointed out that Conrad wrote as a man in authority, a Ship Captain, and to him a rebellious sailor was "incompetent," a "shirker," an "agitator," and so on. Gary knowing nothing of the sailor's life in Conrad's time accepts Conrad's view of these men. These men were martyrs, voicing the grievances of the seamen against the deplorable conditions men suffered under at sea, forerunners of the union organizers that later evolved. . . . But of course, publishers and "gentle readers" want a story, not the truth, and what amused me in Gary's letter was that he says he is trying to organize a strike amongst the teachers of the College against the arbitrary conditions imposed on them; so Gary and Conrad's agitators are in the same boat, though I hadn't the heart to point this out.

The same boat, Jack? I was arguing with him as I fell asleep and I was still arguing with him when I awoke the next morning, thirty-seven years after the fact. Maybe it had something to do with Texada, being on the island.

When I said goodbye to Phyllis and Eino and the "Gravel

Sisters" at the general store before embarking, I asked Eino if the population of Texada was still around 2,500. "No," he said, "only half that number, unless you count the hippies out there in the bush—you never know how many until they crawl out." This was a fairly typical island response to that noble if hirsute subculture that had taken to the West Coast like ants to sugar. However, Eino was not finished; he had another recently minted parable about work to share with me, this one ethnically specific and no doubt prompted by the recent arrival on the coast of boatloads of illegal Asian immigrants.

"Last year, a family of Vietnamese came to Texada to pick huck and salal." Eino paused to check the latest figures for the Super 7 Lotto, which had appeared on the screen announcing a jackpot of ten million dollars. "They had no permit. They were pulling it out by the roots and chucking it down the slope for the grandmother to strip before loading it onto their pickup. The loggers put up barriers the next time, but when that didn't discourage the Vietnamese the crew on the ferry 'accidentally' directed saltwater hoses over the whole truckload. It turned the leaves black."

While I secured a bag of groceries to the rear rack of my bicycle before heading back to the boat, Eino mentioned, as parting comment, an Englishman in a baseball cap who'd tied up his sailboat the previous summer in Marble Bay, asking questions and making a lot of notes. A nervous type who had difficulty making eye contact, he was suspected of working for the RCMP or the CIA, since his boat was registered in Seattle.

"Drugs, probably. We got a friend of Mary's to play a little joke on him. Hightailed it out of here first thing the next morning. Strange piece of work, that one."

Three work-related anecdotes dropped in my lap only an hour after I'd awakened from a dream about jobs, in which my delicate subconscious was trying to wrestle with its demons and resolve the contradictions inherent in retiring from one job in order to work twice as hard at another. Trying, in short, to give birth to a new vision of how to conduct my life. This conjunction not only boggled the mind, but was also distracting the skipper of *Groais,* which was edging dangerously close to the ragged shoreline, not far from where I used to gather chunks of rare and aromatic juniper for making cribbage boards, in that ancient time, shrouded in mist, when I still knew how to relax. Dead ahead, and about four miles distant, was Clam Bay where Jack's two cabins still stood. Rather than bulldozing the squatter's shacks, as the community expected, the owners of the quarry with title to the land had wisely struck a deal with friends of Jack, allowing them to use the buildings for a nominal fee each year, thereby confirming the company's title, reducing vandalism, and discouraging a new crop of squatters.

On a bright sunny coastal morning, when I ought to have been taking deep breaths of clean salty air and absorbing the spectacle of the unfolding universe, I was belabouring the tenuous link between work and the perception of place, or how our attitude to place depends upon what we do there— our line of work. Jack had seen a different Plymouth than I had, an ugly one, because he knew something intimate and frightening about that city's principal employer. He was in good company. Charles Darwin, whose voyage on the *Beagle* was delayed because of bad weather, described his time in Plymouth as the most miserable two months of his entire life. Jack was right about my ignorance. Was he also right about my interpretation of Conrad? He may never have seen a copy of *The Nigger of the 'Narcissus,'* only my essay on the subject. It's clear that Conrad admired the heroic cook, Ransome, who made coffee throughout the storm and declared: "As long as she swims I will cook." And the ultimate compliment he could pay his helmsman was this: "Singleton steered with care." But Conrad was also Polish, experiencing his nation overrun by Austrians, Germans, Russians. He had witnessed his own father die in a gulag in Siberia. He had no sympathy for anarchy or revolution, both of which he equated with chaos. A ship was a metaphor, a microcosm of society, where solidarity was necessary to remain afloat, to reach a destination. There might not be time during the storm to examine the motives of Mr. Jenkins or check with the shop steward to see if he had a legitimate list of grievances.

There seemed to me, at the time, plenty of evidence that Conrad could distinguish between a seaman with reasonable complaints and a slacker, although this quotation from *Notes on Life and Letters* doesn't exactly confirm that view: "A man is a worker. If he is not that he is nothing. Just nothing—like a mere adventurer." At one point, Conrad cites Leonardo da Vinci, who was no slouch either, on the subject of work: "Work is law. Like iron that lying idle degenerates into a mass of useless rust, like water in an unruffled pool that sickens into a stagnant and corrupt state, so without action the spirit of man turns into a dead thing, ceases prompting us to leave some trace of ourselves on earth." This is weighty stuff, which Jack would not have approved of; and it smacks too much of duty, of the kind beloved by the Gradgrinds who torment students or the Scrooges who make the lives of employees unbearable.

Jack Leslie had seen too much brutality on ships and in coastal logging camps to tolerate a starry-eyed or reverential view of work. In an article he wrote about logging on the coast, which I subsequently reprinted in *Skookum Wawa*, Jack distinguished between the original loggers and the greedy, ruthless organizations that replaced them:

The work was leisurely compared to the hectic industrial serfdom in the camps today. The introduction of the contract system in the camps spoiled the woods. Hundreds of old-time loggers refused to accept the unfairness associated with it and left. . . . In later years it was quite common to see men on stretchers carried out every day in some camps, the result of the speed-up system introduced amongst fallers and buckers by contract falling.

Conrad's devotion to writing, his chosen work, was something that appealed to me profoundly when I was young and needed a heroic cast for my ambitions. At its most whimsical, this idea is expressed by Marlow in *Heart of Darkness:* "No, I don't like work. I had rather laze about and think of all the fine things that can be done. I don't like work—no man does—but I like what is in the work,—the chance to find yourself." Conrad thought of writing as a vocation involving sacrifice.

While carrying on this silent debate with Jack and checking my strip chart for reefs ahead, of which there were far too many, especially extending out from Savary Island, I recalled an essay by Ursula Le Guin that had appeared in the *New York Times Book Review.* It was a spirited rebuttal of Conrad's heroic posturing about "wrestling with the Lord" for his creation, especially his reference to eating the food left outside his door, unaware of the life going on around him in the house, which was kept perfectly silent so as not to disturb the resident genius. Le Guin reminds her readers that Virginia Woolf had rejected heroic status for the writer and demanded nothing more than a little income and a room of her own, then she lets Conrad have it with both fists:

A woman who boasted that her conscience had been engaged to the full in such a wrestling match would be called to account by both women and men; and women are now calling men to account. What "put food" before him? What made daily life so noiseless? What in fact was this "tireless affection" which sounds to me like an old Ford in a junkyard but is apparently intended as a delicate gesture towards a woman whose conscience was engaged to the full, hour after hour, day after day, for twenty months, in seeing to it that Joseph Conrad could wrestle with the Lord in a relatively "great isolation," well housed, clothed, bathed and fed?

I'd been thinking about Jack Leslie and the significance of work because it was something I'd never sorted out in my own life. I'm still trying. Jack worked hard, then turned his back on paid employment, as he had on organized religion. He devoted himself to friends and creative activities and self-improvement through reading and observing the world. A friend once suggested to me that religion is nothing more than what you learn to do with your solitude. Jack would have agreed. My own progress had been slow, even halting. I'd been ruthless in my pursuit of certain ideas, in my chosen work. A writing fanatic is no less dangerous than a religious or a political one, at least to those close at hand. And at some point the questions would be asked, if not by me, then by someone else: What was he trying to prove? Did it justify the cost to others? And I was thinking, inevitably, of my eldest daughter Jennifer Leslie, proudly carrying Jack's surname into the twenty-first century, who paid a high price for my ruthlessness, for that tremendous expenditure of creative energy that may have brought forth only a mouse. Jenny had survived—miraculously, and as a tribute to her mother—but not without scars and with too little help from me.

As I sat in the cockpit, my left hand on the tiller, and turned to look back at Texada where I'd experienced so much yet learned so little, I thought of George Vancouver and Juan

Francisco de la Bodega y Quadra and their very different ways of conducting their lives on this coast. While Vancouver relentlessly and humourlessly charted the coast, his Spanish counterpart turned his quarters at Nootka into a pleasant sanctuary, providing food, wine, and hospitality to the officers of foreign vessels as well as to local chiefs such as Maquinna. Granted, their assignments were totally different. Some will argue that Vancouver's legacy, whatever the cost, was a set of invaluable charts in use until recent times; others will insist that Bodega y Quadra, born in Lima, Peru, set a more important example in terms of diplomacy and in answering the eternal question: how should I conduct my life—in general and in this particular place?

Heading north, with my own set of charts and contradictions, it seemed significant to me that so many of the smaller islands on Vancouver's maps—San Juan, Valdez, Galiano, Saturna, Gabriola, Quadra, Cortes, and Texada—had retained their Spanish names, a modest but hardly unconscious tribute by the great English explorer to that other, gentler, way of connecting with the land. I'm not religious, I thought, but is it too much to hope for a wiser use of my solitude and the possibility that this voyage, even without a fixed point of reference, might result in some genuine wisdom?

About half a mile from the ferry terminal in Blubber Bay, where the *Atrevida* had deposited me for my first full-time job in 1962, I brought the boat around and set my course northwest towards Cortes Island. Harwood stood immediately ahead, then Savary Island, where John Wayne owned property and visited each summer on his converted minesweeper, and where he was reported to have had Gary Cooper once as a house guest. Astern, the great open sore of the quarry stretched to the highest point at the north end of Texada, leaving only a narrow strip of road for traffic to and from Vananda and other points on the island. Heavy equipment and more efficient methods of extracting aggregates enabled the mine to operate with a fraction of the staff required in Jack's time, although the visual blight and noise level had quadrupled. It was almost high noon. As the work went unrelentingly on, sunlight reflected off the windows of Jack's cabin.

✳ Eight

Although I'm the kind of person who feels more at home in a book than on a boat, my relationship with *Groais* had been shifting perceptibly. After two weeks of brain-crushing collisions with the boom and hatch cover, I noticed I'd developed new ways of moving. I'd been transformed by necessity into a version of Rubber Man, capable of turning myself into an S-shape to avoid the table and other protuberances and, even more amazing, capable of executing the gravity-defying spiral leap that enabled me to emerge from the bathroom without damage to my skull. This was a complicated manoeuvre which involved deliberately losing balance so that I virtually fell out of the bathroom, caught the door frame with one hand, then propelled myself upward by sheer leg power so my head would emerge unscathed in the space created by the forward hatch.

I'd also figured out, belatedly, how to operate the windlass. In Howe Sound, techno-peasant that I am, I was unable to read the depth sounder or make the simple anchor-hauling mechanism work, so I had to pull up the hook and length of chain hand over hand from a depth of well over a hundred feet. It was like trying to raise the waterlogged bodies of three dead Crusaders in full armour. And I had visions of getting my leg caught in the rope and ending my brief and not-very-illustrious sailing career as crab bait in a hundred fathoms of water. However, by the time I had to repeat the performance in Gorge Harbour, at the south end of Cortes

Island, I was wearing protective work gloves, the lever was in the proper spot for cranking, rather than on the release mechanism, and the anchorage was only thirty feet deep. Within minutes, *Groais* was hanging on just the right amount of rode, a length seven times the depth of the water, and looking, to all intents and purposes, as if its skipper actually knew what he was doing.

Gorge Harbour is less than twenty-five miles northwest of Powell River in an area of islands and protected waterways known as Desolation Sound, one of the major destinations for boaters on the West Coast. To get there from Texada, I had to plot a careful course between the reefs extending out from Harwood and Savary islands and some drying rocks a mile offshore. If I'd gone up the mainland coast, I'd have had an easier time of it and would have passed the notorious community of Lund. Once a thriving Swedish settlement of loggers and fishermen, Lund now prides itself on being the end of the road. The village has a sign that proudly claims you can drive south from Lund all the way to Tierra del Fuego, the southernmost tip of Chile, where the vast southern continent tapers off to a finger called Cape Horn, rudely pointed towards Antarctica. It's true that you can't drive farther north along the coast of mainland Canada (although the highway on Vancouver Island now extends all the way to Port Hardy and Cape Scott), and you can only reach the mainland coast again by road at two other points: four hundred miles north at Bella Coola, or twice that distance at Prince Rupert. So Lund has a legitimate claim to fame as the gateway to absence and ecstasy.

It's a tiny port that consists of an old hotel, several restaurants that can be reached along raised walkways, a marine repair shop and rental, and a lift for hauling out boats. The good citizens of Powell River and Westview who can't manage the time, money or steam to go down to Vancouver for a good piss-up will occasionally make the short hop north to Lund for a soupçon of decadence. For all its reputation, Lund is actually a rather quiet outpost, a jumping-off spot where you can take a water-taxi to several of the islands, including Cortes. You won't find rancour, or any of the other nasty abstractions, in Lund and there are no latter-day ethnic, religious or political squabbles to trouble the tranquil waters of the bay: only low tide competing for aromatic primacy with the smell of fish and chips with vinegar. During my previous visit in 1997, however, it was overrun with Hell's Angels, looking as unkempt and mean as a tribe of marauding Vikings, which gave this quaint but shabby little Scandinavian cul-de-sac an apocalyptic touch quite in keeping with its claim to being the absolute terminus of the world on wheels.

The very inaccessibility of Desolation Sound is what makes it so popular to boaters and the guru-crowd. They have it pegged as a piece of handy wilderness to be milked for its spiritual, aesthetic and commercial possibilities. George Vancouver spent more time here than he intended. It rained continually and his boat crews, out on survey and discovering the rapids at Yaculta and Seymour Narrows and open water farther north, took longer than expected to return to home base on *Discovery* and *Chatham*. His health was poor and he was also privately ticked off with the Spanish, who were accompanying him on two ships at the time, because they had already charted much of what he considered *his* coast. Unlike his upbeat Chamber of Commerce-style boosterism farther south, all George's references here are to the dreariness and gloom of the region, which he eventually took his revenge on by calling it Desolation Sound. Dismissing the surrounding area for being "as gloomy and dismal an aspect as nature could well be supposed to exhibit," Vancouver went on to complain: "Our residence here was truly forlorn; an awful silence pervaded the gloomy forests, whilst animated nature seemed to have deserted the neighbouring country." Ironically, as was the case with Iceland, which had been deliberately misnamed to keep people away, Desolation Sound is now synonymous with beauty and solitude, two of the very words guaranteed to bring the madding crowds at a gallop—or close-hauled and fully rigged.

Although on the map it looks like the outline of an egg that has fallen and splattered inimitably on the floor, Cortes Island is the jewel amongst the pieces of jigsaw puzzle that make up Desolation Sound. It has been a home to Coast Salish people, whalers, loggers, fishermen, and farmers and now plays host to a secondary population of back-to-the-land and spiritual-renewal types. It lies between Quadra and West Redonda islands, with jagged reefs guarding it to the south, a thick covering of second-growth forest, local waters that are balmy in summer thanks to minimal tidal activity, and, unlike Quadra, just enough remoteness from larger centres such as Campbell River to make it, if not inaccessible, at least requiring a serious degree of commitment to reach.

I spent my first morning on Cortes Island tidying the boat, using the shower and laundry facilities ashore, and looking for a spot where I could get a signal on my newly acquired cellphone. Gorge Harbour was, indeed, gorgeous, a high-walled, protected basin with a very narrow entrance between two cliffs, on one of which, if you're clever enough to be able to navigate a boat in tricky water and sightsee at the same time, you might find the faint remnants of aboriginal pictographs. I wasn't, but I did recall that the original villagers used these same cliffs to hurl large rocks down onto the heads of unwelcome intruders. There were a few dozen boats tied up at the marina, another eight at anchor, and a few local craft moving back and forth in a soft rain between the dock and the floating fish farms. I managed to wrap my legs around the bicycle in the dinghy and half row, half splash my way to the marina, where I set out on two wheels for Whaletown, a spot I'd been told was in cahoots with BC Tel and cyberspace.

The absence of phone contact had reminded me abruptly that I was moving beyond the reach of friends and family. I was conscious of being remote, islanded, out of touch. The paved road to Whaletown was circuitous, with enough dips and inclines to keep me hopping on and off the small bike. A single car slowed down and inched past me in the other direction, two small gargoyle faces in the back seat squashed and distorted against the fogged windows, getting a good view of my ambulatory spectacle. I arrived at my destination red-faced and sweating, laptop, cellphone and notebooks jammed into my backpack, just as the clouds released a deluge. Whaletown seemed to have vanished as surely as the whales. Here and there amidst the second growth could be seen the weathered corner or roof of a derelict building, one or two still inhabited and releasing a ribbon of heavily creosoted smoke into the branches and mist that enclosed them like surgical gauze. A portable, but unmanned, fast-food canteen was parked by the roadside just above the ferry terminal, as if to remind new arrivals of what they were leaving behind.

"So, what's it like out there alone, Dad? You okay and all that? Your joke about asterisks, a.k.a. rocks, disturbed me."

"Cozy and uncomplicated so far. A few minor dramas, but nothing to worry about. Everything's working like a charm."

"You sure?"

"You know me, always angling for sympathy."

Tea, blueberry muffin and 110 volts later, I was ensconced

in Kirstie's Craft Shoppe, overlooking the small bay and talking to my eldest daughter Jenny in Charlottesville, Virginia. I was sending and receiving signals as easily and clearly as the endangered finback, blue and humpback whales that once plied these waters. Kirstie was laughing with two women at another table on the veranda while the rain cascaded off the overhanging roof. Jenny had lived in the States for twenty-four years, since moving south with her mother from Toronto at age nine. She had just completed a doctorate and was editing a new ethics magazine called *The Hedgehog Review* at the University of Virginia.

Our visits had been good but infrequent and I had never quite learned how to handle the guilt she called up in me. She'd travelled around the world with us, as part of my second family, and had developed close ties with her two half-sisters and their mother. On one occasion I'd asked her how she felt as a child about my absence. I hadn't expected the reply I got: "It wasn't your absence that troubled me, it was your presence. I didn't know what a father was or how I was supposed to relate to you. And I saw how disturbed my mother was when you were around."

I'd gone down to visit Jenny once while she was still an undergraduate. She had arranged for me to do a reading for the English Department. Charles Wright, a poet and professor, phoned to ask if I would be willing to read with one of the local poets. Yes, I said, of course. The local poet turned out to be Jenny, who read her poems first and related a surprising story. She told the audience how she'd been standing in the schoolyard with a friend, aged six or seven, when she saw me coming to meet her with my beard and long hair, wearing a tattered leather jacket. She used to ask her mother if I was a hippie, but was told, no, dear, hippies don't have jobs. I flung my arms about in greeting. When her friend inquired who was waving, Jenny said: "Oh, just some man." After she finished this anecdote, she announced to the assembled audience, "And here he is again—just as wild and woolly, and still wearing an old leather jacket—but I'm happy to introduce him now as my father." Then she gave me a huge hug. It was one of the few occasions in my life when I was speechless.

Waiting out the rain, I had a second pot of tea and purchased a straw sunhat from Africa, thinking it might be useful later, but mainly as an expression of my gratitude to the store owner for the electrical plug-in which had enabled me to recharge both sets of batteries. I scribbled a few lines in my notebook about Whaletown while I contemplated the fate of species, fathers included.

"If you're still interested in a ride to Gorge Harbour, one of my friends has agreed to drop you off, as long as your folding bike will fit in her hatchback."

I thanked Kirstie profusely, paid my bill, gathered up the equipment and new straw hat and followed my good Samaritan out to her car. The bicycle, which proved to be such a nuisance on the boat and which I'd left standing in the rain, behaved itself and went to sleep immediately in the dry interior of the hatchback, while the owner, if I'd heard correctly, was questioning me about my dental habits. I fastened my seat belt and looked at her dumbly.

"Dental group?"

"Yah, the Addie Group in Colwood. Isn't that where you have your teeth fixed?"

Teeth again. Were my incisors turning into fangs? Did I look as if I was wearing dentures? Could my teeth be advertising a certain style in dentistry? I was not driving, so I couldn't look at myself discreetly in the rear-view mirror.

Then I remembered that the last cleaning I'd had done had taken so long, I told the assistant I'd have the upper teeth done on another occasion. Maybe the difference showed, like one scoop of vanilla ice cream topped with another of maple walnut. I stopped smiling and ran my tongue across my teeth. I was a writer, sure, and some of my words were still in print, but did that explain how a complete stranger could be in possession of intimate information about the terrain and architecture of my mouth?

"The Addie Group in Colwood? I know who you are, you see. I was in the office one day when your name was mentioned. You were on the other end of the phone. I also know you teach in Bellingham. I shouldn't have asked, but I told them I knew you from before, a long time ago. You're Gary, right?"

Who was this person? It suddenly crossed my mind that perhaps I was being kidnapped by a strange woman, an escapee from the thought-control crowd.

"Right. And you?"

"I'm Dale. From Texada. I wasn't going to tell you, but—" She dabbed at the fogged-up glass and turned the defrost knob to the fast position.

"Dale Sellentin? Jackie's sister? I don't believe it. How—?" Jackie was one of my best grade twelve students at Vananda high school, a bright, promising young woman with no end of writing talent. I'd lost track of her and the others for more than a decade, until she started having chronic bouts of depression and would sometimes call me in the middle of the night, three thousand miles away, to tell me she'd written a letter to Prime Minister Pierre Trudeau, demanding immediate action. Action for what, she did not say. I never knew the object of her calls either, other than an attempt to touch base with a sympathetic voice from the past. In those days, I was too caught up in my own problems and fantasies to be able to offer anything in the way of comfort or advice. The calls eventually stopped. I felt badly about it, but knew my limits. Having just come from Texada, where I'd met none of my former students, I was stunned by this chance encounter, brought on by rain, dead batteries, a bicycle, and a straw hat.

I bought Dale lunch at a restaurant in Gorge Harbour called the Floathouse and she reciprocated by showing me around Cortes Island. She was a teacher, on temporary disability. She'd had a rocky row to hoe: losing her mother while still a teenager, a ten-year marriage to another teacher that ended after trying to juggle lives and jobs in two different cities, and another ten-year relationship with a man who apparently had too much time on his hands. She had also been diagnosed with a rare disease, a thyroid condition in which the body absorbs too much iron, causing muscles and joints to become inflamed and making it painful just to be touched. As is so often the case, the doctor dismissed it all as part of the aging process, a current equivalent to saying it's all in your imagination. Dale was healing. She had lived intermittently on Cortes and thought the island would help in the mending process. She found the winters too foggy and wet and the isolation severe, but loved her property, which she said was like living in a park. So she came and went, like the tide, like the birds. I asked her if she thought there was such a thing as an island mentality.

"You mean the small-mindedness?"

"Nothing specific." I was thinking about my experience of living on Texada years ago and now on Vancouver Island.

"Island people—and I guess I have a right to say this, since I've spent so much of my life on islands—are small-minded, but with a difference. You expect the gossip, since there's nothing else to occupy people's minds. But to compensate for the lack of privacy, there's no corresponding sense of community."

We were coming to Hollyhock, the healing centre which had once been part of Cold Mountain Institute, a high-class mind-expanding centre which had attracted gurus, psychiatrists, healers, mystics and poets from all over the world, Allen Ginsberg and R. D. Laing amongst them. Now it was an escape valve for ailing but well-heeled city folk who wanted to experience nature and the inner reality. I mentioned Australian writer Peter Conrad's comment, from his book about his birthplace on the island of Tasmania, that "an island is a misanthrope's last retreat."

Dale seemed fragile, walking with a slight limp and carrying herself as if she were much older. She used to kayak, she told me, years before it was in vogue, and once spent a summer with a girlfriend in Shanghai, completing the final six credits required for a B.Ed. degree that had taken twenty-one years. She was feeling understimulated, anxious for new things to do. She was funny, too, telling me a story, yet another one, about false teeth, this time belonging to a male friend who'd left them at his girlfriend's house the night they had a fight and split up. He asked Dale to retrieve them from the girlfriend; instead, at a bridge game, she presented him with a package of loose yellow teeth she'd unearthed that day in her garden, obviously part of an ancient grave.

Dale gave me a guided tour of the grounds at Hollyhock, passing a direction sign that announced the way to Mayan ruins and the healing centre. The Mayans never made it to British Columbia, but it did not surprise me that someone would have been insensitive enough to transport genuine Mayan artifacts this far north for commercial purposes. It can't be all bad, though, I thought, because the bookstore contained a good selection of poetry, including a book by a friend of mine, and various texts on meditation, T'ai Chi, aromatherapy and what is now called, without irony, "life writing," as if the whole of literature had been concerned only with extraterrestrial matters. Right on cue, a deer appeared on the lawn and a solitary heron was seen to be standing in the shallows, speculating on matters aquatic and spiritual.

I recommended to Dale *The Invention of the World*, a novel by Jack Hodgins I'd been rereading on the boat. One of Jack's characters, Julius Champney, fitted Peter Conrad's definition of the misanthrope to a T. Julius was drawn to islands, but had no use for islanders: "It may surprise you that I loathe the ocean. And that I have little use for the kind of people who move onto islands like this. Whatever their original reason might be, they end up the same. This is a place where people have two goals: to take life slow when it means helping out the other fellow; and to take it fast when it means grabbing a piece of the pie. Island people think they can make their own rules." Julius also describes Maggie Kyle, the main character, preparing for a trip to what could only be Cortes Island: "He'd seen her amongst all those others on the float waiting to crowd into the waiting planes, among three-foot-long beards and fat caftans and at least a dozen pairs of black glasses. . . . He was not there, of course, when she returned two days later, like a sent-home discipline problem. She wouldn't talk about it. Those people knew too much for their own good, was all she would say, and 'I was scared from the minute I put my foot on that island. I didn't belong with those people.'"

As I watched Dale struggle to find a comfortable position in the car, I mulled over her point about there being neither privacy nor a compensating sense of community on many islands. Islands attract two obvious groups: workers who settle there to make some sort of living, to build a community; and others who come to escape, to find some sort of refuge, but are ultimately disappointed. So there's this collision between

small-town politics and disappointed idealism, those who
welcome new business and those who view it as an invasion by
all they've left behind in cities. Cortes, like so many islands
and remote communities, had not solved this dilemma. Larger
island communities, such as those found on Saltspring and
Quadra, had a different set of problems—not attracting industry, but keeping the numbers down and protecting the environment, especially as their educational and medical facilities
had made island living possible for all ages.

Although I was not what James Michener calls a "nesoma-
niac," one who is mad about islands, I'd been attracted all my
life to islands, where, it seemed, all the old rules and restric-
tions might not apply. I'd anchored off Darcy Island, a former
leper colony near Victoria; camped on drying rocks with seals
but no trees or fresh water; considered buying property on
Malcolm Island, a failed utopia farther north. Hong Kong,
Tenerife, Ireland, the Orkneys, New Zealand, Tasmania,
Newfoundland, Prince Edward Island, Fiji, even Isla de
Mujeres off the Yucatan Peninsula, once an uninhabited and
scarcely touched paradise with a few fishermen's houses,
suddenly turned into a crassly commercial hotel strip—all
had proven irresistible. Now I was living on Vancouver
Island, another place reeling from invasionary forces.

Islands make up seven per cent of the earth's land surface,
so they're by no means insignificant. On the West Coast,
thousands of islands shape, obstruct and adorn the Gulf of
Georgia and the Inside Passage; you can't turn around or
swing a cat without seeing or bumping into an island. And
islands—Lesbos, Elba, Bikini Atoll, Skye, Alcatraz—are
central to the mythologies of love, politics, religion and
justice that we have constructed. According to Iain C. Orr, a
consultant who works for the Foreign and Commonwealth
Office in London and is making a database on islands and

their lore, U.S. millionaire Forbes Kiddoo made his own floating island with a huge concrete barge, perhaps inspired by the Floating Islands in Lake Titicaca in Peru.

Would-be islanders, those who have wrecked their own lives and environments and yearn for escape to someplace quiet and pristine, even have a magazine devoted to the dream. It's called, unashamedly, *Islands*. I'd picked up a copy at the ferry terminal in Tsawwassen, a glossy full-colour *mélange* of advertising and upbeat travel articles, one of which was about the recent explosion of media interest in Hawaii, which had brought a fading "Baywatch" sitcom back to life by relocating it and calling it "Baywatch Hawai'i," a sop to the aboriginal pronunciation. The same article outlined the island's film and television history: *South Pacific, From Here to Eternity, Tora! Tora! Tora!, Blue Hawaii*, "Gilligan's Island," "Hawaii Five-o," and *Jurassic Park*, for starters. Sex and war—they both thrive on islands.

But islands, emerging from and disappearing into the sea, have their surprises too. Sometimes they erupt, spewing discontent. Captain James Cook's last bit of R and R on Hawaii cost him his life, hacked to pieces and eaten by angry but admiring natives. Perhaps that's why George Vancouver, who had been a midshipman on that voyage responsible for collecting and giving a proper sea burial to Cook's incomplete remains, was never terribly forthcoming with the aboriginal inhabitants of the West Coast or enamoured of its plethora of islands.

A quick row back to *Groais*. Everything was ready. Dishes stowed, bicycle wiped with oil and folded in the dinghy, the latter secured at the stern, but with a short line until underway so as not to foul the propeller. My strip chart only went

as far as Cape Mudge at the south end of Quadra Island, so I'd
have to ad lib the rest, using the advice and rough drawings in
my cruising guides, all with the warning: NOT TO BE USED
FOR NAVIGATION. Watch for the green barrel and red
buoy that mark the boundaries of Wilby Shoal and expect
turbulence below Quadra, where the fast-moving tide in
Discovery Passage encounters the slower waters of the Strait
of Georgia and the Quadra shallows. A dozen cranks of the
windlass lever and the anchor will be aboard and I'll be on my
way through the entrance in style, perhaps sufficiently organized this time to be able to have a good look at the
pictographs. But first, start the engine. Flip the master switch,
turn the key. Presto!

Zip. Not a peep. As dead in the water as the USS *Arizona*
after the Japanese attack on Pearl Harbor. The phrase "dead
batteries" had been cruising the backwaters of my brain for
days, not so much because of the dangers accompanying such
a predicament as from fear of having to cram myself into the
two narrow lazarettes in the cockpit to inspect the new
twelve-volt beauties, a cranking battery reserved for starting
the engine and a separate "house" battery for all other operations. I'd repressed all thoughts of electrical failure, pretending the batteries didn't exist. And now my worst nightmare
had come to pass. I'd seen Bruce, who sold me the boat, wiggle
himself in there last summer, but I knew my terror of
enclosed spaces would never permit me to do that. He was
slim, six inches shorter, and obviously did not suffer from
claustrophobia. What foolishness; it was just a question of
mind over matter. I dropped my legs into the emptied space
and started to ease my hips through the narrow aperture of
the storage locker under the seat of the cockpit. But it was no
use. Even the thought of ducking my shoulders and head into
that confined space sent me bolting out of the hole gasping for

air, my heart pounding, my shoulder stinging from the impact. I couldn't get both arms in there; and it was so dark I could not distinguish the positive from the negative terminal. I'd have to demolish the lazarette with a saw to get the goddamn batteries out.

Back in the dinghy, doing my Houdini routine with the bicycle, which I came close to chucking overboard, I set out again for the marina, only to be rescued by a hapless Oregonian who made the fatal mistake of saying hello and received a plaintive account of my predicament for his efforts. Together we extracted the starting battery, but his jumper cables had corroded in the salt air and proved useless. This required help from a Seattle boat, getting the state of Washington into the act as well. Before long, I thought, we'll have to call in the marines, if they aren't still busy doing mop-up operations on distant Pacific islands. Once the connections were secure and the key turned, Lister stirred from its enchanted slumber in response to the shock of an electrical kiss. It stuttered, it purred, it sang hallelujah. My gratitude was so excessive, it was embarrassing. I almost forgave the United States for its foreign policy.

I quickly weighed anchor and headed out, knowing the marina operators would not let me fuel up with the engine still running. My only hope was to make it to Campbell River, where there'd be fuel aplenty and an abundance of qualified electricians. I motored towards the Gorge with my tail between my legs and a couple of fenders still dangling inelegantly in the water. The sun was knocking itself out to make this setting perfect; the reflection of trees danced in the water stirred by my passage. I felt like Adam being expelled from Eden. I still couldn't make out the painted images and I half expected a huge rock to come hurtling down at me from the cliff. Since I was hogging the narrow entrance, an incoming boat had to jockey to hold its position in the fast current. Skipper and crew gave me a cursory, dismissive glance, as if I were a fading and no-longer-decipherable pictograph.

Not exactly the grand exit I'd envisaged.

✳ Nine

Nothing's the same after Campbell River, gateway to the central and north coasts. Even the tides move differently there. Instead of ebbing south, the waters of the northern Gulf of Georgia make a dash for the nearest exit, pouring north through a slim gap called Seymour Narrows, where the infamous Ripple Rock, only a fathom below the surface at low tide, sank many ships before being blown up in 1958, in what was, at the time, the world's largest non-nuclear explosion. The city of Campbell River is located halfway up the Vancouver Island side of Discovery Passage, looking across at Quadra Island. That portion of the Inside Passage is a geographical bottleneck through which must funnel huge volumes of water, and the currents in mid-channel run from six to nine knots at full flood or ebb, requiring the Quadra ferry to set a course well above or below its mark. Campbell River, then, is the ideal abode for wall-eyed mariners and for irony; even the long-time residents have a devious look about them and a way of saying one thing when they mean another.

"Ya, sure, it's the genuine item. Hundred per cent." The clerk at the First Nations crafts store in the new plaza bent over to straighten one corner of the nine-by-twelve rug I'd been coveting. I couldn't afford it and it was the last thing I needed to add to the clutter on the boat. I figured I could ask them to store it for me until my return; besides, the interlocking black-and-red totemic figures on a tan background, done in a tightly knit wool weave, would be gorgeous in my dining area back home. I examined the rug carefully. Then I noticed on the label that it was made in India.

"India? I thought you said this was genuine," I blurted out, scandalized by my discovery. Plastic beavers and Mounties made in Taiwan were one thing, but Native crafts? The young woman, who had been twisting her red lips to one side in imitation of the grotesque Hamatsa mask mounted on the wall beside her, gave me a bemused look.

"That's right, designed in Canada by a local Kwak-waka'wakw artist and manufactured in Calcutta. You can't get more Indian than that."

The city of Campbell River is famous in fishing and literary circles, especially amongst readers of fisherman, naturalist and magistrate Roderick Haig-Brown, the latter-day Isaac Walton who wrote so lyrically about its waterways. I had never learned to read or appreciate rivers. The North Arm of the Fraser River, which separated Vancouver from Rich-mond, had not played much of a part in my growing up, but the waterfront, with its complex smorgasbord of natural and industrial smells (creosote, diesel, fish guts, grains, salt water, and the always surprising ripeness of low tide), was comfort-ingly familiar. In Coal Harbour or at English Bay and Spanish Banks, the tides rose and fell with a quiet regularity, with seasonal highs and lows, carrying yet another catalogue of assorted goodies such as driftwood, dead cats, the wreckage of boats, condoms, rubbish, the occasional Japanese fishing-float. The waves varied in intensity, lapping or pounding the sand, the rocks and the sea walls, but there was little of the sense of danger, the constant and dramatic movement, that I associated with rivers or with the powerful currents surging through Discovery Passage.

Despite its fast currents, Campbell River turned out to be a crass but welcome oasis. Ripple Rock was nothing in comparison to the population explosion here of prairie farmers and pensioners fleeing the Canadian and American winters in search of sun, wild spring salmon and a piece of the coast. What they got instead was rain, frozen Atlantic salmon grown locally and cramped living quarters. The sleepy hamlet had been transformed into a mass of shopping malls, ugly condos and bursting marinas. I loved it. While an electrician cleaned my alternator and switched a couple of wires that he said had been reversed, I topped up the batteries and attached them to the new charger I'd purchased. Within hours, Lister was up and running, its pulse regular and strong. *Groais* might be ready to go, but I had no intention of quitting this marine haven so soon and wasted no time abandoning my persona as Sinbad the Sailor to become Sherman the Shopper. Within a couple of days, I'd called everyone I knew in town, done several loads of laundry and sampled a variety of restaurants, including an oyster bar housed across from the marina in a former double-decker bus. The cooking oil must have been as old as the bus, if not from the crankcase itself, as the fries gave me a dreadful case of indigestion. I spent the second morning weaving through traffic on my bicycle, steering with one hand and with the other desperately trying to balance the weight of five or more plastic bags laden with groceries, mostly canned goods and containers of juice. As I careened through an intersection just past the Quadra ferry, my Chinese imitation of a Tilley hat blew off. By the time I'd unloaded my bags on the sidewalk and retrieved it, a larger four-by-four had run over the hat, giving it the appearance of zebra skin.

I was enjoying the protection and all the amenities of Vancouver Island, that convenient 350-mile offshore parenthesis that keeps the Lower Mainland from slipping into or feeling the full brunt of the Pacific Ocean. Vancouver Island began as an underwater disruption in the earth's crust, originating somewhere in the vicinity of Peru, and appears to have spent its first 375 million years on the road. During the Cretaceous period in the Mesozoic era, this crusty nomad threw in its lot, albeit reluctantly, with the North American continent. While the Yukon, Southern Alaska, and other parts of Wrangellia cozied up, some of them adding to the existing confusion of the Coast Range, the Vancouver Island portion kept its distance, much as its future inhabitants would do when British Columbia decided to join Confederation, flying their flags at half-mast and never quite admitting that their destiny lay with the rest of Canada. The other Wrangellian holdout was the Queen Charlotte Islands, also known as Haida Gwai, equally determined to stand alone.

Geologists can't resist describing the northward journey of this vast underwater terrain in epic terms, focusing on Wrangellia as a protean shape-changer whose multiple guises included a brief fling as a string of erupting volcanoes, followed by a sedentary period of accumulating bulk, and a brief .35-billon-year stint of adolescent destructiveness, spewing green lava onto the ocean floor in the form of deep carpets of ash and large building blocks called "pillows." Exhausted, it lay back periodically and allowed itself to be compromised and colonized by various marine animals, including crinoids, brachiopods and bryozoa. According to Chris Yorath and Hugh Nasmith, the Plato and Aristotle of coastal geology, the continental plate tried to subsume everything in its way, sucking much of this upstart plate back into the earth's molten core. They compare the speed of the sea floor's spreading, four centimetres per year, with the rate of growth of fingernails; in other words, four metres or thirteen feet of the Pacific plate are subsumed every hundred years.

If the slow but perpetual colliding of landmasses and the consequent upheaval of mountains aren't obvious enough, there is more dramatic evidence available of the tremendous forces at work on the coast. In 1964, one side of a central street in Anchorage, Alaska, not far from the earthquake's Prince William Sound epicentre, dropped twenty-four feet and the town of Valdez was completely destroyed by the resulting tsunami, buildings sheared off foundations and large boats deposited a hundred yards up the hillside. I remember that event because an uncle in Vancouver, Art Bates, purchased for next to nothing a new Porsche that had been swamped by the residual tidal wave in Port Alberni, seven hundred miles farther south. I was no geologist. I'd like to have been able to identify all those igneous, sedimentary and metamorphic rocks as I ploughed my way up the Inside Passage. Unfortunately, I was, at times, so preoccupied with trying to keep from being subsumed myself, I scarcely noticed the shapes and colours of countless rock faces, bluffs and promontories as I passed. I was too busy imagining the ones I couldn't see, growing down there, incrementally, like granite fangs or flint-edged fingernails, towards the bottom of my boat.

On my third morning in Campbell River, I'd awakened around 0530 at first light. I was a wreck. I'd wrestled half the night on the narrow bunk with a cheap sleeping bag that kept bunching up under my shoulder blades or trying to gravitate to the floor. I could just make out above me the mahogany ribs—overhead frames, they were called—outlined against the white paint on the cabin ceiling. With the stale, bilgey smell of diesel, the primal funk of low tide, and the nearby fish dock, those dark ribs made me feel like Jonah in the cramped belly of the whale, or Pierre Aronnax, the narrator of Jules Verne's *Twenty Thousand Leagues Under the Sea*, after being dragged on board the *Nautilus*. So much for the joy of intimate spaces. However, it wasn't just the confined quarters that had kept me awake. I was having second thoughts about the trip north. Everyone I met seemed to have some disaster story to tell me, even my old acquaintance, Justus Havelaar, who taught English in the local high school.

"You can't tow a sailboat faster than its official hull speed," Justus was saying. He and his wife Sandy, a piano teacher, had spent a couple of years on exchange in Quebec and their kids had gone through French immersion in Campbell River. They were amused to see my most recent incarnation as the Old Man of the Sea. The story he was telling me involved a disabled sailboat under tow by the Coast Guard. "Otherwise, the keel comes to the surface, causing the boat to flip. My friend barely had time to cut the tow rope and get himself and his wife into the water before the boat went down."

"Did they—?" I didn't need to ask. As much chance of compensation from the Coast Guard as there was from the Chilean government two years earlier, when one of their submarines on manoeuvres with the Americans had accidentally rammed and sunk a Canadian sailboat in the Strait of Juan de Fuca. At least they heard the bump and stopped to rescue the skipper of the craft. The U.S. marine on board as an adviser blamed the half-drowned sailor for not noticing the tiny eye of the periscope coming towards him at twenty miles an hour in the dark.

Trevor McMonagle, a high school teacher and former student of mine, had joined me on the boat the previous day for coffee and crackers. He'd cycled down and was looking quite breezy in shorts and T-shirt, clearly a harbinger of good tidings. He looked around the boat, nodding, making approving noises. Then he asked me about my Orkney poems, a few of which he'd heard me read two years earlier at the University of Victoria. He was interested in a long poem about Venetian captain Antonio Zen and Henry St. Clair, the Earl of Orkney, who were alleged to have sailed together to Greenland, Iceland, Newfoundland, Cape Breton Island, and what is now Boston during the summer of 1398, almost a hundred years before Columbus. Being modest men, and knowing that the Vikings, the Irish priests, and scores of others had preceded them, they simply conducted some research, exchanged trade items, and returned home. Trevor was keen to share with me the fact that he knew the current Earl of Orkney, a personal friend and a university professor in Winnipeg. I was delighted to have this information, but before I could learn more, Trevor blurted out something he'd just heard on the news that dispelled all thoughts of the wayward earl.

"Local news this morning. I just heard it. Coast Guard alert. Young couple on a sailboat. Reported missing, somewhere between Cape Scott and the Charlottes. Twelve days—" He paused, suddenly aware of the disjunction in our conversation, and pieced together an awkward grin. "Twelve days since anyone heard from them."

I might have attributed these stories to the neuroses of landlubbers had not the only fisherman I'd met in town been fully equipped with his own string of cautionary tales for mariners.

"It's common knowledge," Steve Martin said, "that a strong westerly wind and an ebbing tide will turn Johnstone Strait into a deadly stretch of water. Steep waves at very short intervals can flip even a large troller or seiner, especially one that doesn't slow down and take evasive action." The area around Kelsey Bay was one of the most treacherous. Steve was putting the season's finishing touches on his troller, *Ocean Fury*, which was moored across the float from me, giving it the royal treatment—undercoat and an expensive white enamel. For the trim, he used an oil-based alternative to varnish, which was supposed to penetrate the wood and act more as a preservative. He didn't like the effect, though, or the fact that it was so absorbent; you couldn't wash off the spilled white paint as easily as from a coat of varnish.

I was sitting in *Groais*'s cockpit in the shade of a plastic tarpaulin I'd rigged as a boom tent. I hadn't quite recovered from the ordeal of fish and chips, grocery shopping and "Indian" culture. Steve cast a disapproving eye at my laundry still pegged and drying on the lifelines. He'd told me the previous day he never let his crew do that. Some of us have lower standards, I said. I asked him what I might expect on the north coast.

"Lots of fog and too many boats."

I rolled up my sleeping bag, stuffed it behind the backrest, and thrust my head out the forward hatch. Feeling embarrassed by the shabby appearance of *Groais*, last winter's winds in Bellingham having whipped a procession of plastic tarpaulins into a paint-stripping fury of their own, I'd let Steve's industry inspire me to get out the brushes. Unfortunately, I was downwind from two young guys using a propane torch and scraper to remove black paint from an ancient seiner that someone was obviously hoping to patch up and sell to an unsuspecting pensioner from Alberta. The gunwales and planking above the deck had rotted off and the entire vessel had an air of doom about it, as if John Wayne and his helmeted crew of deep-sea salvagers had just raised it from a watery grave. It wouldn't have surprised me if it had been called the *Red Witch*. I had to put up not only with the fumes, but also with drifting flakes of black paint that were determined to settle on the fresh cream colour I'd used to touch up the cabin.

I'd decided, out of solidarity, to tie up with the workers at Finger A, Fisherman's Wharf, rather than amongst the glistening craft in the adjoining yacht basin, but my loyalties were under severe strain and I had a different finger in mind for these early morning strippers, who were already at work, laughing and oblivious, ghetto blaster cranked up, country-western torch songs slicing the morning calm as they incinerated black paint down to the waterline.

I closed the forward hatch, sat down to a cup of tea, and spread out the two dozen photographs given to me in Pender Harbour by Bill Turner, Uncle Tom's cousin. Bill and Tom had both been in the RAF and had been quite close. They agreed, if they survived the war, to go into business together when they returned to Canada. Bill had the money to purchase land, so he and Tom became partners in Garrow Bay Boat Rentals in Howe Sound.

When Uncle Tom rented space at Whytecliffe and went into competition, Bill and Doris did not stay long; they sold the business and bought a farm in the Fraser Valley. Bill spent some time as a social worker until, as he explained, a "different philosophy" came to prevail in government, by which he meant chronic handouts rather than helping people find work. He must have been a good scrapper in his time, certainly a good worker. He had such a pleasing way of pronouncing my name, making the *g* and *r* sound less nasal and harsh by forming the word farther back in the mouth and dragging lots of air across the consonants in the process. I don't know why, but it had always made me feel better about myself to hear him pronounce my name; and after more than forty years, it still did. When I asked him about Tom carrying coal in the winters, he laughed.

"We both did, Gary, but not for long. Nancy's family was able to get us jobs loading coal on the waterfront. We put all our money into steel-toed boots for the job, but after only one day we both decided to quit. Never had much use for those boots again, though Tom may have used his cutting Christmas trees over in Washington."

Bill went through his albums ruthlessly removing photographs from their old-fashioned corner-mounts and offering them to me. Photos of my mother and Auntie Pat as young girls with ringlets, as teenagers with shorter hair pulled across the face in the twenties style. There they were sitting on the running-board of an early model "Star" touring car, the kind with wooden spoke wheels, a canopy, two rows of seats and a windshield, Pat looking at the camera, my mother gazing off into the distance. In a more bucolic shot, the girl who would become my mother stands in the long grass, her arm resting on my grandfather's shoulder, while he squats holding an infant Uncle Tom in his arms. She's wearing white socks, a huge white bow above her ringlets, and knee socks that almost meet the hem of her cotton dress. In one shot, my mother is seated in a field of flowers holding a new puppy up to her face, so only her eyes are visible to the camera, above the puppy's mottled stomach and small bud of a penis; in another, she is stretching the pup's abundant jowls to simulate a smile. She looks happy in that picture, though she's not smiling, not exactly. She doesn't smile on demand like Pat, but always seems to be thinking, weighing the situation, sizing up the photographer.

What did I expect to find in these photographs? Bloodlines, familiar bone structures—they're all evident. I was trying to reconstruct something more than a series of names and begats. I wanted to know how it felt to be Irene Turner on a given day and whether it seemed, at least part of the time, worth having been born into this family. I wanted to know the forces at work behind these photographs, the moods and grievances and agendas. Here is my mother who will die when she is thirty-four. Can some foreknowledge of that fact be seen in her serious face? And what about Pat's fate? She was injured during her teens in a car crash that left her with the mental capacity of a child. She was a simple, fun-loving soul, an innocent. I recall her as a grown woman sticking out her thumb to hitchhike on Forty-first Avenue, after taking me to the dentist. She had my cousin Tommy, my brother Jim, and me in tow. A garbage truck stopped to pick us up. She sat in front laughing with the driver while the three of us kids rode in the box amongst the bottles, tins, loose paper, and several rotting cabbages that rolled back and forth each time the truck braked or accelerated. We loved every minute of it and groaned in disapproval when the driver dropped us off at Forty-first and Maple. With Pat, you never knew what to expect. In her later years she had a second automobile accident, which cost her a leg, but this did not slow her down. She remained attractive and good-natured, never without a partner. She once escaped a house-fire in the nick of time, but her wooden leg went up in flames.

When Grampa Turner died, Pat was in the bow of the rowboat that carried his ashes out to the reef off the point at Whytecliffe, her new wooden leg notwithstanding. Uncle Tom, still sporting the mustache he'd grown in the war to make himself look older, was at the oars; and, for some unknown reason, my father, who had divorced Tom's sister so many years earlier, had been invited along and was ensconced uncomfortably in the stern. It was a sunny day with a slight westerly blowing, so the rowboat was a bit unsteady from the light chop. My father and uncle were in suits, trying to keep their good shoes out of the water that was spilling over the gunwales and sloshing around in the bilge. Pat, typically, was dressed for a picnic, in floral dress and sunhat, a large family Bible tucked under her arm. She had consulted my brother Jim, a psychologist and former Baptist minister in Saskatchewan, over the phone about what to read before Gramp's ashes were tipped into the sea. Jim had suggested a brief passage from the First Epistle of St. John, but Pat misunderstood and would have read the entire Gospel of John had the wave action not increased and my uncle insisted on abbreviating the text. With a unanimous amen, they chucked the ashes overboard, container and all.

The photograph I kept returning to showed my mother at ten or eleven in a cotton dress, sitting on a huge rock at the beach, in a pose similar to that of the Copenhagen mermaid. The photo, a bit blurred, is not that interesting in its own right. But it contains on the reverse side the only sample of my mother's handwriting I'd ever seen—"This was taken at Bowen Island when I was at Mrs. Gordon's Camp." Signed "Rene." I hadn't noticed the brief inscription when Bill first gave me the photographs a week earlier in Pender Harbour, while Lewis waited on board *Groais*.

Though I'd had little sense of her presence while I was in Howe Sound or Fisherman's Cove, I felt strangely close to my mother at this moment in the cabin of my boat at Finger A of the fish dock in Campbell River, with all the debris of the trip—papers, computer, books, photos, dirty dishes— strewn about. I had these images spread out on the table and I was weeping, because of fourteen brief words written by my mother so long ago on the back of a black-and-white photograph, the discoloured corner-mounts still attached. It's as if something in the handwriting were more real, more authentic, than the image itself, her own observations on the occasion rather than someone else's efforts to compose a world with her in it.

To have made this discovery in Campbell River, in Discovery Passage no less, was especially gratifying, as this was where I'd reconnected with my mother's best friend, Ann Gill, after a thirty-seven-year absence. A chance encounter at a garden party in Cumberland, an eight-page letter she'd sent me about my mother, as well as a box of keepsakes: a Royal Doulton cookie plate with Cairo pattern, a cameo brooch, a Chinese tea canister, a plastic cigarette case and box made for my mother by her second husband, Jim Friesen. I read Ann's letter over and over—how they walked their babies together in prams along Victoria Drive in Vancouver, how my mother loved to sing, how she had promised, during the final days, to send Ann the smell of strawberries from beyond as a reminder of their friendship. I had great hopes of filling in some of the blanks from what Ann might still tell me, but before I could arrange a second visit she, too, had died of cancer.

The strippers had signed off early, but Steve Martin was still working on the final touch-up of his gunwales and trim. He remembered the good old days when you could make a bundle in a few short months of fishing. He'd had six weeks on prawns so far, but didn't expect much from the sockeye. He and his wife bought, renovated, and rented houses, so they could afford to be philosophical about reduced fish stocks and shorter seasons. Fishing, for Steve, was a way of life that was fast becoming little more than a hobby. He spent a lot of time at the dock, fussing with the *Ocean Fury*, and seemed to enjoy showing me the ropes, the lockers lined with hundreds of carefully stowed flashers and pink hoochies that were supposed to lift off in perfect order as the lines were paid out.

"Hey, don't be so pessimistic, Steve. How could any self-respecting sockeye resist a boat like this?"

"I mentioned your name to Patrick Lihou. He's working on that old wooden classic down the way. He collects your books." All this said in a tone slightly accusatory.

I'd talked to Patrick earlier. Aside from his dubious taste in books, he was a lovely man, with just the kind of smile and light in his eyes to make a student content, if not wildly enthusiastic, to be in his classroom. He was redoing the interior and superstructure of the *Selima*, a yacht built decades earlier for Eric Hamber, the lieutenant-governor of British Columbia, and then sold to handloggers who used it for years in Rivers Inlet. Patrick had lived from age ten to fifteen on Cortes, where his father was a teacher, when the island still had hand-cranked telephones and private generators, and before it was discovered by the cosmic set. We talked about a possible reading and workshop at his school some time in the fall.

Whether it was the fact that I was a writer or that he'd quickly assessed how frightened and incompetent I was—all those nervous questions about weather—Steve had come to the conclusion that I needed looking after, one of the stranger fish to haul up in his net. The previous night he'd invited me home for dinner, on the pretext that he had a couple of books of local history that might interest me. I could see him announcing this news to his wife through the glass of the phone booth at the head of the pier. The call took longer than it should have, so I knew he was getting shit for not giving her more warning. Although I'd already eaten, I was grateful for the diversion and a chance to escape my monkish cell for a few hours. I enjoyed meeting Elsa and their three bright kids and inspecting the menagerie of cats, birds, and tropical fish.

The youngest son told me they'd just gotten rid of a turtle that devoured all their tropical fish and generally tyrannized the tank.

"When you're that slow," I said, "you make up for it by being a bully."

They were a religious family and the eldest, a daughter, sang in the church choir and took voice lessons. She'd be in Justus Havelaar's class in the fall, she confided, obviously pleased. When I asked about their family background, Elsa showed me a portrait of her parents in a frame studded with tiny shells. Steve hauled out a hardcover book—*Robert Martin of Brand*—written by a member of the clan who was important and owned a large house in England. Even the Martins, it seemed, were looking for self-authenticating stories beyond the official ones offered in the Bible.

This scrambling after roots, what's it all about? Do the stories we spin, the family romance, make us more authentic? I'd expended a lot of energy gathering stories that might constitute a memoir, an autobiography, but I seemed no closer yet to any essential truth about my family. I knew less about some of my relatives than I knew about complete strangers; and the fragments, however tantalizing, seemed more likely to resemble a drawing by Picasso—everything distorted and out of kilter—than anything consistent or coherent. My predicament reminded me of the receptionist at Copp Clark Publishing Company in Toronto, who answered a call by someone wanting the autobiography of Bertrand Russell. The receptionist's surprising question—"Who is the author?"—was the source of considerable amusement for me and my friends, feeling ourselves superior and in the know. Now I wonder if she did not have some special insight it has taken me thirty years to grasp.

Ten

"Water baffles us. Contained, it can be measured, given shape and colour, harnessed to cut rock, illuminate cities. Lacking form, it calls to things inside we'd thought forgotten." Those lines, written almost thirty years ago in response to my grandfather's emigration from Scotland and eventual death by drowning off Point Atkinson, had been turning in my mind as I prepared to take the back route to the north coast via Cordero Channel, which winds through several rapids but is otherwise protected from the westerlies that sometimes whip to a boil the lower reaches of Johnstone Strait. I'd been trying to resist a clichéd gendering of seascape, but the umbilical anchor rode and the amniotic lapping—not to mention the legacy of evolutionary thinking about the ocean as the womb of all life—were becoming more difficult to ignore. Expelled, skidded into air, even my lungs, humming a Stan Rogers tune about raising the hulk of the *Mary Ellen Carter*, seemed to be confusing tideline and songline, speaking a restlessness born of moving water.

There was more moving water ahead than I needed or bargained for, however basic and primitive its attraction might be. Yaculta Rapids had assumed mythic proportions in my imagination because of stories told by my father and brother, who took that route home from the fishing grounds in Rivers Inlet. They made the rapids sound like Hell's Gate on the Fraser River and the whirlpools seem the size of the Grand Canyon. My brother described a trip south when he and my father went through Yaculta against a full ebb and were only able to make progress and stay afloat by having their boats lashed together, my father's four-cylinder gas engine and Jim's single-cylinder Easthope at full bore. Suction from the whirlpools on either side was so strong that the boats inched through the tidal maelstrom at a terrifying angle, their masts like crossed spears overhead and the ropes strained to bursting. Logs sucked into the vortex would be tossed several metres into the air, if you weren't unlucky enough to have your hull punctured by a direct hit.

"You've got a guest waiting for you on the boat."

Steve Martin, paintbrush in hand, seemed unusually pleased to be making this announcement from the bow of the *Ocean Fury*. Having picked up on my inexperience and anxious inquiries, he must have been relieved to know I'd have company, however briefly, on my trip north. Given all the disaster stories he and others had eagerly told me, I was beginning to share the sentiment.

Geri was reading a book and listening to classical music on the radio. There was a bottle of beer open on the table. The one bag she'd brought with her would contain at least two items, binoculars and a book on coastal birds, though she hardly needed the latter. Now that she'd arrived, my awareness of flying things would leap from the generic to the specific.

"How's the Bird Lady of Alcatraz?"

"Good. The drive from Duke Point wasn't too long. You don't look nearly as ragged as I'd expected."

"You should see my nerves."

Geri had driven up from Bellingham, where she worked at the university. We had been introduced in the elevator of the administration building, an uplifting moment, on my way to the personnel office. Since I was camping overnight on *Groais* at Squalicum Marina, much to the amusement of my colleagues and boss, Don Alper, this fact was mentioned to Geri, who was an experienced sailor. When I asked what she sailed, she blurted out that her ex got the boat. It turned out we had both been previously married and were nursing wounds from subsequent failed relationships. The plan was for her to spend a week on board, exploring Desolation Sound and, since she was an avid student of anthropology, visiting Village Island, site of the last great potlatch in 1921, and Alert Bay, where many of the items confiscated from that potlatch—ceremonial masks, blankets, coppers, baskets, cedar boxes—had now been returned and were on exhibit in the new museum. Port McNeill was her final destination before heading home.

The first three days together were a delight. We dined out, enthused over the stunning array of Kwakwaka'wakw masks for sale in the crafts shop, and caught the morning flood tide that swept us past Cape Mudge towards West Redonda Island. In spite of her reservations, I think Geri was relieved by the few signs of competence I'd shown as a boat owner. On the domestic front, I'd made curtains. I purchased three custom-made valances, those twelve-inch borders that run across the top of a kitchen window. Two of these did for the main cabin. The third I cut in half, hemming the ends by hand, and hung over the portholes in the galley and above the chart table. The jazzy, abstract design was perfectly coordinated with the new green upholstery. While I didn't stow gear or ropes properly, I did manage to foster the illusion of knowing how to handle the boat, even under sail. I had not yet memorized all the buoys and markers, but I was less of a hazard to shipping than I'd been a month earlier or during the winter, when I insisted on telling her friends and family my story about not knowing that asterisks on the chart represented rocks.

"Look, over there!"

"What?"

"Rhinoceros auklet." I made the effort, but always seemed to look too late or in the wrong direction and couldn't tell one floating ball of feathers from another. I'd had a near miss earlier in the day, though, when I tried to identify a black-headed gull.

"Napoleon?"

"Close. Bonaparte."

The day before, we'd been sailing between Cortes and West Redonda islands. The light westerly scarcely justified hoisting sails, but it was the perfect day for such glorified drifting. Even the training schooner *Maple Leaf* off our starboard bow, full of kids in uniform, was making little way. Geri had years of sailing experience and had taken a power squadron course, so I was glad to let her worry about the set of the main, tension on the jib sheets, and the fact that the bulky knots I'd tied kept catching on the shrouds each time the boat came around on a new tack. She pointed out that I was using a genoa rather than a normal foresail and that the aging jenny had "bagged," meaning it had permanent stretchmarks from too much wind-bearing. I smiled appreciatively. I was pleased to be able to relax and go below to make sandwiches or crack open my box of fishing tackle.

We agreed there was not enough wind to blow out a match and decided to pack it in. As soon as the sails were down, I flipped the master switch and turned the key to activate the starter. Kaput—and only five days after having the generator repaired. I checked out the fuses, the connectors, even gave the starter motor a few bangs with the wooden handle of the hammer. *Rien.* Geri seemed more amused than surprised, as if she'd been expecting something like this. So much for the illusion of competence. I made a quick call to the nearest marina and a local mechanic, Jan Hansen, arrived alongside in a sixteen-foot runabout with an outboard motor. There was juice in the batteries, but he couldn't get Lister to turn over. After towing us into Refuge Cove, aptly named, where the floats were jammed with American boats, he disappeared up the gangway with the starter motor under his arm.

This spot on West Redonda Island was one of the few harbours in Desolation Sound with a fuel dock, store, post office, telephone and café, though not a single road connected it to the rest of the island. While we were cooking dinner a classy fibreglass sloop called *Ginger Lady* from Redmond, Washington, made a somewhat more elegant entrance than our ignominious one two hours earlier. It was skippered by a distinguished-looking gentleman with a long grey ponytail.

"Software type," Geri said. When I gave her a glazed look, she explained that Redmond, a Seattle suburb, was Silicon Valley North. Oodles of money.

While I admired the lines of the boat and its extravagant equipment, which included dacron sails, radar, solar panels and auto-helm, the skipper threw his engine into reverse without first hauling in the dinghy, the result of which was seventeen wraps of nylon line around his propeller. For the next hour, there was a scurry of activity at the dock as one of the local boys in a face mask had a go at the tangled line with a knife, while his mother hovered nearby, worrying about the cold water. Several nautical mascots, which Geri had identified as a Scottie, a Shar-Pei, and a Great Pyrenees, were chasing a tabby cat back and forth along the floats. Eventually, Geri's programmer donned a wetsuit and finished the job himself.

Jan Hansen arrived at the boat at 0900 the following morning with the starter motor overhauled, the solenoid cleaned and its points resoldered. He made a few adjustments to the wiring, so that the gauge in the cockpit finally registered positive when the battery was charging. The motor fired immediately. Since I paid him more than the modest sum he'd requested, Jan insisted on doing a free oil change and showed me how to crank-start the engine by flipping two decompression levers I hadn't even noticed protruding like antennae from Lister's green head. A diesel engine, he explained, once you get it going, will run even without help from the electrical system, but you have to make sure you flip both levers back at the same moment after firing or it will put the engine out of whack. Second, cranking will work only in a mild climate or if the engine is not too cold; otherwise, you need to put a modicum of ether in the carburettor or air intake to enhance combustion.

Before making a run through Yaculta Rapids, we stopped for several hours to wait for slack water at Dent Island Lodge, where the manager Henry Moll could hardly have been keen to see us, since his establishment is private and he was about to host executives from Weyerhaeuser, the new American czar of the B.C. forest industry. Henry was most gracious, however, showing us around the establishment and letting us come ashore to photograph a young black bear that was becoming a pest and had been treed by the lodge's ancient, emphysemic, no-brand dog. As if to confirm my belief that every second person in British Columbia is a writer, Henry confided that he'd lived for many years outside Kingston, running a similar business on Wolfe Island, and had once won the *Whig-Standard* short story competition. Before the ebb whisked me north, we toyed with the idea of hosting a writing workshop at Dent Island Lodge during the off-season months.

Though I'd read all the cruising guides and digested so many horror stories in advance, our passage through the Yaculta Rapids was by no means anticlimactic. Even at so-called high-slack, the currents are tricky around Dent Island, where the constricted waters can't decide whether to take the direct route past Devil's Hole or the indirect route through Tugboat Passage. I had less trouble making that choice. As I steered into the quieter channel, hands seemed to be reaching out to *Groais*'s hull from every direction, one minute swinging her towards the rocks, the next into mid-channel. Judging from the noise and vibrations in the driveshaft, the force and fluctuations of current underneath the boat were ferocious enough to retard or accelerate the action of the propeller. Several kelp beds torn loose and adrift on the troubled surface provided another danger to be avoided, as this was no place for a fouled prop or rudder. I had to brace myself to hang on to the tiller, which was swinging like a baseball bat in the hands of a deranged infielder.

Although the passage took less than fifteen minutes, by the time we were expelled into the broader channel, flushed like refuse from an unblocked storm drain, I was so wiped out from nervous exhaustion I could have fallen asleep at the helm. Since there were two more obstacles ahead, Greene Rapids and Whirlpool Rapids, which, at our snail's pace, would have to be encountered at the next slack water, we decided to spend the night in Blind Channel. I'd had enough moving water, thank you; in fact, I was ready to chuck my Darwin books, revoke my aquatic origins altogether, and crawl out permanently onto the land like a disgruntled tetrapod. Besides, Blind Channel seemed the perfect destination for someone who could scarcely read a chart.

I turned the boat into Blind Channel Marina. Geri, of course, had been unfazed by all this watery commotion. She had the binoculars out and was busy examining several bald eagle nests, which seemed to be spaced at regular intervals of about five hundred yards. She had also made sandwiches and coffee. We'd had a disagreement about cormorants earlier, about why they stretch their wings as if yawning or doing a "Me, Tarzan" muscleflex for display purposes.

"They do that to dry their wings," Geri said.

"Not according to my sources."

"What, then?"

I should have dropped the matter. I rationalized my determination to continue by telling myself she would appreciate any signs of interest I showed in birding, but I knew it was just as much a cheap grab for power, a way of diverting attention from my nautical and emotional inadequacies. I ducked into the cabin and pulled out my *Guide to Marine Life*, published by the B.C. Provincial Museum.

"It says cormorants extend their wings as if to dry them, but that, and here I'm quoting, 'this action helps restore the trapped air which has been expelled from the feathers by water pressure.' Unquote."

"You've become quite the authority." It was obvious that the process of drying involved removing the water from feathers, in effect replacing it with air, a fine discrimination Geri didn't need pointed out. I felt stupid. I made a lame joke about a cormorant, at a depth of seventy-five feet, sticking its beak into an armpit for a quick hit of oxygen, but passing out from the smell. I was in deep water myself. She put her binoculars away.

"When was that article published?" Instead of chucking the drab government document overboard and watching it become part of the marine life, I pressed blindly on and flipped to the copyright page.

"1963."

"Hmm."

One of the things I'd done in Campbell River was acquire a complete set of maps. I'd not only had enough close calls and surprises, but also seen the folly of maps with insufficient detail to realize I'd never survive the trip north without proper aids to navigation. A wing and a prayer would not suffice. After the initial shock of finding out I'd need at least twenty more overlapping maps to take me to Bella Bella, the farthest point north I intended to sail, including all the side trips I expected to take into Knight and Rivers inlets, I was hardly prepared to learn they would cost twenty bucks a pop. I searched for a lower price in three different marine supply stores to no avail and then decided, given the amount I'd already blown on this dubious escapade, that my life was worth another four hundred dollars. I tucked this expensive security bundle—a huge tube of rolled-up charts that looked like a cigar for Goliath—under my arm and headed back to the boat, confident, at least, that my demise would not be attributable to a foolish shortage of maps, only to an inability to read them properly.

I'd been somewhat scornful of the mapping process, linking it to the colonizing impulse, to imperialism. What were Cook and Vancouver, after all, but a couple of real estate sharks in the employ of king and capital? I knew maps were useful, that aboriginal peoples kept elaborate maps in their heads, maps they could reproduce in words or with scratches on the ground. My view of written maps, however, was not unlike Claude Lévi-Strauss's view of written language. "If my hypothesis is correct," he wrote, "the primary function of writing, as a means of communication, is to facilitate the enslavement of other human beings. The use of writing for disinterested ends, and with a view to satisfactions of the mind in the fields either of science or the arts, is a secondary result of its invention—and may even be no more than a way of reinforcing, justifying, or dissimulating its primary function." His hypothesis emerged, interestingly, from observing how quickly an illiterate Nambikwara chief in Brazil grasped the gist of this new form of magic after he'd seen the scribal antics of the foreigners. The chief made some meaningless scratches on paper with a pencil, then proceeded to "read" them to his assembled tribe, holding them in thrall by the power of his new "scriptures."

Mapping, of course, is as natural as breathing or naming. We are constantly mapping our passage through the world, whether it's a trip to the back country or to the shopping centre—recording obstacles, easy routes, the location of food and water supplies, bargain prices, and dangers—so we can find our way back easily, then inform our family and friends of what's "in store" if they make the same journey. You might say we do the same thing in our interpersonal relations, carefully noting which people are safe company, which ones can take a joke (not enough), and where the power resides in given situations. We are mapping the social, psychological and political climate constantly. In fact, the term "mapping" has become so common that it has infiltrated all the arts and sciences to the point that it needs to be outlawed for at least a century. Critics speak of a literary text as a map, the author of which has laid out a set of behaviours, landscapes, ideologies, all of which can be studied as easily as Vancouver's charts of the west coast of North America; all these little verbal notations in the text, which we used to think of, quite happily, as characters made of words and phrases, are now called signs or signifiers.

Nothing, it seems, has escaped the scourge of the mapmaker. You can map pig's bristles or the genes that cause halo blight in beans; you can even map the way pheromones bind with the protein in mouse urine. Psychologists and neurologists use functional magnetic resonance imaging (FMRI) to map brain activity, to see how the mind processes information, which parts of it respond to faces, movement, colour. Eleven researchers collaborated on an article that appears in the *Journal of Neurophysiology* under the title "Spatiotemporal Activity of a Cortical Network for Processing Visual Motion Revealed by MEG and FMRI." If you want to know about eye movements—maybe someone's winked at you lately—or which signs "point to a localized electrical dipole in occipitotemporal cortex evoked by visual stimuli"—and who in their right (or left) mind wouldn't—just check out M. W. Greenlee's article in the *International Review of Neurobiology* entitled "Human Cortical Areas Underlining the Perception of Optic Flow: Brain Imaging Studies." No wonder the natives were made restless in Hawaii, and on the West Coast, by the spreading plague of ships' artists, and later by photographers; rightly worried about losing their souls, they intuited, correctly, that these technologies were the advance guard of retinoptic mapping techniques. And who's surprised to find psychologists and neurologists using the term "mapping" to describe their researches, since the human brain has long been divided, like the earth itself, into "hemispheres"?

The Watery Road to the Deep North took us through rapids, whirlpools, a fourteen-mile stretch of Johnstone Strait, and a narrow slit between East Cracroft Island and the mainland called Chatham Channel that looked so much like a river it reminded me of the line in *Heart of Darkness* where Marlow describes chugging up the Congo River in a tin-pot company steamer: "Coming up that river was like travelling back in time to the earliest beginnings of the world, when vegetation rioted on the earth and big trees were king." The riot was still there, in the form of kelp beds and snags, but none of the monarchs the coast was famous for had survived. Greed and bad logging practices had stripped much of the coastline of trees, although second growth had reduced the blight. A nature walk, advertised at Blind Channel Resort, had turned out to be a course by Interfor in rationalizing logging practices, taking us through several stages of planting and regrowth, all the while reminding us that this regrowth was not being done for its own sake—and certainly not for aesthetic purposes—but for future harvesting. By the time we'd gone a mile, I was so furious that, without Geri's patient instruction, I wouldn't have noticed the huckleberries, the belted kingfisher, the delicate fretwork of deer fern, the blue fireweed's small white cross with curled arms, and the devil's club, so tall from reaching up for light, with its umbrella-like horizontal leaves resembling my grandmother's starched doilies.

Minstrel Island, a two-day's run from Blind Channel and Yaculta Rapids, was a place out of time, a stage set for a Jack Hodgins or Graham Greene novel. This jumble of floats, barges and derelict buildings seemed to have been abandoned by the very forces that spawned it, civilization leaping ahead to other, more promising locations. Everything was in a state of disrepair, helter-skelter, old equipment abandoned and upturned, generators, stainless-steel counters defying nature in the tall grass, an out-of-date radio receiver sprouting a beard of loose wires. Several dogs, part wolf, patrolled the ruins, their glazed eyes seeing through the fabrications of man to some deeper, more enduring truth. They had half returned to nature; the buildings and docks would be close behind. Once famous as an entertainment centre for loggers and fishermen, Minstrel Island had boasted a hotel, music hall, and large population. Men came from miles around to drink, gamble, fornicate and listen to itinerant musicians, many of whom were black. The floor of the harbour was said to be entirely covered with discarded bottles, a unique environment for the crabs and other bottom-feeders. Or bottle-feeders.

Len Clay in Victoria had told me a number of stories about Minstrel Island, but the one that really touched me concerned a lonely bachelor named Einar Johnston, who bought a monkey at an auction because no one else wanted it. The monkey got depressed when Einar drank and paid it no attention. Its response was to raid the beer supply, grab a bottle and run across the boom logs where Einar, in his cups, could not follow.

Fire destroyed the original hotel and general store and the current owner had dreams of chucking it all for a mobile home in Mexico. His lacklustre marina was attracting fewer boats each year and the government was trying to wash its hands of maintaining the wharf. Apparently, three branches of government flew in each year at the taxpayers' expense, and often with their families, to inspect the situation, but nothing was ever done. I thought it was a gem that ought to be maintained as a historical site.

Kurt Wetzel, another boater, was not so sure. I was having trouble placing his accent.

"Round Up."

"Seriously?" I was putting a new roll of film in my camera and watching the way Kurt's nostrils moved when he talked. "It sounds like a new shampoo. Or a weedkiller."

"Actually, it's a small town in Montana. I get back there every year or two to visit the family."

Kurt, a transplanted American, taught labour relations at the University of Saskatchewan and spent his summers on Hornby Island. His boatmate, John, a retired Englishman who had been involved in the construction of the Comox Hospital, where my father recovered after triple bypass surgery, told me he had a daughter studying English at

Concordia. A small world, made even smaller with maps. Kurt and John were tied up in a twenty-foot yellow fibreglass sloop that made *Groais* look like a floating palace. I'd been up early photographing the oddities of the place, including a set of plaster of Paris figures of Snow White and the Seven Dwarfs, almost lost in the creeping ivy and salal at the head of the pier. I thought a dwarf had fallen or been knocked over by one of the ghostly dogs until I remembered Sleepy. Kurt, who looked a bit sleep-deprived himself, had been up since 0430, when a gang of ten sport fishermen from Kamloops awakened the entire community with their shouts and engines starting.

Kurt was sitting in the cockpit of his boat with John, sucking at a mug of coffee. I sat on the dock, trying to cozy up to a small black kitten I'd enticed down from the pier. It was having nothing to do with me.

Kurt was still talking about Snow White, flexing his nostrils with every other word. I'd finished loading my camera, but resisted the temptation to take a close-up of his nose.

"Did you notice the eighth gnome?"

I hadn't. "Chomsky?"

I was about to ask him how you teach labour relations—was it a course for would-be mediators or a history of nasty confrontations between labour and management—when Geri emerged, rubbing her eyes and pulling her dressing gown tight around her to hide the array of bruises inflicted by *Groais*. She hadn't reached the bruised-banana stage yet, but the trip was not over. The previous night we'd shared a barbecue with the sport fishermen, one of whom had started a computer mail-order business as a retirement project, selling rare and sometimes signed photographs of great wartime aviators to a new generation of yuppies with the time and money to develop a taste for arcana. He couldn't contain himself when he learned her maiden name was Foss and that her father was a second cousin of the famous Second World War American air ace who later became governor of South Dakota.

"A near relative of Joe Foss! My God, that's amazing. And here on Minstrel Island." His eyes narrowed. "Are there any photographs left in the family collection?"

Geri aptly described living on a small sailboat as getting used to someone walking on your kitchen counters and falling asleep on your dining-room table. Aside from the bruises, she seemed to have adjusted to the confined and intimate spaces of *Groais*, if not to my moods. Her parents had been undemonstrative, a mother whose passions were fishing and Solitaire and a father who, though a professor of accounting, never quite balanced his needs and desires. "When I told him I was depressed or having a rough time," Geri said, "he'd be just as likely to change the subject and ask: 'Have you checked the oil lately?'" An avid gardener, curious about the world, and an indispensable resource at the university, she was reputed to have the Midas touch, the ability to transform an ill-conceived and badly written grant application into a winning proposal.

Shortly after we met, Geri related an incident from her life that still haunts me. The way she told the story conveyed so much of her feeling towards animals—the horse she used to own, the three cats who try to run her life, the colony of worms at work in her compost, and the shorebirds she braves the weathers to count each New Year's. She was galloping along a stretch of beach on the coast of Washington, somewhere south of Bellingham, when her friend's horse went down in an unexpected tidal depression and could not get to its feet. The mare panicked, its chest heaving, its legs thrashing in the shallow water. The situation seemed ridiculous, so easily remediable, but with each stroke of its powerful legs, the horse dug itself deeper into the loose gravel. Its eyes were frantic and bloodshot from the salt water. There was nothing they could do, wave action further destabilizing the sand and stones underfoot. Before they could go for help, the mare choked on salt water and her heart gave out. Geri's friend wrestled the head and neck back out of the water, thinking the mare might only be unconscious, but it was too late.

Geri was bent over in the companionway, stroking the black kitten that had followed me down the ramp and along the string of floats, but had refused my invitation to come on board *Groais*. It rubbed itself against her bruised shins, then stood on its hind legs to be gathered into her arms.

What draws us to one another, beyond the usual genetic maps and biological imperatives? I think it's related to my reasons for writing and for returning to the coast in search of my watery origins. As I watched Geri comb out her hair in the cockpit, I thought of a piece I'd read in the *Times Literary Supplement*, where reviewer Ian Pindar argued for a link between love and the construction of stories, how we relate to one another—and, of course, to the dead—by means of the stories we have in common, stories rescued from oblivion and stories shaped and constructed to explain our all-too-brief passage.

"What is a relationship, after all," Pindar asked, "if it isn't in some sense a narrative that must be sustained?"

Eleven

By the time we arrived in Knight Inlet, grizzlies, with their huge bulk, thirteen-foot reach, almost human footprints and Latin name—*Ursus arctos horribilis Ord*—had been very much on my mind. It was the *"horribilis"* part that caught my attention, then the fact that these amazing creatures of the wild were omnivorous, with a healthy appetite for berries, grass, herbs, ants and carrion, but unlikely to turn up their ultra-sensitive noses at whatever live fish or mammals they could catch. I knew they were supposed to be as fast on land as racehorses, but was startled to learn grizzlies are also excellent swimmers. I'd counted on being able to sprint to shore and make a quick splash for the safety of the boat, leaving the shaggy giant scratching its head at water's edge. Now I was wondering at what quiet anchorage I would hear those long claws scrape across my hull, feel the boat heel over under fifteen hundred pounds of unequally distributed weight, and see a damp nose and hairy concave face peering at me through the plastic of the forward hatch cover.

Rather than chuck my garbage overboard, I was storing it—another no-no—in the hindmost lazarette in the cockpit for later disposal. I suppose, following the advice to campers, I could have hoisted it up the aluminum mast, except that the steps on the mast made that a simple target for a bear, even a grizzly who does not climb so easily as its black cousins. I'd read the precautions in the "Bears in Provincial Parks" brochure, published by the Ministry of Environment, about not walking alone, not smelling like a fish cannery or fast-food restaurant, about making loud noises to scare them off, and carrying a big stick or branch which you hold above your head to make you look larger and more threatening. Or merely ridiculous. These procedures made sense to me, but I could not—not even vaguely—grasp the logic embedded in the contingency plans the brochure recommended in the event that a grizzly should decide to attack. First, you were advised not to run away unless you had a secure spot near at hand; second, you were offered the half-hearted consolation that grizzlies sometimes "bluff their way out of a confrontation by charging, then turn away at the last moment." If this last-minute change of mind did not happen, you were advised not to fight back for fear of further arousing the bear. In fact, the fetal, or "cannonball," position was highly recommended since "such attacks only last a few minutes." A few minutes seemed to me more than enough time for the Horrible One to dispatch a grovelling and terrified poet, however tight the ball into which he'd rolled himself. Playing dead sounded too much like asking to *be* dead. Disconcertingly, the next paragraph advised *not to play dead* if a bear attacks by surprise or while you are sleeping. This seemed to me a rather fine point to argue. In the case of a night raid, the brochure advised, either run to a secure place—that is, if you have a spare car or building handy—or come out swinging with rocks, branches, bazookas and any other weapons you might have tucked away in your backpack or sleeping bag.

The only course of action that made any sense whatsoever was to stay home, with doors locked and windows barred. The subtext of the provincial government document given to me by Tom Sewid was simple enough, at least for this mariner: If you think the sea is a dangerous place, try a forest full of cougars, grizzlies and black bears. If you think wilderness means being somewhere in Canada where you can't pick up CBC on the radio, think again.

The brochure was face up on the folding oak table in *Groais*'s cabin, where I'd left it, beside a copy of Robert Bringhurst's *A Story as Sharp as a Knife*, in which he revisits John Swanton's neglected transcriptions of Haida myths and makes a strong case for the importance of Skaay and three other mythtellers as major poets. Tom Sewid, who'd provided the grizzly brochure, was neither a Haida nor yet a major poet, but he worked daily each summer caretaking and trying to improve his storytelling techniques at Mamalilaculla, an abandoned Kwakwaka'wakw settlement on Village Island at the mouth of Knight Inlet, home of the grizzly. Mamalilaculla was the site of the last great potlatch, many years after the practice had first been outlawed by a government committed to the acquisition and hoarding of its wealth and by a Christian religion which had abandoned at least two of its first principles, that it is better to give than to receive and that the rich will have a tight squeeze getting into heaven. Families and delegations from as far south as Cape Mudge on Quadra Island and as far north as Smith Inlet had gathered for this splendid and clandestine feast and gift-giving cere-mony, which included drum music, masked dancers, speeches and dramatized narratives.

Mamalilaculla was strategically located at the mouth of Knight Inlet, but protected from view and from the winds that pound Blackfish Sound by various smaller islands called the Indian Group. A shallow, heavily weeded trough called Canoe Passage, which boats like mine might navigate at their peril, separated it from Tournour Island. A natural breakwa-ter of shoals, islets and reefs gave the village the appearance of being in a quiet lagoon. One of the smaller islets, where the dead had been buried for generations, was a sacred site and out of bounds to boaters; it had suffered from vandalism and the curiosity of amateur anthropologists on the prowl for artifacts. A ghostly stillness pervaded the place. Although the living had departed for Alert Bay and the larger centres, the dead were very much present, and felt, as you anchored and rowed ashore in this remote Kwakwaka'wakw hideaway.

The cove in front of us would have been alive with fires and banners, as well as several hundred boats of all sizes, from dugouts and small gas boats to large seiners. In fact, one of the most coveted gifts to be distributed to an honoured guest that evening in 1921 was a brand-new, fully equipped commercial fishing boat. The Cranmer festivities were what is known as a repayment potlatch, which takes place several years after a wedding, often when there are offspring to endow with special names and privileges. On this occasion, the bride's father returned the blankets and other wedding gifts that had been paid by the son-in-law; he, in turn, dispersed these gifts and more to those in attendance. At one level, the potlatch was a vote of confidence in the marital union; at another, a way of more closely bonding the two domestic units and the larger community. Gift-giving and storytelling, in short, were important cultural glue, entertaining and morally uplifting, a means of redistributing wealth in the community. Not so, according to the infernal trinity of poet, cop and Indian agent who were responsible for convicting many of the participants and confiscating coppers, masks, and other ceremonial regalia, much of which ended up at the Royal Ontario Museum in Toronto and the Victoria Memorial Museum in Ottawa.

In 1913, Duncan Campbell Scott, deputy superintendent of Indian Affairs and one of Canada's major poets of the period, was committed to the total assimilation of the First Nations; and the bee in his bureaucratic bonnet was the potlatch, which he believed stood in the way of absorbing *his* Indians into the fabric of the Great Dominion. He suppressed important papers, many of them testimonies by famous anthropologists and public figures asserting the cultural value of the potlatch and the wrong-headedness of destroying it. Scott's melancholy temperament, no doubt exacerbated by a clerical job in the nation's capital, seemed to demand the demise of the First Nations as separate entities, although his poetry shows much in aboriginal culture that he admired. His man Friday at Alert Bay, Indian agent William Halliday, has been described as a fanatic in the pages of *Prosecution or Persecution*, written by Daisy Sewid-Smith, one of Tom's relatives. However, Halliday seems to have been somewhat ambivalent about the potlatch. Before the anti-potlatch campaign began in earnest, he had dismissed the ceremony as a "comparatively harmless institution." When pressure from Scott's office increased, Halliday stepped up his efforts to bring about convictions amongst the offending potlatchers, but seemed quite content with the idea of suspended sentences. His personal opinion, less fanatical and less rigorously asserted than Scott's, was that the potlatch was largely a waste of time and substance. When Halliday published *Potlatch and Totem and Recollections of an Indian Agent*, in 1935, his text was full of contradictions, indicating that although he was racist in some of his views regarding the Kwakwaka'wakw, he may have shared public opinion that the potlatch should not (or perhaps could not) be suppressed. He was also determined, of course, not to lose his comfortable, if not always pleasant, government job.

Aptly named for the job, Sergeant Daniel Angermann, of the newly established RCMP detachment in Alert Bay, was less ambivalent about the potlatch. In fact, he conducted a vigorous campaign to enforce the laws against the practice, gathering information from paid informants and laying charges as broadly as possible in order to intimidate the people into signing a non-potlatching agreement. It's not surprising that he was aware of plans to hold a potlatch on Village Island. However, despite Angermann's efforts, the potlatch did not die; in fact, forcing it underground—another chapter in a long saga of suppression and intimidation—may have strengthened resolve to keep the practice alive. Numerous arrests were made and several of the more important participants were charged and held briefly in Oakalla Prison in New Westminster. The bulk of the confiscated ceremonial masks, blankets, coppers and other regalia were not returned until 1979.

As I sat on the freshly cut grass at Village Island with Geri and half a dozen boaters and kayakers, listening to Tom Sewid and his back-up chorus of crows, I was off in a historical time warp—Christmas 1921. I was fascinated not only by the potlatch but also by its prohibition, since it seems to embody the early Christian practice of giving away all worldly goods—volunteer bankruptcy, not as a means of eventual salvation, but as social practice. Or, in the old familiar, abbreviated terms: Give and it shall be given unto you. First Nations spokesmen had wasted no time in pointing out these parallels, as well as the contradictions inherent in the anti-potlatching law and convictions. In fact, the Cranmer potlatch at Village Island had been advertised informally as a Christmas party, a legitimate disguise, but one that had not worked.

"So that's a bit of stuff on our social and economic system," Tom said, slipping on his ceremonial blanket. "If the white man had used the potlatch as a method of exchange and social insurance, the crash of 1929 would never have happened."

There was some laughter and scattered applause as the sprinkling of boaters and kayakers adjusted their raingear and shifted their bottoms on the two uncomfortable planks that served as bleachers for Tom's performance. He'd given us a bit of history on the now-abandoned village, which has attracted a wide assortment of visitors, including actors Tom Selleck and Sidney Poitier. All that remained of the original Native dwellings were the front- and rear-support posts and crossbeams that held up the roof of the lodge. Other than a tuft of grass sprouting from one of the crossbeams, time had hardly touched the enduring cedar. On either side, as if exhibits A and B to the tastelessness and fragility of the invading culture, were the leaning remains of two wood-framed and shingled houses, doors and windows gaping. The whole area was overgrown with salal and salmonberry, but Tom kept a sizable patch cut back with a weed-eater. As a token of their appreciation for making access to the berries easier, the bears had left the path to the second cove, where *Groais* was anchored, littered with fresh scat, undigested red berries still intact and glistening in the steaming piles.

"Mom, will you bring the bear-claw necklace when you come up from the boat?" Tom was talking on a portable VHF. He had his library, a cardboard box of reference books, spread out on the weathered picnic table and was trying to protect it from the sporadic drizzle with a plastic tarp.

The books were bounded at one end by a high-powered rifle for scaring off bears. One of the titles was Hughina Harrold's *Totem Poles and Tea*, which I'd purchased in Campbell River, a compelling account of two years spent as a teacher and nurse at Mamalilaculla in the thirties, at a time when the village was reaching the nadir of its decline, with tuberculosis and poverty increasingly prevalent. As Tom recounted a legend about the mischievous Raven, I couldn't help smiling at the image I remembered from the book, a description of the village cow loose in the empty schoolroom, devouring notebooks and children's art with that look of utter contentment only the bovine species has mastered. In those same pages reference was made to the drowning of three Sewid brothers in a storm just off Cormorant Island in Blackfish Sound, one of whom may well have been Tom's grandfather or great-uncle.

Tom was wearing running shoes, jeans and a ceremonial blanket with abalone-shell buttons outlining, on a blue background, a red mythic creature whose upraised arms ended in the heads of two grizzlies, each equipped with what looked like a tasselled nightcap. I'm sure my misguided reading of Kwakwaka'wakw iconography would have amused Tom. He seemed well aware of the irony of his situation, reconstructing and explaining aboriginal history for the benefit of those whose ancestors had done their damnedest to destroy it. In fact, his infectious smile resembled the toothy grin lingering on the face of the carved grizzly on one of the two remaining totem poles collapsed and rotting amongst the bushes at water's edge, tender salal shoots sprouting from its mouth and eyes.

As we passed the shell of the old residential school, there was a rustling in the bushes that elicited from me superfluous clapping sounds and loud talk. It was unnecessary for two reasons: the large number of humans in the vicinity would have discouraged the bears; and Tom's partner for the day, James Brotchie, was ahead of us on the path, talking to a tourist who was working the squelch button for the weather channel on his portable VHF. James was no longer wearing the ceremonial ermine-skin and cedar-bark headdress, which was a bit large for him and rested on the metal frame of his prescription glasses. He had told me, in response to my question about his family name, that his grandfather, a massive and legendary figure on the B.C. coast, originated in Orkney. James wrote his Port Hardy phone number, in case I wanted to get in touch later, on the cover of my grizzly brochure. Geri, of course, had made an unannounced and unaccompanied trip earlier along this same path, just in time to rescue the dinghy, which I'd secured to a beached log that was now adrift.

A detailed commentary on aboriginal history on the West Coast would include startling population figures, suggesting that at one time there were hundreds of small communities ranging in size from a few families to extended clans of several hundred individuals, a total tally of well over 150,000 on the Canadian portion of the coast, not counting the large settlements in Washington, Oregon and Alaska. Nowhere in the world was there more abundant sea life to be harvested: shellfish, salmon, cod, halibut, seals, sea lions, even whales, as well as birds and their eggs. Art flourished, including weaving, basket-making, wood carving—most notably the totem poles or "talking sticks"—and highly refined storytelling. With no shortage of food, tribal boundaries remained more or less constant, except for the occasional raiding party to capture slaves and reassert authority. Thanks to greed, disease, dispossession of lands, residential schools, various kinds of restrictive legislation, and outright murder, these wealthy and proud peoples were decimated, their numbers reduced in the first 150 years after Cook's and George Vancouver's friendly visits to fewer than twenty thousand over the entire coast. Villages abandoned, art plundered, stories lost.

Before setting sail from Vancouver, I'd made a couple of visits to the Museum of Anthropology at the University of British Columbia, which has a stunning collection of artifacts from most of the major language groups on the coast, including Salish, Kwakwaka'wakw, Haida, Tsimshian, and Tlingit: masks, poles, blankets, coppers, baskets, cedar boxes, house-posts. These items were given a position of prominence in the museum, benefiting from space and natural light. Tucked away in the back rooms and mostly consigned to shelves were thousands of pieces of aboriginal art from Borneo, New Zealand, Australia, Fiji, New Guinea, Brazil, and Mexico, to name only a few source countries, in such abundance that no single piece would ever be given the attention and pride of place it deserved. Out of context, these pilfered items provide shocking evidence of a feeding frenzy amongst collectors and anthropologists. I could not look at these artifacts for more than a few minutes at a time without a feeling of deep shame and revulsion settling upon me. I had experienced similar feelings thirty years earlier in the British Museum in London as I wandered amongst Egyptian sarcophagi and Grecian marbles.

Walter Benjamin comes closest to explaining this legacy of shame in an essay called "Theses on the Philosophy of History," which appears in his book *Illuminations*:

Whoever has emerged victorious participates to this day in the triumphal procession in which the present rulers step over those who are lying prostrate. According to traditional practice, the spoils are carried along in the procession. They are called cultural treasures, and a historical materialist views them with cautious detachment. For without exception the culture treasures he surveys have an origin which he cannot contemplate without horror. They owe their existence not only to the efforts of the great minds and talents who have created them, but also to the anonymous toil of their contemporaries. There is no document of civilization which is not at the same time a document of barbarism.

An obvious answer is to return these artifacts to the communities where they belong, where they can nourish and inspire surviving generations and provide them with whatever revenue might be extracted from the world's cultural industries and curious individuals. I, for one, was happy to pay fifteen dollars to Tom Sewid for the privilege of anchoring at Village Island, visiting the ancient village of Mamalilaculla, talking with him and providing distraction for the otherwise bored grizzlies.

I tucked the grizzly brochure and Tom Sewid's business card inside the Bringhurst book. I was on my own again. Geri would be safely back in Bellingham by now, having taken her first flight in a float plane from Port McNeill to pick up her car in Campbell River. As the plane took off, all that watery turbulence followed by such seemingly effortless flight, I had mixed feelings. It was good to think of Geri aloft, up there amongst her beloved birds; at the same time, I was feeling rather bereft. I had no excuses for not getting on with the trip, though I'd doubtless find one. Our departure from Mamalilaculla had proven difficult. By the time *Groais* was well into the mouth of Knight Inlet, a huge bank of fog had crept along the far shore, obliterating all the bays and points of land I'd chosen as aids to navigation. Jan Hansen may have told me, after he fixed the starter motor at Refuge Cove, that corrosion is a boater's number-one enemy, but I was still prepared to argue with Lewis and his pilot friends that fog ranks right up there. Even without radar on board, as long as I can see where I'm going, I figure I'm okay and have a fighting chance. But fog was in the same category as disease—unpleasant, always unexpected, and likely to prove fatal.

I also worried about fog, even when I'd memorized points on the shoreline and their compass coordinates, because of the huge cruise ships encountered along the way, four of them in less than an hour outside Campbell River. We'd sighted a huge black floating island of a Holland America liner in Johnstone Strait and a streamlined white immensity called *Visions Ocean*, which I thought as demented in its shape and course as in its oddly worded name. It was a designer special straight from *Star Wars* and seemed to be heading right for us, like those staring billboard eyes you can't shake no matter which way you turn. When I started heading to port, the ship's bow would turn a little to starboard. We continued this way for ten or fifteen minutes as if locked in a deadly embrace, like iceberg and *Titanic*. It's terribly unnerving until that moment when the funnels go out of line and the floating monster broadens on the horizon and you know, at last, it's given up on you to go in search of worthier prey.

An extra night at Village Island, waiting out the fog, had meant that Alert Bay and its famous museum were out of the question for Geri. With the north coast and its uncertainties ahead, I was too preoccupied to concentrate on museum exhibits. I spent two days in Port McNeill shopping and getting a new VHF installed by an electrician named Lindy, who was delighted by my breathless account of my attack of claustrophobia and nearly having to dismantle the cockpit with a saw to get at the batteries. I'd left my bicycle in storage in Campbell River, but Port McNeill was quite manageable on foot and I was able to persuade the food market to deliver my groceries to the dock. That's when I first noticed a man draped across the bow and propped up against the windshield of a tiny clinker-built motorboat, reading a copy of the *New Yorker*. He was short and elfish, quite in keeping with the diminutive size of the boat. With a slouch hat on and a straw between his teeth he could be taken for an aging Huck Finn. As I staggered past him, precariously balancing ten plastic bags of groceries on a low-slung courtesy wagon, I told him the impression he made.

"I'm going to take that insult as a compliment. But you really should be more careful about how you address hermits, as they're an unpredictable lot, especially the old ones." Only when he'd finished speaking did he look up from his magazine and peer at me fiercely over his glasses. He was working hard to keep a straight face, but the eyes gave it away.

"Come by my boat for tea in half an hour," I said, as I dragged the wagon back to its place beside the ramp. "Second from the end, same side. Just give me time to put the groceries away. We can discuss etiquette and exchange lawyers' addresses."

Between the cups on the table and Christopher Bracken's *Potlatch Papers: A Colonial Case History*, the nautical elf placed on the table, a business card:

BOB STEWART
Hermit
Lower Potts Lagoon

It also provided a post-office box in Port McNeill and specific coordinates—50° 33.48 N, 125° 27.00 W—but no phone number. Bob's friends had the card printed as a joke. He lived in a float house on West Cracroft, just around the corner from Minstrel Island, where he spent his time reading and writing stories, some of which he had placed in magazines, but most of which he sent to friends. He told me about a neighbour named Weaver who complained that other coastal characters had had books written about them, but no one had ever written about him. So Bob composed a three-hundred-page novel, handwritten in three notebooks, and gave it to his friend. It included an epic cast and a picaresque plot that made my head spin, depicting Weaver's various exploits in sometimes outrageous and unbecoming ways. Needless to say, it proved a great hit with the protagonist.

Bob was retired, having designed boats and been a special-needs educator with two master's degrees, one of them from Western Washington University where I was teaching. Although he was a Canadian, he had lived in Bellingham for twelve years and had owned over the years a total of eighty-three boats, of which his little lapstreaked hull with the ninety-horsepower outboard motor was number eighty-two. I didn't catch the significance at first, then realized he must have bought back number eighty-two from the man he sold it to. His mind was wiry, more so than his thin body, which was fidgeting uncomfortably on the straight-backed cushion of the spare bunk that also served as both settee and dinner bench.

"Too bad about that seat," I said, offering him a couple of pillows. "It's worse than the pews in a Baptist church."

Bob declared himself an atheist and promptly delivered a diatribe against organized religion, which he dismissed as ignorant balderdash and bad myth. He preferred his myths home-made, although he allowed for one or two exceptions from amongst the Greeks and Romans. He liked religion's underlying morality, however, and explained that his own parables about animals at work and play often dealt with issues of responsible stewardship, how to be creative and helpful in the environment.

"*Hamlet* is about indecision, *Othello* about jealousy, *Macbeth* about ambition, power." He was quite animated by now and, oblivious to his discomfort, was bouncing up and down on the green cushions. "My little pieces run the same gamut of emotions and moral issues, but in a non-literary way. I also illustrate them when I can with cartoons."

Having refused my offer of beer or wine, Bob Stewart, hermit of Lower Potts Lagoon, seemed to be enjoying the coffee I'd brewed especially for him and was breaking open another apricot from my store of supplies. He was far too social and voluble to be a genuine hermit, although I thought his exaggerated eye movements and compulsively delivered arsenal of stories suggested a certain vulnerability. Before I could weigh this hypothesis, he launched into a tale of personal woe that was so bizarre I couldn't help hooting.

"Sure, go ahead and laugh at my expense. Everyone does, you might as well join the club. One day, at the store in Port McNeill, Myrtle told me the debit-card machine had broken down and I needed to pay for my supplies with cash. I said, 'You mean I have to go to the bank and say, "Myrtle is kaput and I need real cash?"' I was trying to be funny, but she just nodded. By the time I got to the bank, I was exhausted and irritated, so when the teller asked how I was, I raised my voice a little—you know the way you do, when you want to be heard over the din? At that precise moment, all other conversation stopped in the bank.

"'Okay, I'll tell you how I am. Two wives have left me, my kids are disasters, my body is deteriorating, my boat's too small, and now Myrtle tells me she's kaput and I need real money.' The entire staff and several customers burst out laughing. Since I lost Phoebe a couple of years ago, I suppose my role in life is to be comic relief for the whole of Port McNeill, not to mention"—and here he paused dramatically—"some of its more insulting nautical drop-ins." Bob was happily consuming the last of my six apricots waiting for me to take the bait. I hesitated, then inquired about Phoebe, who turned out to have been neither sweetheart nor third wife, but a dog.

"That dog was a source of more joy in my life than any woman. Did I ever tell you about the old Indian? When I was nineteen in Alaska, I went into the post office. Everyone in the line was complaining. The butcher complained about the quality of meat they were shipping him. The minister complained about alcoholism amongst the youth. The mechanic complained about the unavailability of parts. Since this seemed to be a national pastime, I thought I'd play it safe by complaining about the weather. The old Indian in line behind me, who'd said nothing so far, suddenly tapped me on the shoulder.

"'You have woman?' No, I admitted rather sheepishly in front of the assembled audience. The old Indian made a harrumph noise deep in his throat.

"'You have boat?' No, I confessed even more reluctantly. I did not have a boat either, but I did hope to own one someday. In fact, I was already thinking of designing and building my own boat. There was another guttural harrumph.

"'No boat, no woman. Nothing to complain about.'"

Each of Bob's stories had the shape and authority of a tale that had been refined and rattled off many times before. However, a threshold now seemed to have been crossed and I was offered the details of his loss in a different, less shapely manner. Phoebe, it turned out, after more than two thousand dollars' worth of medication and treatment, suffered a slow, painful decline and had to be put down by lethal injection. As Bob told me this, his face streamed with tears. I decided to read him a poem of my own about a similar experience. We'd come full circle from puns to pathos.

I'd run out of apricots, but Bob's supply of stories showed no signs of diminishing. He compared aging to an old Plymouth rattling down the highway with parts falling off and continually losing power. The pillows I gave him did not appear to be working. I assumed he was suffering from arthritis or lower-back problems. Scotch would have been more useful than coffee. The only consolation, he continued, shifting the metaphor, is that as you grow older you have more stories to tell; you also hope to acquire a modicum of grace. Eventually he dropped the spoon into his cup, signalling his imminent departure. All that emotion and laughter and talk had left us both exhausted. I gave him a copy of one of my books and promised to visit him at the hermitage in Lower Potts Lagoon on my way back. As he rose to leave, he confided that he sometimes had conversations with imaginary beings, including Jesus, about decisions needing to be made. All he ever got from them was smug smiles to indicate he knew damn well what had to be done. As he stepped onto the float, he turned to shake my hand, telling me there was one Greek myth he still found meaningful and compelling, the one about Charon rowing the dead across the River Styx, where a loved one was always waiting to receive them. "Whenever I think of this," Bob said, "I know it will be Phoebe waiting for me."

I slipped his "business" card alongside Tom Sewid's, which I was using as a bookmark. One of the stories Tom had shared was about grizzlies and why they are not found on Vancouver Island. There was a jumping contest, apparently, and Grizzly had bragged, before lying down for a nap, that he could jump across the waters separating the mainland and Vancouver Island. His competitor, I think it was Raven, managed the jump easily by taking advantage of low tide, when the distance was greatly reduced. By the time Grizzly awakened from his nap, the tide had come in and he could see his competitor on the far shore. Try as he might, he could not make the jump and was confined thereafter to the mainland and the small islands dotting its shore.

It seemed, after all, that although grizzlies are good swimmers, they don't have the stamina for long distances. A small consolation, I thought, but it would have to do.

✳ Twelve

"It is a great day to die."

This line, which appears to have become somewhat of a sacred joke within the aboriginal community—whimsical, ironic, prophetic—was spoken by Chief Dan George when he starred with Dustin Hoffman in *Little Big Man*, the movie that catapulted Hoffman from national to international stardom. I'd heard it the previous day when listening to a CBC radio documentary on the life and legacy of the famous West Coast personality, and it was the first thing that popped into my head in the morning when I woke up. My daughter Bronwen would have happily pointed out its significance, but I didn't need any help figuring it out. I was worried about what lay ahead, wondering whether I had the moral fibre to go through with it. And I'd become superstitious of so-called random happenings, significant input. I couldn't even turn on the radio, it seemed, without some trite song or sentimental aside ringing a bell.

I was rafting alongside two "boats" near the cannery in Port Hardy. A rotting gillnetter covered in grime, which looked as if it had given up the ghost years earlier but still figured in someone's dreams or investment plans, since the pump came on each time I crossed the deck and disturbed the water level inside; and, at the spot next to the float, in the shape of a rectangular biscuit tin, a huge derelict steel hulk that must have served as floating barracks for a logging or salvage operation. There wasn't a soul aboard or any sign of recent habitation, not a thing to soften or humanize the empty metal compartments. What human industry could not provide that morning, however, nature did, casting a soft gauze of fog over the proceedings and giving the fleet of gill-netters, seiners and large trollers a brief air of intimacy and solidarity, sufficient, almost, to belie the economic reality of an industry on its last legs. I could feel the pulse of anxiety and frustration seep back into the assorted dreamers, as they awakened in their bunks to the drone of the cannery starting up and the grating, impertinent cry of a scavenging gull.

I was leaving the south and central coasts behind, but not their ghosts—not my mother, dead for more years than she had lived; not my drowned grandfather, his swamped body never recovered from the currents around Point Atkinson, perhaps still searching for his missing false teeth; and not my favourite uncle, permanently AWOL, the blunt lozenge-shape of his ghostly Lancaster glimpsed periodically through cloud cover like the hulk of the *Flying Dutchman*, like retri-bution itself. Where I had sped so heedlessly and with such arrogance over surfaces and lives as a young man, I moved now, amongst these silent companions, with the slow deliber-ation of an ancient mariner in whose heart the dark flower of fear had not just taken root, but was in full bloom. Or so it seemed that morning in Port Hardy, to whatever remained of the self-indulgent poet, as I laced up my runners, sucked at my third cup of tea, and waited for the fog to lift.

Vancouver Island, from Port McNeill north, tapers off rapidly until it disappears beneath the sea from whence it came. In another hour, it would be gone altogether. It's an amazing ridge of land, a vast natural breakwater sheltering Western Canada from the full force of the Pacific Ocean. British

Columbians are grateful for whatever subduction and plate tectonics produced this natural (and national) barrier, thereby creating twice as much coastline and a submerged valley that offers 350 miles of unbroken and relatively protected passage to the northwest coast. As my travels so far had shown, this vast trough that includes the Gulf of Georgia, Johnstone Strait, Queen Charlotte Sound, and myriad interconnecting waterways can, at times, be anything but tranquil and safe for navigation. Winds find ways of changing direction, funnelling along the steep inlets; fast currents impede movement and can swamp a boat; and thousands of jagged rocks, which didn't quite make the grade as high ridges or mountaintops, take revenge by thrusting themselves just close enough to the surface to carve up each year a flotilla of wood, fibreglass, and metal hulls.

Despite the dangers of these relatively protected waters, I was reluctant to leave them behind for the uncertainties of the north coast. I'm not an offshore sailor. In fact, the thought of being either out of sight of land or exposed to the full force of the ocean is enough to put my blood pump into overdrive. Queen Charlotte Sound is a nasty and dangerous stretch of water, subject to constant swells from the Pacific and strong winds from the west and northwest. And it was doubly sobering, as I turned to port out of Christie Passage and left behind the last safe harbour on Hurst Island, called, all too appropriately, God's Pocket, to recall that George Vancouver's ship *Discovery* went aground in these very waters and was within inches of sinking as the tide receded and left it tilted precariously—"sewing" is the term he used—into the water. Only the quick action of the crew, who dismantled the topmasts and spars to use as props and supporting posts, and the fact that there were no waves at the time, kept it from perishing. The next night the same thing happened to its sister ship, *Chatham*, also without permanent damage.

So, I was out of the pocket and into the drink—the salt-chuck, that is—though I might get to the other kind of drink before long. By taking this route, I'd missed the Gordon Islands with their rusty band of intertidal seaweed; in the distance they looked like cupcakes for a leprechaun's birthday party, the paper wrappers still intact. On my immediate right was the Deserters Group, picturesque enough to inspire photographs but not settlement. I didn't have my reference book on place names handy, but I had no trouble spelling out what my own reason for wanting to jump ship there would be: one last grab at the continent. The Deserters, the Storm, and the Tree islands had so many drying rocks and reefs scattered about, only a few of the latter detectable as a result of breaking surf, that it looked as if God, his pocket overflowing, had given up trying to put the jigsaw together and chucked the remaining pieces of the puzzle overboard.

Vancouver Island was not the only refuge that was disappearing. The absence of transmitters meant I could no longer pick up any further signals on my cellphone. No calls, therefore no e-mail. I'd comforted and consoled myself along the way by keeping in touch with family and friends. Now it was just me and the cormorants; and on this day even they seemed to be otherwise employed. The new VHF had already gone on the fritz by the time I reached Port Hardy, my last port of call on Vancouver Island before heading to the north coast. I tried it out in the harbour, but the needle on the control panel indicating voltage levels would drop to zero when I flipped on the switch for the radio, or any other switch for that matter. A quick call to Lindy in Port McNeill did not improve my disposition. "It's not the radio," he said, "we had that working just fine yesterday. Your battery's dead." He gave me the names of several electricians to call, but because of the bank holiday no one was answering the phone.

I poked and prodded the wires, about as pointless as a car buyer kicking the tires and opening the hood for a peek. Then, while waiting for someone to return my call, I decided on a little excursion into town to do some sleuthing and have my last supper in a restaurant. I'd been told that someone from Orkney operated a B&B in Port Hardy. Lindy's wife was in the same business and had given me a list of local proprietors, each of whom I began phoning. There were no obvious Orkney names—Isbister, Mouat, Dyer, Gunn—on the list, but one of the proprietors, a young woman who had Scottish connections, was intrigued by my Orkney research. I was so encouraged by her interest, I revealed my predicament.

"Dead batteries. Can't find an electrician to answer the phone, let alone make a boat call."

"I have a neighbour who runs a kayaking business." I could hear the divine wind rustling her wings. "He used to be an electrician at the mine. Maybe he'll help."

I must have sounded so pathetic that Pat Kervin of Odyssey Kayaking agreed to come down and have a look. "I'm not a marine electrician," he warned, "but I might be able to tell you what's wrong. Have you tried cleaning your terminals and connections?"

So I wouldn't appear totally ignorant, I extracted both batteries and put them on the charger, checking to see that the terminals were clean. There seemed to be no corrosion where the ground wire attached to the engine, either, so it had to be something else. When Pat and his brother arrived, they ignored my efforts and set about cleaning the battery terminals again, this time with a wire brush and sandpaper, pointing out that the ground to the engine was covered with green paint, applied after it had been reconditioned. Once this paint was scraped off, they went to work on the master switch that controlled the passage of electricity from the cranking battery to the starter and from the house battery to radio, running lights, depth sounder, and pump. While they worked, I rattled on half-heartedly about various writing projects. I was not only skeptical about their diagnosis, but also concerned about the delay and the cost of this pointless two-man cleaning operation. I think I was more worried that it might work, thus eliminating my last excuse for delay. To my surprise, Lister perked up immediately, acknowledged the tickle of current, and burst into applause.

"I don't believe it. The terminals looked just fine to me. There was no rust or corrosion evident. How could you tell they needed cleaning?" I was blathering, my excessive gratitude competing for airtime with my embarrassment.

"Corrosion's your number-one enemy on a boat," Pat intoned. Not that again, I thought. This was beginning to sound like a Greek chorus. I was having enough trouble keeping track of my growing number of adversaries—storms, fog, cruise ships, swimming grizzlies and now corrosion—never mind trying to rank them. It was enough to petrify the faint of heart.

After packing up his tools, Pat responded to my question about cost by asking how much their three hours of work was worth to me. Well, it was certainly worth a hundred bucks. He gave me back twenty-five dollars and invited me to come by for coffee if I were ever in the area again. He also told me his ex-wife's family was from Orkney, but I was too nervous at that point to be thinking of connections other than the electrical kind.

Someone else who was having trouble—though not the cowardly kind—was Steve Martin, my fisherman friend from Campbell River. When I made my way down Heart Attack

Hill to the pier that evening in Port Hardy, after picking up the various spare parts Pat had recommended—locker nuts, washers, clamps, a voltage meter—I noticed *Ocean Fury* moored farther along the same dock. I climbed aboard the sparkling troller and rapped on the cabin door, but Steve was nowhere to be found. The opening for sockeye had not come, so I assumed he'd gone back home to be with his family. I was wishing I could do something similar. If I couldn't talk to Steve, at least I could amuse myself and further procrastinate by playing a small joke.

Back on *Groais*, I unshipped my laptop from its plastic ziplock bag. At Port McNeill, the day after meeting the Hermit of Lower Potts Lagoon, my internal mouse had crashed, so I could not get into my files or use any of the computer's functions. I phoned a local hacker who worked part-time at the mine and was told all I had to do was plug in an external mouse. I spent hours going in and out of retail and service shops to no avail; not even the indomitable Lindy could help me. No one seemed to like Macintosh products in Port McNeill and it would take two or three days to have a mouse shipped from Vancouver. I didn't know what to do. Along with all my other setbacks, the thought of wasting three days, or having to make all of my notes by hand, then transcribe them later, was just too much. I leaned on the counter of the post office, while the clerk wrote the addresses of several northern delivery spots on a piece of paper, and uttered an audible sigh. She stopped writing and looked up, eyebrows raised, wondering what had inspired this rude expression of impatience.

"No, no, it's not you," I said. "It's my deteriorating equipment." She offered a sympathetic shrug.

"I know just how you feel."

"And there's not a mouse for sale in the whole of Port

McNeill." She laughed. My predicament seemed to amuse her.

"Mice for sale? That's an original way to get rid of them, a lot cheaper than traps. But who would you get to buy them? Cats, maybe?"

After she'd written a few addresses for mail pickup on the north coast, this second ministering angel, disguised as a government employee and stand-up comic, phoned someone who taught at the local high school, where there just happened to be a Mac lab. A car arrived at the post office ten minutes later with a selection of mice for me to choose from. It was high summer, schools were closed, and you'd expect teachers to have been either away on vacation or, at least, incommunicado. No identification was required, no deposit; all I had to do was promise to return it before the start of school in September. While the teacher waited, I pulled the laptop out of my backpack, sat on the sidewalk and plugged in the external mouse, a grin as stupid as Sylvester's appearing on my face as the cursor began to move across the screen.

I composed the following letter, printed it on twenty-pound bond paper, and taped it to the door of Steve's wheelhouse, the letterhead enlarged in bold and italic Palatino type:

SOCKEYE STANDARDS ASSOCIATION

August 1, 1999

Steve Martin
Skipper
Ocean Fury

Dear Mr. Martin:
It has been brought to our attention that your boat, *Ocean Fury*, is, despite its rather aggressive name, the most attractively

maintained boat in the harbour at Port Hardy, which means that we will be biting when you set your lines. We sockeye are particular about the boats we patronize, preferring beauty and cleanliness above mere efficiency and slavish hours.

You will receive in the mail, in due course, a copy of our Certificate of Fishy Merit, which we hope you will have framed and give a position of honour in your wheelhouse.

We would like to bring to your attention, however, that a small smudge has appeared on the starboard bow of your vessel, doubtless the result of some low-life rafting alongside without due care and attention. We are confident that this blight will be quickly eradicated.

Sincerely,

U. R. Scales, Inspector

For the trip across Queen Charlotte Sound past Cape Caution, the cruising guides all advise giving yourself plenty of time, leaving Port Hardy early and paying close attention to the weather reports, especially with boats as slow as mine. I couldn't leave early because I noticed the belt that drives the alternator was breaking down from being adjusted so tightly. Three-quarters of an inch is all it should budge when thumb pressure is applied; if you can turn the alternator by hand, the belt is not tight enough. Rather than fiddle with the adjustment, I decided I needed a spare. I called the emergency number on the door of the auto parts dealership and convinced a reluctant employee to delay his family outing for ten minutes in order to sell me a belt. As a result, it was noon before I took my leave of the *Ocean Fury*, the rest of the unemployed fleet and the shoaling harbour.

In addition to ignoring the advice to depart early if you're

sailing past Cape Caution, I'd obviously not read the navigation literature carefully or hobnobbed enough with local
boaters and fishermen to learn that northern waters, even on
a clear day, often get boisterous during the afternoon, so that
there can be a lot of surface wave action on top of the swell.
Judging from the increasing chop and the three hours it had
already taken me to reach Pine Island, I realized I couldn't
make it to my destination, Millbrook Cove on the north shore
of Smith Sound, before dark. I considered turning east to
Miles Inlet, one of the recommended anchorages, but it
seemed too far afield and would require some deft manoeu-
vring between reefs and islets if I didn't want to share the fate
of *Discovery* and *Chatham*. Then I noticed on my chart a
place called Burnett Bay, located just below Cape Caution.
Not only did I remember the high recommendation it
received from several boaters quoted in the guides, I also
recalled mention of a famous painting by the same name by
Emily Carr, done before the village's decline, all of which
made this seem the perfect alternative.

I altered my course slightly, no longer heading for Egg
Island, which was clearly a good four hours off. Burnett Bay
required a more northerly route, which I found especially
gratifying as my entire journey so far seemed to have
involved travelling west rather than north. I studied the
coastline. Even with the binoculars, I could pick out no boats,
no signs of either habitation or harbour in the distance, only
grey coast and the blunt outline of Cape Caution. Well, at
least I'd find good anchorage for the night. A three-foot chop
had developed and a brisk westerly, which would have made
for perfect sailing if I hadn't been so nervous about the wind
increasing and finding myself trying to lower the sails while
bouncing around a few hundred yards from an unfamiliar
coastline. I was still not confident that the electrical system

had run out of surprises and wouldn't choose the worst possible moment to crap out again. So, cowardly lion that I am, I stuck with Lister, who was pounding away faithfully below deck and was best not discouraged.

As I drew closer, my doubts increased. Even from a distance of ten miles, I could see there was clearly nothing in Burnett Bay in the way of protection. It was barely an indentation in the coastline. What were the guides talking about? When I checked them again, I noticed that both entries mention chart 3,548, which I'd filed away two days earlier, not the chart I was currently using. Then it hit me: I'd been confusing Burnett Bay with Blunden Harbour, at least ten or fifteen miles southeast. It was too late to retrace my steps before nightfall; the only solution was to make a run past Cape Caution and take my chances on finding anchorage. Meanwhile, a heavy swell was running, combined with a six-foot chop, and the wind showed every indication of increasing. I had about two hours of daylight left, maybe more, but certainly not enough to navigate safely amongst the constellation of rocks guarding the mouth of Smith Sound like a set of rotting teeth. No wonder that portion was called Radar Passage, an option I didn't have in my bag of navigational tricks.

The chart was not just discouraging, it was positively scary. Where were all those comforting, if innocuous, English surnames imposed by Vancouver and his shipmates when you needed them? Instead, I discovered that Cape Caution was in cahoots with a nasty snout of land called Neck Ness; that the small bay just beyond Neck Ness contained a ghastly scimitar-shaped obstruction known as Hook Reef; and that somewhere offshore, not visible even at low tide, lurked a menace called South Iron Rock. This fiendish roll call was not exactly inviting. I had no one to blame, only my own stupidity, and I wanted nothing more than to crawl into the bunk and pull my sleeping bag over my head. The words of the young captain in Conrad's *Shadow-Line* rang in my ears: "And I am shrinking from it. From the mere vision. My first command. Now I understand that strange sense of insecurity in my past. I always suspected I was no good. And here is proof positive, I am shirking it, I am no good."

I tried to think of Chris Law, *Groais's* original owner, who had braved gale-force winds in the English Channel, "tikker" fog in the North Atlantic, and a hurricane in the Pacific. He was made of the right stuff. *Groais* was made of the right stuff, too, like the original *Golden Hind*. According to Nuño da Silva, the Portuguese master who had been pressed into service when the English pirates looted his ship, Francis Drake's *Golden Hind* was

in great measure stout and strong. She has two sheathings, one as perfectly finished as the other. She is fit for warfare and is a ship of the French pattern, well fitted out and furnished with very good masts, tackle and double sails. She is a good sailer and the rudder governs her well. She is not new, nor is she coppered nor ballasted. She has seven armed portholes on each side, and inside she carries eighteen pieces of artillery, thirteen being of bronze and the rest of cast iron, as well as an abundance of all sorts of munitions for war, for none have been expended. She also carries workmen and a forge for making nails, spikes and bolts. She is water-fast when navigated with the wind astern and not violent, but when the sea is high she labours and leaks not a little, whether sailing before the wind or with the bowlines out.

How all of this might have been fitted into a ship little more than twice as long as *Groais*, I couldn't imagine. *Groais* had two sheathings as well, British plywood with a fibreglass skin; it also had the advantage of a diesel engine. It was armed reasonably well for the weather, too—no radar, but at least a GPS and an occasionally functioning depth sounder. What it lacked, and this might prove its undoing, was a competent skipper.

Both cruising guides had mentioned Jones Cove, a small indentation just beyond Cape Caution, as a possible place to hide in the event of bad weather. On the chart, clenched in my hand and soaked from spray, it looked like a skin-tag, a tiny piece of skin flaking off the continent. It also appeared to be my only choice before dark. The problem was that the route to Jones Cove required holding a tight course between South Iron Rock and Hook Reef, the proverbial rock and submerged hard place. I was half a mile off Cape Caution, a blunt, expressionless outcrop of rock that takes its colours from the sea, this hour all grey with a beard of white surf. Ahead, I could see waves exploding over Hook Reef, sending spume fifteen feet into the air. Judging from the chart, the reef was two hundred yards in length, curving out from shore like the Grim Reaper's scythe. This was the dreaded moment when I wished I'd stayed home to putter in the garden or taken the power squadron course. Or at least paid attention to the warnings. I didn't have anything ready in the event of running aground. The survival suit loaned to me by Hank of Holland was stuffed in the forward compartment under suitcases and extra bedding; the flares and smoke bomb were stowed away in the chart table. There was no survival kit of food and medications within easy reach. And I couldn't start rummaging around for this stuff without heading out to sea again, losing precious time. If I made it to shore from a sinking boat, I'd be dead in a few days from starvation; that is, if Grizz and his feline pals didn't do the job first.

Groais was already taking water over the port quarter as I fought an awkward yawing motion to hold the boat on course. I had to maintain an undeviating line a hundred yards off Hook Reef and hope to hell the charts were accurate and

that South Iron Rock hadn't migrated shoreward. If continents can migrate, I thought, what's to stop a mere reef from
doing the same? For some reason, I recalled the sea lion that
had flopped about clumsily on the rocks at the tip of Pine
Island before slipping into the water when I passed—so
awkward out, so graceful in—and the golden brown of his
coat. As I gripped the helm, held my breath and watched my
painfully slow progress along the length of the reef, its black
shapes writhing and animate in the swirling water, there was
a terrible crash below decks. I didn't have time to investigate.
Whatever it was that had ripped a hole in the bottom did not
seem to have impeded the forward movement of *Groais*,
which was still yawing crazily in a following sea.

When I was clear of Hook Reef, I held the tiller in place
with one foot and peered into the cabin to see if there was any
sign of water. To my relief, only the peanut butter jar, not
properly stowed for rough weather, had crashed against a
bulkhead and broken, its contents slowly oozing down the
finger hole in one of the plywood floorboards. According to
the chart, Jones Cove ought to be just ahead. Protection Cove,
off to starboard, might do in a pinch but, despite the encour-
aging name, its depths weren't charted and it was not
mentioned in the books. It was a bit too exposed; besides, I
wanted to put some distance between myself and Hook Reef. I
had no time for moorage by trial and error.

Twilight is far too pastoral a term for what was happening on
the north coast at that moment. Everything had become flat-
tened out in the growing dark. I could barely make out the
charted indentations. When I came to the spot where Jones
Cove was supposed to be, there was only a slight dip in the
coastline, the bared fang of a drying rock guarding its entrance,
and beyond that a vast uninterrupted wall of solid trees and
rock. Animate and inanimate realms fused by darkness.

I'd gone a quarter mile past the familial-sounding Turner Islands before I could admit I'd missed Jones Cove. I turned back, inched *Groais* around the drying rock at a crawl, and headed straight for the wall of darkness, which suddenly opened up on my right into a cove 150 yards long and 75 feet wide. I dropped my hook dead centre in four fathoms of water, a few shadows of treetops dancing in the last light. An eagle, which had been watching my progress from a snag at the head of the cove, lifted off and made a low sweep over the boat before disappearing into the shadows.

I heated up a can of turkey soup on the stove, chopped an onion and green pepper and dropped them in. To perform these simple tasks, I had to step around the oily peanut butter, which I didn't have the energy to clean up. What was a little domestic chaos at a moment like this? Jones Cove was so well protected I did not need the sternline I'd attached to shore. Though Lister had been at rest for half an hour, my ears still rang from the noise of the engine and from the blood pounding in my temples. I could feel silence spreading like a mantle around me, the soft probes of light from my portholes all but swallowed by the growing dark. The green pepper was okay, but the onions had not cooked properly. They should have been browned first. I didn't care. I lifted the spoon to my mouth, but my hand was shaking so much I had to eat directly from the bowl.

Fifteen feet below, although I wouldn't know it until the following morning, a brilliant orange sea creature two feet in diameter and with more than twenty arms, officially known as a Sunflower Star, had taken a shine to my anchor, half-buried in the mud and murk. Having glided with seeming effortlessness through the wall of dark water, it was slowly attaching itself to the length of chain. When I weighed anchor, grateful but reluctant, and prepared to take my leave of the sanctuary of Jones Cove, this stellar concentration of grace and light and colour, resembling a child's drawing of the sun, would hang from *Groais*'s bow, momentarily suspended above the water, like a badge of honour, a precious mandala, a chain of office.

Thirteen

"If there's low fog or it starts to get dark, always steer for the white mark on the hill. It's just above Wadhams. You can't miss it."

This is the advice I remember my father giving to me as we made one of our regular trips across Rivers Inlet. He was standing beside me, supervising my erratic efforts to steer the boat. I could feel the texture of his woollen sweater on my bare arm and smell the smoke from his cigarette, which was being sucked out the window of the wheelhouse. Trixie, our spaniel, was standing on the bow, using the anchor to brace herself, her black nose sifting the bouillon of unfamiliar smells, her generous ears lifted slightly by the west wind that always rises in the afternoon. The white patch above Wadhams could have been a marble formation, or an outcrop of limestone. I did not know about such things then. But I could see it was unique. I filed the information away. Somewhere in the recesses, surviving the repeated slaughter of brain cells, this image would await its moment of recall.

Rivers Inlet, 375 miles north of Vancouver and well beyond the protection of Vancouver Island, is exposed at its mouth to the full force of Pacific westerlies; the rest, to a maelstrom of competing air currents, much like the wind-tunnel effect created by huge office towers in an urban centre. It's a vast, labyrinthine network of inland waterways that includes three other inlets: Draney, which branches southeast, Moses, which runs fourteen miles north, and Hardy, which jogs westward for six miles from Moses. The mountains plunge from heights of 2,500 to 4,000 feet to troughs so deep that if you're in a small boat, you'd best not think about it. As a young poet, I was hard-pressed to describe the severity of this dramatic conjunction of land and water:

> Whether the land had made
> headway or the sea
> inroads, it was a place
> of no compromise,
>
> a harsh geometry of triangles,
> steep mountain slopes disappearing
> into cold green water.
>
> No fooling around with beaches
> and pleasant meadows, the only
> way to go was up.

I'm still hard-pressed. It's the kind of elemental encounter to crack open your mind, or at least permanently rearrange the molecules. Definitely not a place to be classified as "landscape," a term so often applied by Europeans and inhabitants of the industrial heartland of Canada and the U.S. to any piece of rugged, unfarmed nature outside the city limits. Sylvia Plath had a taste of what I'm talking about when she travelled from the polite landscapes of Boston to Rock Lake, Ontario, where chummy horizons and recognizable vegetation had vanished: "Here on the last frontier of the big brash spirit . . ." she said, "it is comfortable, for a change, to mean so little." Even Plath, who courted oblivion, might have found herself less than comfortable here, the difference being that in Rivers Inlet you don't just "mean little," but grasp at once your utter insignificance in the scheme of things. The scale and "awful silence" of such a coastline profoundly disturbed George Vancouver. Blind to Native occupation and culture, he lamented the absence of familiar human forms: roads, buildings, farms, gardens, anything cultivated. Only the work of mapping kept him from getting bushed, from rowing ashore and shaking hands with the cedars.

Although I had not been to Rivers Inlet for forty-seven years, I could feel something of the same old excitement welling up at the sheer physical spectacle that awaited me—its overwhelming sense of place, unremitting place, with virtually no signs of human habitation left to qualify its grandeur or mitigate its indifference. With the decline of the salmon fishery, I was expecting that most of the small canning operations that dotted the shoreline like last bits of melting snow would have been torn down or reabsorbed by the imperial forests.

Setting out from Duncanby Landing, after my troubling encounter two days earlier with Cape Caution and the whims of an unfettered Pacific, I was delighted to find the names on my chart less than threatening: Goose Bay and a series of small islands called Bull, Cow and Calf. They were bucolic names endowed with humour, all signs of there having been, at least once, considerable human traffic in these parts. As a matter of fact, shortly after the turn of the last century there were seventeen canneries operating in Rivers Inlet, each with hundreds of boats in its employ, mostly small skiffs, some equipped with sails, that were towed to the fishing grounds every morning, then gathered up again in the evening. Nets were set and hauled by hand. Steamships from Vancouver plied the coast, arriving and departing at least twice a week to deliver passengers and supplies and to take out cases of canned salmon destined for a world market. Prospects for the industry seemed boundless.

According to Ken Gillis, that bounty is kaput. Ken ran the store, the marina and the café at Duncanby Landing, all purchased several years earlier with a dream, a mortgage, and considerably more enthusiasm. Indiscriminate logging and overfishing had destroyed the salmon that were once so plentiful. I remembered gillnetting with my father in 1952 during a run of pink salmon. Our net was so full it began to sink, whole stretches of black cork floats disappearing into the water. We had to row along the net and remove the excess fish by hand, until both gillnetter and rowboat were in danger of sinking. Five hundred salmon in a single set, a lot of fish for such a small boat and the price all of three cents a pound! By the time the packer came to relieve us of our precious cargo, we were bailing furiously to stay afloat. Ken was bailing, too, he said, and might soon have to throw in the bucket along with the sponge.

"Look at that," he said, pointing at the dock. "Half a dozen boats and not a goddamn fishboat amongst them. Most of those guys bought their supplies in Port Hardy—or Seattle. And then there are the sailing types like yourself—the wind-bags—whose little diesel engines run on air. Or is it prayer?"

Ken was waxing poetic. The previous night he'd regaled us with several of his compositions, one about a local character named Henderson who achieved a degree of notoriety by running off one year with Ken's cook, the next year with Ken's partner and sweetheart. This ballad was followed by several requests for favourites from the repertoires of other minstrels, including a song about trucking chickens over the Great Divide, as well as a tasteless and politically incorrect piece about Barnacle Bob trying to blow out a candle, which involved imitations of a lisp, a cleft palate, and Prime Minister Jean Chrétien. Appropriately, Ken's first set concluded on a lament with the refrain, "You picked a bad time to leave me, Lucille."

The restaurant-bar was called Jessie's Place, after the black Labrador who'd spent much of the afternoon fetching a large stick from the chuck and was now pegged out in the corner. In addition to a couple of boaters like myself, the half-dozen students from *Seebreeze III*, an old forestry boat built in 1939 and currently used for whale research, were the principal patrons. *Seebreeze III* was skippered by William, who was working on his doctorate on greys and humpbacks at the University of British Columbia. Funding was short, so he had hired out himself and the boat during part of the summer to interested parties, including two Israeli tourists, a Québécois and several undergraduates in marine biology who wanted to jump-start their studies with some first-hand encounters in the wild. William told me he and his crew had set up several base camps, including one at Jones Cove, though I'd seen no signs of human presence when I took refuge there. One of his crew members, Eileen, was surprised by my interest in the ancient village of Owikeno, located on flatlands at the head of Rivers Inlet.

"I was born at Owikeno. If you plan to visit, get in touch with my grandfather, Howard Jones, and his new wife, Irene. Channel Six on the VHF. They'll take you upriver, show you around." She brushed back her hair and turned her plastic chair in my direction. "And tell them hello from me."

Eileen was drinking a Coke. As a regular deckhand on the whaleboat, she'd heard Ken's songs and anecdotes several times. She wanted to talk about plans to finish her schooling in Port Hardy in the fall and go to college. There was an urgency in her narrative, as if she'd heard all the possible impediments to fulfilling her dream—marriage, childbirth, lack of funds, family illness—tapping, like grizzly claws, on the hull of *Seebreeze III*. To drive home the point, there was a full-sized adult cougar skin pinned to the wall behind her and, hanging from the ceiling, a mallard, a heron and an owl, all stuffed.

"So, let's have a round of applause for this evening's bell-ringer. The man with the golden arm and the stuck accelerator."

Ken had not finished ragging the captain of a Bayliner from Oregon who'd almost swamped *Groais* and several other boats when he ignored the courtesy rules and roared up to the fuel dock at half speed. There were shouts, a finger or two, then a conspiracy of silence when he decided to stay overnight. Although he'd promised to ring the bell for his crimes, signalling his willingness to buy a round of drinks for the house, his appearance in the bar had prompted an unending string of jokes, all at his expense.

"The American poured drinks for the three of them, then tossed his half-empty bottle of bourbon into the water. 'Shee-it,' he said, 'in the U-nited States we never drink twice out of the same bottle.'" Ken was warming to his role as host and raconteur, colour high in his cheeks and three empty beer glasses on the table.

The atmosphere in the room was charged. Even the sleeping Jessie seemed suddenly infused with energy, as she was vibrating on her mat and making short, muted whoofing sounds.

Ken cleared his throat. He paused for a mouthful of beer, casting a discerning eye over his audience.

"The Australian sliced enough beef for three plates, then chucked the roast overboard. 'Bugger that, mate. Down under, we've got so much bloody meat we never look at the same roast twice.' Then the Canadian took out his fish-whacker and bonked the American over the head, causing the Aussie to leap backwards from the table and spew out a half-chewed mouthful of beef. 'What the hell you do that for?' he stuttered. 'Well,' said the Canadian, 'we've got so goddamn many Americans in this country, we don't have to drink with the same one twice.'"

As I made my way past Cow, Bull, Calf and other pasturing islands, I decided to celebrate my arrival in Rivers Inlet by putting out a line, and not the poetic sort. I was tired of my boring fare of cheese and eggs; and having noticed all the fish, prawns and crab being cooked and consumed at the dock, I'd been hankering for a couple of small salmon steaks. An army-truck hoochie, which was a rubber replica of a squid with camouflage markings, and a large green-and-chrome flasher with twelve ounces of weight ought to do the trick, I thought. That late in the morning the salmon would be deep, doing their overdue school assignments. I hadn't done my own homework, though, and was not sure I could remember how to distinguish one kind of salmon from another, though I used to do it so easily. Coho, I knew, were *verboten* this season, for sport as well as commercial fishermen. To top it off, I had no idea where I'd stashed my fishing licence either.

Even at its most sluggish pace, *Groais* moves too fast through the water to troll properly, causing the fishing gear to rotate maddeningly rather than sweep back and forth in an enticing, rhythmical arc. In order to compensate, I had to make a series of sharp S-turns, following, wherever possible, the outline of the small bays and protuberances. This movement caused the gear to speed up and rise closer to the surface at the peak of the turn, then sink and dawdle during the lull, approximating the movement of the salmon and giving them a chance to check out the merchandise at more than one level. A good marketing procedure, I concluded. And it worked. I hadn't put my strategy to work for ten minutes when there was a strike and the line peeled out from the reel with a familiar and exciting whine. Fifty yards to port the fish broke the surface. I tried not to overplay my hand by bringing it in too fast; however, I didn't want any slack in the line to allow it to slip off the barbless hooks that are now mandatory.

I hadn't fished much over the years. I wasn't exactly rusty, but I was uncertain how I'd manage to haul in a fish with the sailboat's rigging, boom and lifelines in the way. Lister was idling in neutral, but the fish had taken off again, this time under the dinghy, forcing me to pass the rod around the afterstays to the starboard side, an awkward manoeuvre that could have proven costly. The hand net, meanwhile, was lying under a heap of line on the stern where I'd stowed it weeks earlier, not exactly ready for action. I had about twenty-five feet still out when I saw it again, flashing silver past the boat, taking another fifteen feet in its break for freedom. A tighter rein, fifteen feet, ten, and it was alongside, bigger than I'd expected, and furious. I'd made the leads from the flasher quite long, so it was going to be difficult maintaining the tension while I eased the net underneath, the damned stays impeding my every move.

Suddenly it was in the cockpit, thrashing, both hooks free, head and tail sawing at the small apertures of the net. Fins, gills, rudders, ailerons. I'd forgotten how beautiful salmon look, gods of the deep, so streamlined that their dynamics serve as the model for all of man's fastest inventions in water, even in air. According to my chart, it was a spring salmon (which Americans refer to as king), with the characteristic black spots on its back and upper and lower tail fin, and at least eighteen pounds, the biggest fish I've ever landed. It was also about ten times as much as I could hope to eat, given my lack of refrigeration, even over a couple of days. Sunlight reflected off the overlapping network of transparent scales, highlighting the greenish blue of the back as it graduated to silver sides and a white belly. I remembered the excitement of watching salmon emerge over the stern-rollers of the gillnetter, especially at night within the intimate cone of light above the drum, black noses first, then the full body drawing form and substance from the modest glow of the lantern.

I lowered the net and its precious contents back over the side of the boat. Before I had a chance to reconsider what I was doing, the fish had exited the net gingerly, nursing its bruises, not quite believing it was free to go. Too long out of the water? Injury to eye or gills? You can't play this game without causing damage, and there was a trace of blood in the cockpit to prove it. Then, with a wink of tail, it vanished. Having learned a useful lesson—who knows? Fish are often described as eating-machines, single-minded, capable of taking the same lure twice. At least it wouldn't have to make that decision today. I was relieved, grateful for the option of releasing it. My own vulnerability on this journey, my tentative status above water, had made me reluctant to kill anything. I'd had enough sport.

What I hadn't had enough of, though, was a real dose of nostalgia and that's where I was headed. Wadhams Cannery, where my father had worked, renting his boat and net and buying all his supplies from B.C. Packers, was a few miles up the inlet. It had been a booming affair, a huge, rambling conglomeration of floats, net-lofts, machine shop, packing plant, company store and bunkhouses, some of the structures balancing on creosoted pilings, others jammed into the hundred yards of unusually swampy shoreline at the foot of the mountain. From the bow of the SS *Cardena*, the Union Steamships vessel that delivered my stepmother, two brothers and me to Wadhams Cannery in Rivers Inlet in the summer of 1952, the cluster of white buildings in the distance seemed pretty small change, especially after the lights and attractions of Vancouver.

We'd just arrived by bus from Saskatchewan, where my father had tried construction and then farming, using up his veteran's allowance to purchase a small Massey-Ferguson tractor. Not even good equipment could make the land deliver. We were hailed out, frozen out, then moved out. He said he'd send bus fare when he found work. A few letters arrived from the Marble Arch Hotel on Richards Street, one eventually containing a money order and an address. As poor as we were, when she saw this hotel a month later, with its seedy rooms and dubious clientele of drunks, prostitutes and hustlers, my stepmother Marge, still young and impressionable at twenty-six, was embarrassed to be associated with it. The name became synonymous in her mind with everything ugly and to be avoided in the city. When we'd set out from Yorkton, the diesel fumes, swaying movement and enclosed spaces of the bus went to work immediately. Before long the pungent odour of my stomach acids permeated every cranny of the Greyhound, inspiring stronger stomachs than mine to conform. I tried directing my projectiles out the window, but had only a fifty per cent success rate. By the time we reached Saskatoon, the sides of the bus were streaked with vomit. By Edmonton a survival routine had developed—all the passengers purchasing newspapers with which to make barf-cones, which they'd dutifully pass back to me and the other unfortunates on board. I'm sure the clerks and porters who sold newspapers thought this the most literate busload of prairie emigrants they'd ever encountered.

My father was waiting for us at the dock at Wadhams when the *Cardena* slid alongside, scarcely nudging the pilings. He had secured a house for us across the inlet, but first we had to meet the manager, his fishermen friends, and a Chinese cook named Lu. Huge vats of copper sulphate dye, "bluing" he called it, lined the pier, and fishermen were soaking their nets, then hauling them out to dry. The dye made the mesh of the net less visible in the water. Several men sat smoking pipes while they mended holes in nets that had made contact with propellers, rocks, logs, even whales. Two others piled cases of salmon, with their brightly coloured labels and bold lettering, onto pallets. Having been sick to my stomach on the *Cardena* as well, I was struggling to cope with a symphony of new smells, which included gas boats, sweaty bodies, fish, human sewage and the detritus of the canning process being flushed out constantly between the pilings.

I'd been told the cannery was bought, several years after it closed, by Americans who thought they'd turn it into a sport-fishing camp, using the smaller buildings as dormitories and the plant itself as a lodge. Whatever its present status, Wadhams was likely to look pretty much as it had more than four decades earlier, a white blur at water's edge that would materialize into a cluster of buildings and pilings as I approached. What I saw instead, when I rounded the point of Johnston Bay, was a tidy stretch of beach and a few barely discernible pilings. I've miscalculated the distance, I thought, Wadhams is farther up the inlet, though the map suggested otherwise. I'd passed the narrow entrance to Draney Inlet a few miles back, so this had to be it.

But the cannery was nowhere to be seen—the whole enterprise had vanished. I'd travelled almost five hundred miles by sea and the one landmark I'd been most confident of finding no longer existed. What I saw in its place were three small dwellings, all new cedar-and-glass constructions, at intervals along the beach. They appeared to be private homes for the use of a few friends during the summer months. I could see movement on the pier—a man, two kids and a dog descending a ramp to the float to which I was heading. I should turn around, I thought, and head for Dawson's Landing, since I'm clearly trespassing here, another meddlesome boater to shatter the serenity and solitude of Rivers Inlet. But it was too late. The dog was wagging its tail as my bowline was being secured to the float.

"I'm sorry to intrude." I wasn't the least bit sorry, but I did feel like an interloper obliged to come up with an explanation. I stepped off the boat and secured the stern. "I used to fish up here with my father when I was a kid, forty-seven years ago, and I'm very curious about the site."

"That's a long time. A bit of a surprise, eh? If you'd like, I'll show you around."

I was talking to Larry Sinitsin, a semi-retired executive in the plastics industry who loved the coast and spent all his spare time between Crescent Beach and Alaska. His wife, Jan, not an avid boater, preferred the comforts, safety and solidity of dry land, so Larry had purchased several coastal properties, which he was fixing up as a hobby and an investment. We climbed the ramp and sauntered along the length of the pier.

"I like building things. I'm also a bit of a bottom-feeder." Larry was rubbing the dog's ears to get it to release a small stick. The dog refused. "I tried to buy this place from the American owners several years ago, but they wanted too much for it. Then the cannery collapsed, because some of the beams had been taken out for other purposes. They couldn't wait to get rid of it after that."

Only one of the original houses had been preserved, serving as a residence while the demolition and rebuilding took place. It was a white two-storey clapboard house, the original manager's dwelling, tucked out of sight behind the pier. Larry described how, while work on the property was underway, a hungry or rabid wolf once kept them pinned inside for three hours, growling at the door.

"At least he didn't blow your house down, the way he did the rest of the cannery." I offered this bit of whimsy for the benefit of the kids, who were ambling along with us. Chelsea was amused, but Matthew, who had not said a word by this time, looked away. They'd seen grizzlies on the property, too, Chelsea told me. Her dad kept a close eye on the kids and on the dozen or so deer that grazed daily on the new lawn. I was curious about the demolition. What had they done with all the rotten lumber—burned it?

"No, buried it. We hand-picked the best lumber, which was salvaged for rebuilding the pier. The rest was buried in a huge pit we dug with an excavator. It brought up the level of the property, which had been low and boggy, by at least ten feet."

Larry was thinking of turning Wadhams Outpost into a fishing lodge, but he couldn't quite adjust to the idea of having people there whom he didn't know. At the moment, the lineup of summer guests included only friends. I suggested it would be a great spot for a writing workshop.

"Fishing for words."

"My wife would love that." He showed me through the cabins, two of which were fitted out with great attention to detail—skylights, potential for adding a sleeping loft in the larger rooms; even the individual planks of cedar siding had been bevelled. "You could use this as a central lounge."

As we looked around, Chelsea extracted from the drawer of an end table some photocopies of archival photographs a friend had sent up from Vancouver. I'd asked Larry if he had any photographs of the old cannery, but all that stuff was still down south. One of the photocopies showed the SS *Cardena* alongside the pier; another, a frontal shot of the cannery, perhaps taken from the ship as it docked, showed a dozen First Nations employees in aprons taking a break. Something outside the picture, at water level, had caught their attention. I was grateful to Chelsea for remembering these photocopies, which ought to have moderated the profound sense of loss I was feeling, but didn't. From the porch I was struck again by the bleak magnificence of the prospect—not a sign of other human occupation anywhere, just water, trees, peaks still dotted in August with last year's snow, and the headlong, precipitous mountains.

Back at the dock, Larry, kids and dog helped me embark. The small dog, which he called his bear-chaser, was pulling at the sternline as Larry tried to untie it, while Chelsea, age seven, was telling me she often visited her friend over at Dawson's Landing, my next port of call. I'd come looking for the past, but found myself pondering the future of this spot I'd visited so many years earlier, wondering if I'd ever see it or its new owners again. The smells and the accommodation had definitely improved. And the inhabitants, if not the wolves, seemed friendly enough.

Larry gave me his business card. This was the third business card in a week. I had none to offer in return, so I gave him a copy of one of my books.

"Any time you need to take refuge here, don't hesitate. You'll be most welcome."

I nodded, mouthed a thank you, and gave the throttle a nudge. A few feet from the dock, I took a photo of Chelsea, who was hugging the dog as if it were the one departing. I wasn't much older than that when I stepped off the gangway of the SS *Cardena* onto the pier where she was standing. I had a tattered brown cardboard suitcase in one hand, my brother Lloyd's small fingers in the other. Our father was running towards us, his shoes echoing on the planks of the pier. He was as happy as I would ever see him.

Chelsea and Larry returned my farewell salute in unison. High above them, and off to the right, I could see the white patch of rock on the mountain that my father had singled out for the purpose of navigation when he was so much younger than I am now.

Limestone? Perhaps. I preferred to see it as a precious arch of marble.

Fourteen

My arrival at Dawson's Landing was somewhat more satisfying than my arrival at the site of the former Wadhams Cannery. After sailing past an islet called the Haystack and around the northeast tip of Walbran Island, I saw a familiar scene—an acre of cedar logs and planking on which were perched a store, a machine shop, a fuel shed, a house and several smaller makeshift cabins. A floating opera of docks, boats, tourists, kids and dogs, attached by chain to the foot of a mountainside that offered no purchase, not even a foothold. For all that, it was a comforting sight that made me think of John Marshall's pithy three-liner, "Seymour Inlet Float Camp: Domestic Scene":

> mother is sewing
> father's
> thumb back on

Tucked away in a small by-channel on the northwest shore, Dawson's Landing was a snug recess at the entrance to Darby Channel, well protected from the fierce winds that played havoc with the rest of Rivers Inlet. To my great joy, the place had scarcely altered in five decades. The one significant change, fresh milk, was cause for celebration, too, as I had grown as a boy to loathe evaporated milk in cans after using it on cereal and in tea all summer.

I spent my first night at Dawson's Landing talking with

Willy, a Japanese Canadian who was doing repair work on the cedar logs and cross-timbers on which the entire establishment floated. Many of the rotten planks he replaced must have dated back to the fifties, when my family and I stopped there in our gillnetter once a week for groceries and mail. Willy's boss, Rob Bachen, who had taken over the business from his father, Lucky, had his own portable sawmill on a separate float, where he rendered into boards any salvaged logs he thought unlikely to bring as good a price later on. When Willy was not called away on a troubleshooting errand, he spent his time beachcombing for stray logs or restoring, slowly and meticulously, the extensive deck and walkways with these rough-hewn two-by-twelve cedar boards.

As a child growing up in Vancouver, I knew nothing about the wartime evacuation of Japanese Canadians. In a society already fuelled by a deep-seated anti-Asian racism, the bombing of Pearl Harbor provided the impetus for official persecution. Thousands of men, women and children were herded into cattle barns in Exhibition Park in Vancouver before being shunted off to internment camps in the interior of British Columbia, their savings, property and worldly goods divvied up for the benefit of neighbours and local authorities or sold off at bargain-basement prices to the first or the loudest in line. An official apology and a token twenty-thousand-dollar settlement to each of a dwindling number of survivors took four decades. Neither my schoolmate Roger Kamakura nor our family friend Toshiko Miagawa, who worked with my stepmother at the cannery in Steveston, had chosen to enlighten me about this missing chapter in the high school textbooks and one of the blackest pages in Canadian history.

Willy's father and grandfather accepted repatriation to Japan rather than face internment in Canada, then returned after the war. As a result, Willy remained an outsider, having little in common with the Nisei (first-generation Canadians) of Vancouver. When his mother died, Willy's father discovered he had been playing hookey for two years, leaving in the mornings and acquiring an informal education on the street. He was thrown out and drifted for several years before heading north to reinvent himself as a logger, beachcomber, and Mr. Fix-it. He had his own rhythms, though, and did not quite approve of his boss, Rob, for being a workaholic.

"I told him, 'I'm going to talk to people while I work. I got no family, I need some sort of social life.'" Willy slid another bottle of beer across the coil of wire on the stern of Rob's steel-hulled tugboat, which he was using as temporary lodging. "Rob doesn't like it, but what can he do? I said, 'Pay me less if you want, but that's the way I am. I'll work hard, but not non-stop. And not in silence.'"

Willy was small, wiry. He smoked too much and his teeth wanted fixing; they were not likely to be a priority, though, as he had bills to pay and needed a tugboat of his own if he were to earn any real money. I made a trite if well-intentioned observation that Japanese-Canadian families expect too much of their kids.

"What do they think of a son and a brother who's a beachcomber?"

Willy's eyes bent around the neck of the upended bottle of beer to see my face. "Hey, man, Bruno Gerussi did it on television." A gull landed on the coil of wire between us, quickly assessed the situation, then hopped onto the fish float to look for scraps. "He earned big bucks, too."

"Ya, but he died young."

"Booze, not logs."

"Or the coffee at Molly's Reach."

"Hey, somebody's gotta collect all those glass fishing floats washing up on the beaches from Japan, right? I'm the runt of the litter. I got in trouble a couple years back and had a blow-up with the family. We don't talk."

Willy opened two more beers while we talked about logging in Draney Inlet. The cruising guides couldn't make up their minds about the length of the inlet, one saying it was eleven miles long, the other twenty-four, just the kind of discrepancy that could get a boater in trouble. As the last light was absorbed by the surrounding forest, Willy told me of spending two sleepless nights towing a boat to Kitimat. He needed rest, but the harbour-master chewed him out for pumping foul water at the docks. The tugboat owner's idea of an oil change had been to let it drain into the bilge, which meant that the boat's pumps were constantly expelling a mixture of oil and water into the ocean. Willy was so rattled and embarrassed, he set out at night from Kitimat and fell asleep at the wheel in Dean Channel. The boat hit a rock, sending his partner flying six feet off the bunk.

"He said, 'Jesus Christ, what's happening?' I told him it's nothing, go back to bed. An hour later it happened again. This time he crashed into the bulkhead. So he took over and I slept. We were lucky. The sides of the channel were steep rock. Not too much damage to the metal hull, only a few thousand dollars. I told the owner to give me five hundred bucks of what I'd earned to get me back to Vancouver."

As the pile of empties mounted, the discussion turned to fishing—the destruction of salmon stocks and the current plague of sport fishing. While motoring into Dawson's Landing, I had seen a middle-aged couple in an inflatable dinghy fighting with what turned out to be an eighty-two-pound halibut on the line, which they'd snagged near the dock. They weren't just having fun, they were serious fishers and had put a harpoon into the halibut so it wouldn't escape if the line broke. Half an hour later, it lay on the dock twitching, blood oozing from the harpoon gash, making a few final spasmodic slaps with its tail, the two topside eyes looking more like a Picasso drawing than anything else to be found in nature. I admired the couple's expertise in filleting the halibut, even removing the cheeks, which are considered a delicacy. A small girl in a print dress was watching too, her eyes large with amazement at the blood and surgical procedures.

"Pastor Jim, why do they look like that?"

Pastor Jim, part of the yearly contingent of Christians to descend on Dawson's Landing, was not reminded of Christ on the cross by this ghastly scene; nor did he wonder why he was participating in such carnage rather than fishing for souls. In fact, it probably had not occurred to him that the girl might be thinking about the pool of blood and the flesh laid open, or the two carvers busy with their dismantling, rather than the halibut's strangely placed eyes. "That's how the Lord made them," he told the girl, "with two eyes on top so they can skim the bottom and see predators above." She didn't look convinced. Obviously, those Cubist eyes had not done the job the Lord assigned to them.

While we watched the gutting of the halibut, a couple of American anglers arrived at the scales, each with large spring salmon, the beloved kings. They weighed the fish and should have had their photos taken with the smug, half-stunned look of prizefighters—or Great White Hunters, in the Papa Hemingway tradition, standing over their kill. But the shortest of the two men, who was holding up a magnificent salmon that had weighed in at thirty-five pounds, seemed irritated and was cursing.

"What's wrong?" I figured he'd cut his hand or was having trouble supporting the weight of the fish.

"Not big enough." He spat, turned on his heel and slammed the massive salmon down on the stainless-steel cutting table. His friend had caught a fifty-five-pounder. Not an ounce of wonder or gratitude for this amazing gift from the briny deep. I wanted to shake the fool or throw him in the chuck for the halibut to feed on.

Willy was outraged when I described this incident and told me about various scams being used to evade quotas in Rivers Inlet, where more salmon than are allowable per person were being bagged, frozen, and shipped home to Calgary, Denver and North Carolina. Fines were high, but there were too few inspectors to cover all the fishing grounds. In addition to the five hundred to one thousand pounds of salmon brought in every day to Dawson's Landing, there were a dozen other official and unofficial fish camps in Rivers Inlet, at least one of them run illegally by American guides. The best fishermen would release all but the largest fish, sticking to their quotas. Others sent fish home with friends or family members and didn't seem able to stop. Willy had seen an angler keep a twenty-five-pound spring in the boat all day, then chuck it overboard after he caught a larger one.

Greed—raw and ugly. It put a new spin on the phrase "spring fever."

"There's not a thing left at Brunswick Bay," I explained to my stepmother Marge on the phone in Garson, Manitoba. A year ago, she had returned to that former inland sea known as the Prairies. She'd never felt quite right living next to the real ocean. There was static on the satellite phone, which I was paying three dollars a minute to experience. Two boaters were waiting for a turn on the only phone available, and Nola Bachen, the proprietor of the general store, was standing next to me with a stopwatch to get an accurate reading of my time on the airwaves.

"Do you remember the ping-pong table? Lloyd used to ride his tricycle around the table while you and Jim played. Trixie would chase after him barking."

"The summer Olympics. Sounds perfectly idyllic for you, a quiet retreat on the coast."

I didn't recall a ping-pong table or tricycle, though I did have shadowy memories of the doctor's residence, with a large living room where there were a hundred or more Hudson's Bay blankets stacked in a corner to be sold for two dollars apiece. My most vivid memories were of the pier, the moss-covered boardwalk and the mission hospital itself, with three storeys and a working dumb waiter, on which I could imagine dead infants or severed limbs being lowered. I found a gold tooth in a desk drawer, one of many treasures, which my father later pawned on Hastings Street in Vancouver when there was no money for food. When I discovered my loss, Marge was peeling potatoes on the checkered vinyl tablecloth in our dreary walk-up above a shop on Commercial Drive. She was wearing felt slippers and a blue apron smudged with flour from the baking-powder biscuits quietly humming in the oven.

"I'm sorry. Your father got seven dollars for it."

"But it was mine." I don't know whether I was offended more by the theft of my property or by her nonchalant attitude. I was old enough not to need a lecture on sharing or family solidarity. Marge swept the potato peelings off the edge of the table into the waste bin, one of them coming to rest across Trixie's nose like a pair of bifocals. The dog sat there without moving a muscle, as if waiting for an idea or an explanation to form in her cocker-spaniel brain.

Eleven years younger than my father, Marge was not yet thirty when she arrived in Rivers Inlet in 1952. When she met him in Winnipeg at the end of the war, dazzled by the uniform and his good looks, she could have had no idea of the difficult years that lay ahead, almost fifty of them.

"What about the pier?" Marge asked. I could hear her two dogs barking in the background. By now there were four people in line behind me waiting to use the phone, looking at their watches and muttering.

"Gone," I said. The pier, the house, the hospital, the board-walk—not a thing left standing. And the whole slope had been logged, clear-cut. All the way to the water. Willy and Rob had warned me not to expect much at Brunswick Bay. Even then, I was not prepared for the devastation awaiting me when I motored past Edna Mathews Island, a small tree-covered ovoid named after the wife of Dr. Darby, the famous founder of the mission hospital. The slight indentation in the shoreline hardly justified its description as a bay and provided nothing in the way of protection for boats. However, it did offer a toehold on the shore. Darby, who was based in Bella Bella, needed the Rivers Inlet hospital to provide medical support during the summer for the First Nations community at Owikeno village and the huge fishing fleet, which he could no longer service adequately from farther up the coast.

The wooden three-storey hospital with a fifteen-bed capac-ity, which had the aspect of an outpost of progress irrevocably reverting back to rainforest, had been closed in favour of a smaller clinic at Wadhams, where the bulk of the fishing fleet gathered. When we first came to Rivers Inlet in early July, we camped in the doctor's residence on the point and made frequent excursions along the twin boardwalks out back, which led to separate staff dormitories for men and women. My brother Jim and I fell through those rotting, moss-covered boardwalks more than once, slipping on banana slugs and ending up in swampy patches of skunk cabbage, which sported huge fronds and phallic pistils. These rank, luminous beauties, with their bright yellow spike and hooded bract—a yellow shield or reflector—are also called, not surprisingly, swamp lanterns. Their lance-shaped leaves, known as Indian wax paper, were used to line berry baskets and steam pits. Here and there, we also found enormous shelf fungi growing on the north side of trees, the poor man's blackboard. The velvety upper surface is so sensitive to the touch that any design or words scratched onto it will remain intact when the fungus is removed and dried. I once immortalized a friend's slip of the tongue—"A mere elephant of contrivance"—by inscribing it on one of these fungi. We also climbed hundreds of feet up the creek-bed—Marge and two-year-old Lloyd inching over a crevice behind us on a fallen cedar log—to reach the wooden storage tank that collected and supplied water to the hospital. There were cracks in the pipe, but it still worked. I don't recall any mention ever being made of the very real danger of wild animals in relation to these outings, though this was grizzly and cougar country.

Marge was the backbone of our lives then—our Rockies, Selkirks and Coast Range all combined. Whatever healing took place in my brother's and my lives, shattered as a result of our mother's death, we owed to her. She was told she'd never conceive because of a tipped womb, but shortly after we exploded into her life she became pregnant with my half-brother Lloyd. At twenty-seven, resigned to being childless for life, Marge found herself with three sons: an infant, a boy only thirteen years younger than herself, and me, a bed-wetter, a squinter, and a general psychological disaster. With her good nature and common sense, she managed, in short space, to get us all on a more or less even keel. Rivers Inlet and the farm years still strike me as a magical period, during which I felt, at long last, secure, loved and free to explore the world around me.

Her early years with my father were fraught with difficulties arising from his drinking, womanizing, and various commercial fiascos, starting with the cancellation of his contract to build custom houses on the U.S.–Saskatchewan border after early frost destroyed the freshly poured but not winterized concrete foundations. The nadir of his subsequent career as farmer-cum-carpenter would be reached when Marge, with the help of her aging parents, had to bail him out of jail for writing bad cheques.

The insecurities lingered as my father travelled from job to job trying to supplement the negligible income from the farm. Even with the help of the Massey-Ferguson tractor, wheat farming proved as difficult and unpredictable as prospecting. I remember crawling under the hay wagon with my father and brother, hailstones pelting down like large marbles, reins wound around the axle to keep the horses from bolting, while an entire summer's work was destroyed in minutes. Although Marge hated to leave the Prairies, my father's decision to return to the coast came as a relief to her, as it meant—if he actually sent for us, and no one seriously doubted he would—that he'd have to take full responsibility for our well-being and not depend on her parents. Whatever his personal failings, my father was always a hard worker and seemed to be able to find and keep a job as long as someone else called the shots and managed the money.

Two years before his death in 1995, I visited him and Marge in Cumberland, a former coal-mining community near Courtenay, halfway up the east coast of Vancouver Island, where she was virtually a prisoner of his deteriorating physical and mental condition, his lifelong insecurities and jealousies exacerbated by a cocktail of twenty-seven different pills. He wouldn't let her out of his sight, insisting she was having an affair whenever she went out to buy groceries, and

standing at the window with binoculars to chart her progress
to and from the Legion bingo games. Marge was not one to
complain, even in the worst circumstances, but now she let it
all out. I was stunned. I remember taking her for lunch and a
walk on the pier in Comox, where we stood gazing at the
boats and the cold, grey surface of the inner harbour.

"You could always bring him down here for a walk and give
the wheelchair a gentle push."

On the second night of my visit, Marge went out, at my
insistence, to play bingo with her cronies at the Legion, above
the disused coal shafts that riddle the townsite like a subterranean warren. I sat in their tiny seniors' apartment with my
father, trying not to listen to the cumulative noise of the
perpetual television and the short-wave radio on which he
monitored police and emergency calls. It was an opportunity to
talk, if I'd been prepared to persevere, to force the issue. I no
longer knew where to begin, there was so much I needed to
know. He was dozing, oblivious to the operatic frenzy of
natural and unnatural disasters being served up in stereo and
technicolour in the room, so I took refuge in the newspaper and
thought of my stepmother two blocks away, wondering what
might be going through her mind as the caged bingo balls
gyrated like whirling molecules. A hundred feet below the
Legion hall, ghosts of Chinese miners hold their breath,
numbers in lieu of foreign names recorded on their graves and
payslips, emigration not the only game of chance. Her first
husband, snagged on barbed wire, unravels in mortar fire in
France. She recalls Johnny Brigadier's crooked grin and the
rosebud he carefully mounted in his foreskin along the road
allowance after school. A membrane of earth encloses her
brother Alvin shortly after diphtheria stitched shut his throat
at age sixteen, hopes of the family dashed, education not for
girls, except the kind you get at a munitions factory in Etobi-

coke, hair done up in a kerchief, the foreman persistent, a smile the only ammo he needs. And meeting husband number two, my father, in Winnipeg after the war, a beached mariner still in uniform. Watch your step, get sea legs first. Adopted sons swimming in the Souris River, attached to her by ropes. Prickly hemp or smooth sash-cord, I don't recall the texture of that lifeline undulating alongside me in the muddy current like a water snake, but I bear the marks of all that caring, anchored to her flesh. The caller with hennaed hair fishes out a numbered molecule under the G. Not ground or grief, but grace abundant.

A full card.

Nola was rolling her eyes, wondering how much longer she'd have to hold the stopwatch for my call to Manitoba. I'd need to win the Lotto to pay for this one. There were now five customers lined up to use the phone, images of tar and feathers animating their angry faces. Marge was so excited to get this call from Rivers Inlet, I could barely extract the fact that she was still having a lot of pain in her knee. The injection had not worked and an operation seemed the only solution. "You have to be dragged in there screaming before the doctors will recommend treatment," she said, and she was too proud to do that. In the forty-seven years since we had lived in Rivers Inlet, Marge had buried both parents, her brother and my father, and watched her youngest son struggle with a series of personal disasters, some self-inflicted, some resulting from bad luck, an industrial accident, and government intransigence. Her move to Manitoba, at Jim's prompting and with his help, was a gesture of self-preservation, an acknowledgement she could no longer support herself and Lloyd on her pension and his meagre welfare cheque. I asked if she remembered the white patch of rock above Wadhams.

"No, but I remember how terrified I was stepping onto your dad's boat and heading across that inlet with three kids. The *Cardena* was bad enough. It seemed like the end of the world. I must be crazy, I thought, to have agreed to this. When we got to the mission hospital and I saw that metal ladder disappearing over my head, I said, Laurie, I can't do this."

"Good pioneer stock, right?"

Farmers, at least, had a piece of land to build on, to shape towns and cities in the image of the Old World, to harness the unknown, grow things, bring the chaos under control. Rivers Inlet, like so much of the coast, defied such futile gestures. Houses and businesses sank back into the forest in a decade or two, the alien growth bursting through walls and floorboards. On the Prairies, Marge knew what to expect; during the war, she followed the seasons, heading home in late spring from the munitions factory in Ontario, where the forty-millimetre shells moved along on conveyor belts as innocent as Coke bottles, so she could help plant the crops. Here, even the water couldn't make up its mind, and changed levels constantly, lapping at the rock and weed one day and stirring itself into a deadly frenzy the next. Everything about this place confirmed her farmer's instincts that she'd made a colossal mistake. As if to justify her worst fears, my father got blood poisoning from stepping on a gaff hook and I was drafted to serve as crew on the gillnetter. When Marge looked out the window of the doctor's residence in the morning, with Lloyd in her arms and Trixie worrying a rubber ball at her feet, and saw the net aground on the reef, the black corks extending like an out-of-control ellipsis towards our boat where it rubbed against the rocks, she was sure we had both drowned, like my grandfather before us. But I'd only fallen asleep on the job, the first and most glorious in a long line of botched assignments.

As *Groais* came in sight of Brunswick Bay, I could see

they'd logged over the old cemetery, cutting right down to the water's edge, leaving a huge gash on the side of the mountain, the original creek-bed devastated. Topsoil had eroded, exposing bald rock. A few pieces of heavy equipment still littered the narrow shelf above the high-water mark. I didn't stay long. A light wind was building and I used it to sail past McAllister Point and the mouth of Moses Inlet, as far as Kilbella Bay and the head of Rivers Inlet. I had the genoa up and was moving along at a good clip, but I paid for all that speed when I had to get the sail down again in the heavy chop created by a west wind meeting the outflowing river. Glacial runoff had turned the water a milky colour. At the mouth of the Wannock River, I couldn't reach Howard Jones, the grandfather of Eileen on *Seebreeze III*, by VHF at his house in Owikeno village, and the water was so rough I didn't dare leave the boat at the government float. In fact, the wind was gusting so strongly, I had to put *Groais* in gear in order to untie the lines and keep it from being driven into the pilings.

Nola's mother had put several freshly baked pies on the shelf behind me. I could smell the crust and steaming apple without turning. Before I rang off and faced the tally from Nola's stopwatch, I told Marge I wished we'd held a glorious cook-up before we left—a honky potlatch—giving away all those Hudson's Bay blankets, along with the cases of evaporated Carnation and Pacific milk I hated so much, something outlandish and extravagant to mark our own brief passage. Do you remember those crazy people who lived at the old hospital site before it vanished? they'd ask years later. You know, the ones with the yapping spaniel and the lucky gillnetter? What a party. More than two hundred boats in Brunswick Bay. You could have walked across the water on them from one end of

the bay to the other and never got your feet wet. Like Jesus
Christ. Dr. Darby might not have approved, but he'd have
enjoyed it. Poker, ping-pong, mah-jong, Monopoly, hot-
buttered rum laced with Carnation milk. Five hundred baking-
powder biscuits, a laundry tub full of salad, and thirty-four
barbecued sockeye. The young woman had three kids—two
almost her own age and a brat on a tricycle running over
people's feet—knocking over drinks. And remember the
husband—at least, I assume they were married—his black hair
slicked straight back, who used to buy rounds of drinks for
everyone at Wadhams as if he were Rockefeller?

No, I don't remember, I wasn't even born then. Well, come
to think of it, my old man did mention something about that.
Happened a long time ago, right?

Outside, the water and the distant mountains were changing colour constantly in the late afternoon light as high overhead, patches of cumulus cloud drifted inland like so many of
Dr. Darby's cotton swabs. I thought of Rupert Brooke's
observation in 1913 as he sat on the edge of the Pacific, ecstatic, and wildly surmising: "Nature here is half-Japanese."

✳ Fifteen

When Charles Darwin set out from Plymouth on the *Beagle* in 1831 for his three-and-a-half-year trip around the world, he was a young man determined to see as much as possible and to prove himself useful to science. Writing later about his adventure in *The Voyage of the Beagle*, he said very little about the difficulties and dangers of such a sea voyage, except to mention the obvious losses—friends, familiar places, space, privacy, rest. He refused to romanticize the sea, whose "boasted glories" he dismissed with the Arabian sentiment: "A tedious waste, a desert of water." A storm, he admitted, was worth seeing, with its gale-force winds and mountainous waves; however, it was better seen from shore, because, at sea, "the ship alone and its inhabitants seem the objects of wrath. On a forlorn and weather-beaten coast the scene is indeed different, but the feelings participate more of horror than of wild delight."

He never forgot his remarkable good luck in being appointed naturalist on the expedition and considered the inconveniences well worth the price. Unlike George Vancouver, who was not the least bit curious about flora, fauna, landforms, and icebergs, or Native customs, culture, and language—and even resented having Archibald Menzies thrust upon him as a naturalist—Charles Darwin was nothing if not curious. He was also endowed with a sense of awe and wonder. You can't read a page of *The Voyage of the Beagle* without coming across phrases such as "I have often admired," "it is admirable to behold," "I was pleased with nothing so much as," and "I did not cease to wonder at." There seems to have been very little that did not provide him with raw material for scrutiny and curiosity. In addition to his well-known observations about plant and animal life, Darwin was a keen student of geology, listing amongst his most amazing sights "an active volcano, a lagoon island, the blue ice of a glacier, the effects of an earthquake, and the Southern Cross." Of these, he was most amazed by the earthquake:

These latter phenomena, perhaps, possess for me a peculiar interest, from their intimate connection with the geological structure of the world. The earthquake, however, must be to every one a most impressive event: the earth, considered from our earliest childhood as the type of solidity, has oscillated like a thin crust beneath our feet: and in seeing the laboured works of man in a moment over-thrown, we feel the insignificance of his boasted power.

Despite his constant seasickness, which he described as "no trifling evil," Darwin seems to have been more or less impervious to the discomforts. He attributes his success to having a purpose, a hobby, an ulterior motive.

Hence, a traveller should be a botanist, for in all views plants form the chief embellishment. Group masses of naked rock even in the wildest forms, and they may for a time afford a sublime spectacle, but they will soon grow monotonous. Paint them in bright and varied colours, as in Northern Chile, they will become fantastic; clothe them with vegetation, they must form a decent, if not a beautiful, picture.

While Darwin's grammar here seems to promise a more

convincing epithet than he delivers on behalf of vegetation, it's clear that, had he travelled to the west coast of North America, he would not have suffered a moment's boredom.

While rock prevails along most of the B.C. coastline "in the wildest of forms," it does so against a background of fern, salal, arbutus, hemlock, sitka spruce, pine and Douglas fir. Since I had been on the water during the majority of my trip along the Inside Passage, often far enough from shore to give vegetation something of the sameness of rock, I had to count on marine life, human encounters, and the gathering of stories for distraction. I was neither botanist nor biologist, but I did fancy myself a connoisseur of seaweed, particularly the kind that clings to exposed rock or grows up around beaches and shallows. One of these, bladderwrack, was very much in evidence in Rivers Inlet and Darby Channel, especially at low tide when it formed a rusty border between the water and the perpetual grey of the shoreline.

Bladderwrack is a short branching seaweed that attaches itself to rock, but manages to grow above the low tideline even though it is exposed to heat and light. The bladders found at the tips of dichotomous branches contain gas, a gluey substance, and sea water; more important, they pop when squeezed. If you apply pressure evenly across the surface, between thumb and two forefingers, you can make an impressive noise, not quite as good as a firecracker but respectable enough to amuse a child, and you can squirt an impertinent friend. At the beach, when we weren't skipping stones or popping bladderwrack, my daughters and I would use the bulbous tips of the bull kelp as microphones and conduct make-believe interviews and concerts. This wondrous seaweed, which grows on tapered rope-like stems fifty to a hundred feet long, is known as the boater's friend, because its presence alerts mariners to the presence of reefs and otherwise shallow water. If you pay attention to the action of its leaf-like fronds, undulating like Ophelia's hair in the water, you can also gauge the speed and direction of the current. The stems of bull kelp attach themselves so firmly to the bottom that you can tie up alongside in calm seas; they're also an ideal spot for dropping a line, as the forest of stems serves as a protective and nourishing habitat for fish. The First Nations people found them equally interesting, using the bulbs to store oolichan oil and as voice-tubes for ceremonial dances.

My daughters and I preferred to transform them into kelp ladies, a role for which these fair damsels of the deep were perfectly suited. They had tresses long enough to make Barbie and Rapunzel weep, the price was right, and they were completely recyclable. All you had to do was scratch small indentations in the bulb, much as you might do to make a face in a miniature pumpkin or snowman, and insert tiny stones from the beach to serve as eyes, nose, and mouth. Then, let the play begin. Sometimes these kelp ladies acted more like sirens or waterfront floozies, as if their naked, serpentine bodies and their watery origins had freed them of all constraints and inhibitions. Between the rhythmic assaults of the waves, I would hear snippets of conversation as my daughters and their friends worked out some of their domestic quandaries with the aid of these aquatic handmaidens. A sort of kelp-help group.

"I'm the one who's married. You're the child."

"That's not fair, you got to be married last time. It's my turn."

"I know, but if you're the child, you get to watch television and eat candy and go to school. Okay?"

"Real candy?"

"Of course not. Pretend. Here are two pieces. You can have one now, one later, if you're good."

"Yuck."

"You're not supposed to put it in your mouth. It's only make-believe. Don't you know anything?"

While imbibing courage for the journey north from a beer bottle and a few phone calls to the family, I discovered that my new VHF had crapped out. No wonder I had not been able to contact Howard Jones at Owikeno. I might as well have been talking to the water. Tycho Horning, who was fishing nearby off the stern of the *Penguin*, had mentioned he was an electrical engineer. He had made a name for himself working in computer software before dropping out. He and his wife Kathy lived aboard an American fibreglass imitation of the Bristol Channel cutter, a distinctive design he was surprised I recognized. I'd seen several of them during my trip to Plymouth the previous year. They'd lived on the *Penguin* for two years, exploring the coast since early April, from Redwood, California, to Klemtu, a hundred miles farther north, and were leisurely making their way back down. I didn't envy them the spring storms they'd encountered en route.

"Radio problems? That sounds more challenging than a hypothetical halibut."

Tycho disappeared below deck and re-emerged with tools and a drawstring cloth bag full of connectors and spare parts. He was not just an electrical engineer, but also a savvy sailor who had carefully assessed everything that could possibly go wrong on his boat and had come prepared. Within minutes, he had replaced the aerial connector attached to my radio, using a butane soldering iron that worked on the same principle as a cigarette lighter. We'd done this without first checking that there was enough slack in the coaxial cable to make up the lost inches, but luck was with us, briefly. The radio still didn't work. Whether as a result of yarding the cable too vigorously through a tight hole in the bulkhead or years of deterioration, Tycho's tests indicated that some sort of rupture in the line was permitting contact between wires in the inner and outer layers of the cable. This was bad news, since it would involve ordering expensive new cable from Port Hardy, then trying to hook it up myself without the proper knowledge or tools, climbing the mast to thread down the new cable or lowering the mast to dockside. Since it was Friday and there were no deliveries on weekends, these technical problems would also oblige me to stay another three or four nights at Dawson's Landing.

As I weighed the relative merits of desertion and self-immolation, Tycho and Kathy sailed off with apologies. *Groais* looked as if a bomb had gone off inside. When I finished putting the tools and boards and cushions back in place, I noticed I was not the only one at Dawson's Landing in a foul mood. Several disgruntled guests were grumbling because fog had delayed the Pacific Coastal Airlines flight that brings in mail and freight and takes out passengers. It was two hours late and not expected to leave Port Hardy until 1600. I made a quick decision and ordered a hand-held VHF radio by phone, the kind Geri had recommended in the first place, from Striker's Electric in Hardy, which they promised to deliver to the dock in time for the delayed flight to Dawson's. In a perverse gesture of gratitude for my neighbours' misfortune, I offered up an uncharacteristic prayer to the God of Fog. Within two hours the plane arrived with my second new VHF in a week. This required a prayer of thanks to the Deity of Plastic Credit. I might be broke and unbelieving, but I was mobile.

Darby Channel, the waterway that stretches from Dawson's Landing to Finn Bay, was named after the medical missionary Dr. George Darby, who was much respected up and down the Inside Passage. This protected stretch of water was, like the Good Life itself, narrow, if not straight, and fraught with several navigational hazards. I took the middle road, straddling an invisible white line and steering deliberately close to a seal in mid-channel, which turned out to be a deadhead, known locally as a sinker. It was either a hemlock dropped during heli-logging which had refused to surface, or some other species that had simply become waterlogged at one end. Most deadheads ride just low enough in the water that they can't be seen if there's any sort of chop. Others you don't know exist until they say hello and introduce themselves through the bottom of your boat.

What went on in the good doctor's mind as he conducted his business on the north coast? After growing up in Ontario and studying at the University of Toronto, did he feel the remoteness of these bays and inlets? According to Hugh McKervill's biography, *Darby of Bella Bella*, the doctor came out as a summer replacement and was asked to stay on. He went back east to finish his medical studies and, perhaps, to strengthen his romantic ties with his future wife Edna Mathews. Then he spent the rest of his life beetling in and out of these channels and estuaries in every kind of weather imaginable, administering to the flock. In those days, every service on the coast was provided by boat, a vast flotilla of dentists, tailors, electricians, salesmen and priests, who would visit the villages, float camps and canneries once, possibly twice, a year. My childhood friend Garry Wickett, whose memories were the source of much of McKervill's material, worked for Darby and, to my great envy, skippered the mission boat, *William H. Pierce*, in the summer. Before I started my journey, Garry had invited me over to dinner in Victoria. According to him, Darby travelled without charts and claimed to know every rock on the coast because, as the doctor insisted, he'd run the *Pierce* aground on all of them. There's no indication that he ever felt lonely or chafed at the remoteness of the north coast. Carlos Fuentes once joked that Mexico was to be pitied for being so far from God and so close to the United States. A Christian or urban pantheist might be excused for thinking that the north coast, while close to God, was a bit too far from Vancouver; but Darby appears not to have unduly regretted the city or separation from his wife and his children during the winter months. He was too busy administering a hospital, making sick calls, being a wharfinger, father confessor, postal clerk and general factotum for Bella Bella and the surrounding communities.

There had been no shortage of excitement or strange characters to make his job interesting. During Garry's third summer on the *William H. Pierce*, they were called to visit a woman at Owikeno village who had gone into labour. The *Pierce* tied up at the mouth of the Wannock River and Garry and the doctor were taken by dugout to the house upriver. All the adults, including the mother, were sleeping off their celebration of the child's birth. Several small children were gathered around the new baby, which had been placed on a pillow in a piece of gillnet hanging by a nail from the ceiling of the cabin, where it was safe from rodents. Darby checked out the newborn, told the kids they were doing a good job, and explained what to watch for in the care of the baby. Before leaving, he told them a Bible story. On the trip back to Bella Bella, they visited an old man who'd been having trouble with arthritis. After checking him over, Darby mentioned his surprise at the improvement. Garry recalled seeing the old man standing on the dock, shouting, with his arms above his head: "Skookum Postum! Skookum Postum!"

"What was that all about?" he asked as Darby stepped on board the *Pierce*, his face contorted with laughter.

"The Seventh Day Adventists in the area told him to give up tea and coffee and to drink only Postum. He was waving his arms to show how much better he feels."

Lucky Bachen, Rob's father and the previous owner of Dawson's Landing, was mangled badly in some cannery conveyor equipment and rushed to the hospital in Bella Bella, where Darby stitched him up and wrapped the foot in plaster. The toes needed to be kept in traction, so Garry and the engineer designed a metal harp that was attached to the cast and to which the toes were connected by rubber bands. Lucky, who was not one to moan or complain, would offer to play them a tune on his toe-harp whenever Garry or the doctor visited.

Darby often visited a recluse who'd once been a trapeze artist in the Barnum and Bailey Circus. Billy had been injured in a fall. He lived with his English wife on a sloping float house anchored in a small cove in Gunboat Passage near Bella Bella. While Billy dreamed of split-second timing, hushed audiences, powdered handgrips, and glorious flight, his wife dreamed of opening a tea shoppe in Victoria and kept several barrels packed with fine English china in the corners of the float house, each covered with a crocheted doily and photographs. Billy eventually became very frail and had to be removed to Bella Bella, where he died shortly after. He was rowed out to the *Pierce*, a heavy blanket over his shoulders in midsummer. As Garry leaned over the rail to help the old man on board, Billy squinted up at him through blue eyes glazed with cataracts.

"And Mr. Barnum was like a father to me."

I woke the next morning, filled my freshwater tank, did a load of laundry, said goodbye to Rob, Nola and Willy, and was about to set off down Darby Channel when I heard a squeaky voice calling my name. It was Chelsea, over for the day from Wadhams Outpost. She was holding the hand of Rob's daughter as they climbed into the new plastic paddleboat Rob had purchased to keep the kids amused and physically active, not the easiest task on a float camp, unless you're the resident carpenter. She and her friend paddled furiously around the far end of the first float. I soon had in my hands a still-warm cherry pie baked by Nola's mother, the kind I'd been ogling for days, a treat to myself for getting this far and solving the VHF problem. *Groais* was a disgrace, a floating laundry barge, with T-shirts, socks, pants and underwear pegged to the lifelines. I smiled, recalling Steve Martin's disapproval of such nautical bad taste.

I checked the weather station on my new radio, untied the bow- and sternlines and put *Groais* in gear. Before I'd gone a hundred yards, Willy roared alongside in Rob's overpowered boat and offered to race me. I was touched by his gesture and renewed the invitation to visit me at French Beach.

As Darby Channel narrowed, I waved to the occupants of several expensive powerboats, but they chose not to notice me and my floating laundry. Then a group of Native kids I'd met the previous day in Nola's store zoomed past in their aluminum skiff, heading back to Dawson's for more supplies. Each of the kids waved to me separately, so my arm was kept working like a metronome. They had pulled into the dock in the late afternoon, drenched from the trip down Rivers Inlet from Owikeno reserve on the Wannock River. It seems unlikely they hadn't anticipated the afternoon westerlies, which I was learning to respect, but, like most teenagers, they had simply refused to dress properly or stay together under the large tarpaulin. The flat-bottomed skiff, dry enough in calm weather, would have been sluggish and wet at slow speeds. They were going camping at Clam Bay at the mouth of Rivers Inlet, where the Owikeno people maintained a small cabin. I must confess that the notion of Native kids on a camping trip struck me as peculiar, especially as their permanent living conditions on the north coast seemed impossible to distinguish from that species of outdoor privation that goes by the name of camping. As they squished through the store, completely soaked, they left little lakes and rivers wherever they passed up and down the aisles, gathering all the adolescent essentials: chips, pop, chocolate bars, wieners and buns. The one adult accompanying them, a woman in her late thirties, joked with Nola, who'd just spent the previous hour sweeping and cleaning the floors. Nola was not thrilled, but she was used to kids and bad weather, a formidable combination. At least there was no mud, one small consolation of living on a float camp. A couple of fishermen, swarming the phone and fresh pies, felt obliged to give the kids disapproving looks and exchange meaningful nudges.

Here was an opportunity to try my new VHF.

"Owikeno, this is *Groais* on your starboard side. Request permission to talk on Channel 73."

No response. I raised the hand-held VHF over my head for them to see, then repeated the message.

"Gross? Ya, man, go ahead."

"How's the weather outside?"

"Peaches and cream."

"Do you know Howard Jones?"

"Of course."

"I met his granddaughter, Eileen. She works on the whale research boat, *Seebreeze III*. She said to send him greetings. Will you do that?"

"Sure, Gross. We'll say hello for Eileen." By now they'd left me in their wake, but the radio transmission was loud and clear. "By the way, nice underwear you got."

My destination was Finn Bay, at the mouth of Darby Channel. Not very ambitious, but a good jumping-off point for the trip north to Namu the following morning. The only place to tie up in Finn Bay was a new float about seventy-five feet long, which I discovered was the property of Pete and Rene. They owned a piece of waterfront near the mouth of the bay. Although it was on a small island, with a place sufficiently cleared to build on, they preferred, like so many maritime gypsies, to keep their options open by living in a float house, one that could be towed to another location if the need arose. The splendid new dock awaiting me had been finished only a week earlier, with freshly hewn cedar boards and extra-strong rails for tying up. The floating complex consisted of a small house surrounded by potted plants, including a riot of sweet peas and an almond tree which Pete was watering when I arrived. There was also a gazebo on a separate float, built with lumber he had milled from old float-logs, the wormholes made by teredos a prominent feature of the design. The gazebo was equipped with a sink, running water, several tables, a supply of chopped wood and an old boiler that served as a barbecue.

"It's actually an ocean buoy," Pete explained. He'd cut it in half with an acetylene torch and suspended the upper portion on chains to serve as a smoke collector and chimney. The setting, in a completely sheltered cove, was idyllic, except for the patch above the house, stripped bare of trees, a blighted no man's land of stumps and old machinery whose eventual transformation into a Shangri-La of gardens and fountains was difficult to envisage. Kew Gardens North. Pete and Rene had both been raised on Lasqueti Island. He had lived in Lama Passage, in Goose Bay near Duncanby Landing, and at various other spots on the coast, logging and beachcombing, as well as hauling freight and barges by tugboat. Now, he said, they were doing very little, which was why he'd decided to make his private dock available for a small fee to boaters.

Rene worked during the summer at Buck's Trophy Lodge, a float camp at the head of Finn Bay with accommodation and boats for twenty guests per week. She had the afternoon off, so they invited me in for a glass of wine. My house gift was the remaining half of the cherry pie. Rene had left home quite young and spent several years on the road across Canada as a helper-trainer in harness racing. It's hard to imagine someone from remote little Lasqueti Island working with trotters. To lure her home, the family regularly sent packages containing shells, a jar of sea water, dried kelp, small fir or hemlock seedlings wrapped in plastic and, eventually, a one-way plane ticket. It worked. She loved her animals, including an orange cat named Fur Ball, which she described as three bricks short of a load.

I'd noticed Rene earlier, when she arrived home from work by boat, playing with her German shepherd on the float, leaping out from behind a potted tree to spook the dog, who would go along with the game, turning tail and running to hide behind the house. She told me her grandmother had sailed from England in 1908, the same year my own grandmother had sailed from Scotland, and had been dropped off at a small agricultural settlement at Cape Scott, the northern-most tip of Vancouver Island. Her grandmother eventually married a German-Canadian fisherman, whose name was anglicized during the First World War, and they migrated steadily south towards his childhood home in White Rock.

While *Beagle* and *Discovery* had been bursting at the seams with botanical specimens, *Groais* was overrun with sticky notes, scraps of paper covered with jottings about this or that individual, stories, anecdotes, taped to bulkheads, tossed in corners, used as bookmarks, or crammed in the kind of airtight zip-lock bags whose blue-and-yellow plastic zippers turn vomit green when properly sealed. I hoped these notes might help to explain what kind of creature can adapt to the severe climate, unaccommodating geography and solitary life of the Inside Passage. Rene had her own inquiries to make.

"How come you're sailing alone like this?"

Rene poured tea, which I drank between sips of wine. Her name and nickname were the same as my dead mother's. She even bore a faint resemblance to the face in the photographs of my mother as a young girl that Bill Turner had given me in Pender Harbour. I liked the easy, comfort-able fluidity of her movements and her interaction with Pete on their post-lapsarian float haven. It was enough to make me ache, aware of something irretrievably lost. What was it I wanted—a mother? Thinking of myself as motherless and adrift, especially at my age, was a bit melodramatic, if not ridiculous. Besides, I had two mothers—one dead, one alive—and both very much on my mind. A companion? After twenty-five years of marriage, I was certainly missing the comradeship and the reservoir of shared experience that allows you to predict and enjoy a partner's reactions to phenomena—a word, a song, another seaside attraction. All this speculation, too, about Darby and his work had reminded me of the confidence and sense of community I once found in a shared system of belief, the loss of which had left me floundering, unfocused, and aggressively acquiring a new discipline, a new vocabulary.

"It's not as though the boat is too small." Rene was nothing if not persistent. All that training of horses. I was feeling mellow, but in no mood to be harnessed.

"I guess I'm a bit of a hermit."

"Right, the gabby, social kind." She poured more tea and glanced through the brochure I'd given her. "A hermit who advertises his services? You sound more like a professional oracle."

"I had company earlier, for a few days. I've got a book to write. I don't need distractions or the cocoon effect of travelling with someone else."

I was talking rubbish and Rene knew it.

The return to Rivers Inlet had not been easy. If the physical effort and dangers of the journey hadn't finished me off, the emotional diving and psychic spelunking just might. The dreams were driving me crazy, which ought not to have been a surprise, given the fear, the constant movement and Joan Skogan's warning in her novel *Moving Water*: you dream more at sea. This certainly seemed to be happening to me, especially after all the increased traffic of ghosts and old memories.

I'd awakened at 0300 at the dock in Dawson's Landing with a full bladder and a pounding headache. I could hear the fenders rubbing against the float as *Groais* fidgeted at her moorings. No one was about, but there was a light on in the tugboat at the far end of the dock. Perhaps Willy had fallen asleep with the light on. I'd been struggling in my sleep, for hours it seemed, to dispense with two bodies caught in my gillnet. I could neither extricate them from the net nor bear the idea of bringing them on board. They were too heavy to haul over the stern-rollers without breaking limbs or damaging the net, so I had to bring them alongside with the aid of a boathook and try to unravel hair and limbs tangled in the square mesh. They were both women, completely naked. I was horrified. I tried to push them away from the boat with an oar—I couldn't bear to touch them with my hands—but they kept drifting back. Rays from the stern lantern, mounted above the drum, highlighted the contours of each bluish white shape as it turned slowly in the current. Frantic, I disconnected the net from the boat and raced over to pick it up from the other end, hoping to reduce the amount of net in the water and, thus, the area of vulnerability. Perhaps I could tow the net until they slipped free. No such luck. The ghostly shapes appeared again as if drawn to me, or to the boat, magnetically. I cut the net adrift and gunned the boat towards a distant anchorage. But it was no use, I could hear them nudging the hull all night.

"A different book," Rene was saying, "that's all."

She took a piece of cherry pie and sat by the window facing the boats that were still visible in the gathering dusk. Her hair was greying and her body had begun to thicken, but she seemed ageless, beautiful. She addressed my reflection in the window.

"A more intimate book. Domestic, not the least bit heroic. People could relate to that. *I* could relate to that."

At the door, Pete placed in my hands a generous bundle of smoked salmon from the deep-freeze and advised me to give the rocks south of Addenbroke Island Light a wide berth. I thanked him and let myself out the screen door, but not before Fur Ball had dashed in.

"You didn't tell me your last name," I said through the steel mesh of the screen, which gave Pete the appearance of a photographic reproduction. With low resolution.

"Darwin," he replied.

Sixteen

As I left Finn Bay and Rivers Inlet astern, I felt some sort of sea change at work in me. I couldn't quite fathom what it was, but I knew something had shifted, a plate perhaps, pushing itself upwards, causing one or two things that had troubled and impeded me to move aside. Not high drama; an adjustment, the geologists call it. To begin with, the voyage itself had assumed a different aspect; I was less fearful of what seas and weather lay ahead and of the personal salvage work that remained. At first, I thought I could pull off this writing trip by resorting to humour, constructing a narrative full of unusual characters and quixotic encounters. But there was always a downrigger, a pink lady, pulling me deeper and deeper into underwater troughs and canyons where God knows what might be lurking.

When I arrived in Namu around noon, after a foggy passage up Fitz Hugh Sound, I decided to spend a few hours exploring the site of the abandoned cannery, which had been one of the largest of its kind on the coast. It began in the late nineteenth century, through the efforts of Robert Draney, as a small operation for canning salmon and clams, a sawmill being added in 1909. By 1911, Draney Fisheries had become a significant player, with a fleet of small skiffs with their oil-burning Primus stoves and little canvas tents called "doghouses," driven only by wind or oars, which the men called "misery sticks." These hardy fishermen were at the mercy of the elements, which could be quite fierce around Namu, whose name translates, roughly, as place of high winds; their only means of warning vessels that might be bearing down on them in thick fog was to beat on a pot or frying pan with a wooden spoon. Although it passed through several hands, the cannery did not experience major growth until it was purchased by B.C. Packers. The company added power, reduction and cold storage plants, so every part of the salmon could be utilized, including head, tail and guts, the foul-smelling offal that had previously been transported by barge and dumped in deep water. By mid-century, Namu had thirty to forty permanent families in residence and employed as many as a thousand people during the peak summer season, producing not only more than a hundred thousand cases of canned salmon, but also large quantities of fertilizer, cattle food, and fish oils that were used for medicinal purposes. I remember my father mentioning it often with a hint of excitement in his voice, as if, compared to its sister cannery at Wadhams, Namu were a city of wonders where anything might be expected to happen.

And, of course, it did happen, dances fired by fiddle music, sports competitions in the gymnasium, small clashes between the various groups of Caucasian, Chinese, Japanese and Native workers, all of them housed in separate ethnic dormitories. With the arrival of a Union Steamships vessel every few days, bringing supplies, mail, salesmen, gamblers and itinerant entertainers, the docks were alive with activity, a Babel of strange voices and accents rising and falling in that rhythm of excitement, denial and understatement that characterizes fishermen—lonely but protective of their privacy, especially their secret times, sets and spots for fishing. A major event in the history of Namu was the fire on January 11, 1962, which was started on the second floor of the cannery, perhaps by a welder's torch, and consumed several other buildings, including the cold storage and power plant.

With the company's radio telephones destroyed, news of the fire had to be relayed to the outside world by fishermen from their boats. Auxiliary power was brought in, the cannery quickly rebuilt.

The bustling port of Namu has other, more ancient, claims to fame, including five thousand years as an important Heiltsuk settlement. In August, 1969, a group of students from the University of Colorado, in collaboration with Simon Fraser University and with the permission of the cannery management and the Bella Bella people, discovered three levels of ancient culture in the extensive middens. The oldest finds included obsidian microblades, inch-long cutting edges probably mounted in wood and used to make tools and utensils; also found were more recent chipped and barbed stone spear points and fully articulated human skeletons. James J. Hester, leader of the expedition, had promised to work closely with Canadian authorities and to keep important artifacts in Canada. There is a photograph in the Provincial Archives in Victoria of Native fishers seining sockeye off the rocks at Namu Creek; only the European clothes and modern nets distinguish them from their ancestors of past millennia.

The trip from Addenbroke Island Light to Namu had taken five hours because of fog and low visibility. I stuck close to shore as I crept past Kwakume Inlet, Koeye River and Warrior Cove, picking out any headland visible through the mist and trying to identify it on the chart. Not only were there no boats fishing, there was not a single boat in sight going in either direction. The chart showed no major hazards to avoid except in the entrance and harbour of Namu itself, including the infamous non-drying Loo Rock and various shoaling grounds around the small adjacent islet. I could see in the distance a large tree adrift in the bay, branches extending several feet out of the water. One of the cruising guides announced itself "happy to report that Namu is coming back to life. To keep the B.C. ferry, Namu's owners are reopening the café, probably with a wine and beer licence. The grocery soon will carry souvenirs and basic foods, new floats will be built, and dangerous buildings removed." They were even promising a B & B and interpretation centre, run in conjunction with the local Heiltsuk band. By the time I arrived, I was salivating and imagining myself luxuriating in a hot shower.

I chose the one float that was not half submerged. Several fishboats were tied up farther along, as well as two sailboats, a ketch preparing to depart and a fancy fibreglass sloop that showed no signs of life. Two kids who belonged to the ketch were having a final romp pell-mell up the ramp and along the pier before surrendering to another day of confinement on board. Every available space on the ketch was covered with debris, bicycles lashed to the lifelines, crab traps, three five-gallon plastic gas cans, a small wooden structure that resembled a doghouse, two inner tubes, oars bungied to the stays and an upturned inflatable dinghy that covered the forward hatch. If they'd been able to stow a rusting car-body on board, it would not have looked out of place. *Groais* was looking a bit shabby, its paint and bright work showing signs of wear, but the cluttered, greasy condition of the ketch made me feel like someone with a severe cleanliness fetish.

I climbed the ramp and explored a maze of paved passageways between the buildings on the pier and a rocky outcrop, looking for a caretaker to inquire about moorage fees. Grass and weeds were pushing up around the base of the locked buildings. As I stopped to examine an antique fire truck with a single wheel at the front and wheelbarrow handles for propulsion, the two kids from the ketch belted past me screaming. A small peppermint mongrel was chasing after them, barking excitedly and trying to nip their pant-cuffs. The cannery and net lofts constructed on the outcrop of rock looked solid enough, but a shed around the corner, supported by pilings, had collapsed and its huge boiler hung precariously over the water. Alongside was a steel-hulled vessel that served as tanker and fuel dock. A woman in overalls was paying out black hose to refuel a gillnetter. The fisherman had an unlit cigarette dangling from his mouth.

"Anywhere you can find a place," she shouted up to me, brushing the hair from her face. "It's fifty cents a foot, seventy-five if you need power."

I started to retrace my path, but took a detour past the old company store. It was dark inside but, to my surprise, open. A young boy about twelve years old leaned on a counter near the cash register, tapping a tune only he knew on the empty glass display case, idly watching a man and woman move up and down the aisles in the gloom. None of the basic foods predicted in the guide had materialized. What had once been a major shopping centre for the coast was now a dusty storeroom with a bizarre assortment of hardware items for sale at reduced prices. The only food consisted of a box of Hershey bars that were five years old—the boy insisted they were still edible—and a plethora of dried soups in aluminum foil packages. When I passed by, the man and his wife were going through drawers of nuts and bolts, whispering about bargain prices and arguing about sizes they might need. At the back of the store, looking like a black-and-white mural depicting ringworm, or some rare chromosomal disorder, was an entire wall of belts for water pumps and generators, thick heavy-duty reinforced rubber and fibre belts for large diesel engines, and lighter belts of the sort I'd purchased as a spare in Port Hardy. You'd have to know exactly what you wanted, or have the original with you, because most had lost their labels. His mother and father, the boy told me without much enthusiasm, had been given permission to sell off the remaining merchandise for whatever they could get for it as part of their benefits as caretakers. He did not look as if he thought his three customers were likely to prove big-time spenders.

The kids and dog and their bedraggled ark had disappeared, but the fibreglass sloop from Vancouver had disgorged a young couple who were hastily washing down with hose and brush their already immaculate white hull, in case it had been exposed to some rare disease from its erstwhile neighbour. They were clad in T-shirts, white shorts and designer running shoes. After a futile attempt to engage them in conversation, I decided on a systematic exploration of the cannery site and made my way back up the ramp. The two women in kayaks I'd mistaken earlier for a tree adrift in the bay were just arriving at the dock, taking advantage of the derelict float by paddling right up over its submerged surface, where they began immediately to unload both craft. I was awed by the amount of gear they were yarding out onto the dry end of the float. I heard them ask the woman in overalls if they could pitch a tent on the only patch of lawn.

Since neither Wadhams Cannery nor Darby's mission hospital and residence in Rivers Inlet had waited for me before packing it in, I was doubly grateful to find Namu more or less intact, despite the unfulfilled prophecies of food. On a separate pier, connected by a boardwalk, were two well-maintained buildings, one containing the Namu Café with its door open and looking as if the last customer had just stepped out. There were six chrome stools, five with green plastic covers and one with brown. On the counter, the edge of which was missing a sixteen-inch strip of arborite, languished a crumpled Coke can, a container of Carnation powdered milk, a half-finished bottle of apple juice fermenting with an island of green mould in the middle, an empty box of lemon tea bags and a rusting but unopened can of pumpkin purée. Through the fishnet decor suspended over the doorway, I could still make out the hand-written breakfast menu on the wall above the serving window that connected the café to the kitchen. The picture was completed by a square green fan, a jar of jam, a metal salad bowl and a cash register, just visible behind the empty cooler. It had the air of a movie set whose actors had slipped away for lunch or been abducted by Martians. I could imagine my father here and the place bustling with activity, heated conversations, jokes, ribaldry, and vigorous repartee between the customers and staff.

"What'll it be, O'Reilly?"

"The usual."

"Bacon and eggs, easy-over?"

"No."

"What, then?"

"Insults, Gladys, hard-boiled. A side order of sarcasm. And a cup of bile. A man cannot live by bread alone, even toasted."

"You sure you can afford it?"

"Anything wrong with my credit?"

"I wouldn't give you credit for breathing, never mind paying your bills."

"Stop flirting married men, Gladys. Bring coffee."

"Give me a break, Bronsky. All I got to choose from here are the married and the dead."

"What about me?"

"You're a sweetheart, but you'd need more than coffee to get that old blood moving."

"Is diagnosis or offer?"

"Leave her alone, Bronsky, you old letch! She's got better things to do, like serving me."

"You tell him, Laurie. At least you shaved this week, not like the rest of these bums."

In addition to the manager's house, which the caretaker's family inhabited, there were more than a dozen clapboard cottages on a grassy rise above the wharves. They were flimsily built, in need of repair and rapidly receding into the riotous undergrowth, but all had a glorious view of the harbour and would be ideal for summer residences. I examined various relics left behind, including a beach ball, a plastic rattle, a baby stroller in one of the back bedrooms, several 1974 issues of *Good Housekeeping*, old prints and floral paper curling from the walls, and a kitchen chair quietly decomposing in the long grass between two houses. The young couple, having washed their immaculate boat, was making the same rounds in the opposite direction in white track suits with a matching poodle on a leash, speculating aloud on the cost of buying and refurbishing one of the dwellings. I didn't think I'd enjoy them as neighbours, so I skipped the last six houses and made my way along the rickety boardwalk.

Three hundred yards of boardwalk followed the shoreline, connecting the docks, stores and houses with a full-sized gymnasium. A red nylon jacket, which looked like a wayward blob of paint, an alien intrusion of colour in this weathered setting, was draped over the rail outside. Although the building was condemned and had warning signs posted at both ends, I slipped inside where light from high windows slanted down onto the hardwood floor and stage. Downstage a large, jagged hole had been smashed through the plywood backdrop, revealing in the shadows a starkly beautiful thunderbird painted in red, green and black. The haughty bird, its pristine shape a reminder of better times when culture as well as fitness prevailed in this out-of-the-way place, cast a look of scorn on the current state of affairs in Namu with its fiercely stylized rectangular eye. I could have sworn I'd heard voices and a burst of laughter.

Farther along, the boardwalk diverged, the path to the left leading overland to Namu Lake, the one to the right following the shoreline to two large dormitories, which had been white-washed and looked quite solid where they extended out over the water on pilings. The green railings were covered with a patina of moss and bird shit. Above the boarded windows of the nearest building, I could still decipher in red lettering the calligraphy of some long-departed wit: NAMU HILTON, Hotel and Conference Centre.

I would have to check out the Hilton's cuisine and service on some future occasion because that portion of the board-walk was leaning precariously. Most of the planks had been stripped off and a barrier erected to discourage access, which meant that the residences for Asian and First Nations work-ers, across a narrow channel of water beyond the hotel, were also out of bounds, except by boat. While I lay on my stomach on the boardwalk, trying to take a worm's-eye photograph of the Namu Hilton, the two kayakers emerged from the gymnasium and picked up the red jacket. They nodded to me and turned back towards the dock.

I ventured out along the boardwalk towards Namu Lake, taking note of the fresh bear scat and tracing the wooden water pipes held together with wire as they appeared and disappeared amongst the ferns, salmonberry and salal. Here and there a solitary foxglove hung over the coiled pipe like an elegant sentinel, its mauve-coloured bells a source of digi-talis—a stimulant for the heart. This was not something I needed. My heart was already racing from the exercise, as well as from the noises I could hear, and vibrations underfoot. There was nothing to grab to make myself look large and menacing, so I began to clap my hands and whistle loudly. A good tactic, perhaps, for a black bear with cubs, but not much use against a grizzly barrelling towards you at the speed of a horse at full gallop. The vibrations on the boardwalk increased. As I considered letting out a piercing scream or diving into the underbrush, hoping the bear was suffering from congested nasal passages, the young couple and their designer poodle passed me at a trot, returning from a jog to the lake. The woman rattled a small bell gaily at irregular intervals. They must have thought I was either daft—clapping and whistling in the forest—or just applauding their fitness, but they all smiled, even the dog.

Back at the dock, a party of three more kayakers had arrived and was already setting up tents on the ragged patch of lawn, in preparation for being picked up the next day by the new coastal ferry service from Port Hardy. They were talking excitedly about a wolf that had chased them from their first campsite. The two I'd seen earlier—twins or sisters in their mid-sixties—told me they'd kayaked around the Goose Islands, which are exposed to the Pacific. They'd had one tight spot with fog, another with high winds, and that very morning had seen a humpback whale breach fifty feet offshore. As it turned out, they were from Sooke, only twelve miles from my home at French Beach.

Two gillnetters were now tied up across the float from *Groais*, one rafting alongside the other. I introduced myself. Gordie and Marie Widston on board the *Tiara II* came from Prince Rupert. Gordie, my age, had spent his childhood in Ocean Falls and remembered my late father-in-law, Bill Macht, who, as a young man, had worked as an electrician at the pulp mill and been the town's projectionist. My second wife Jan's father loved movies and used to collect advertising posters. At the movies, she remembered how he would put his hat over her five-year-old face when he thought a scene was too scary or too explicit. I'd felt closer to Jan's father than to my own, so this brief encounter with someone who knew him many years ago seemed a stroke of luck.

Gordie and Marie were travelling in tandem with Marie's uncle or second cousin, Heber Clifton, who owned the *Cheryl-C*. Heber had grown up on the Tsimshian reserve at Hartley Bay, which was located on the Douglas Channel near Kitimat, but he lived in Rupert. While they prepared supper, Heber joined me on *Groais* for tea. He was immensely fit, drank green tea, swam fourteen laps daily in the pool at home, took long walks, and popped an aspirin a day to break up his cholesterol. He told me that the doctor had heard a bubbling sound in his neck and thought it might be a blockage, but it turned out to be a false alarm. Since one of his nephews had recently died of a heart attack at thirty-two, the whole family was being checked out. That's why his son was not with him on this trip; he was back home waiting for results. His wife, Heber confided, had Parkinson's, but it was under control thanks to some new drug that caused a terrible month of adjustment, including constant sweating and nausea.

"She told me to stay out of the room." Heber had been shocked. He stirred his tea, a man who had learned to school his movements and emotions.

We talked a lot about ruins, about the coast as a graveyard of ships, a vast stretch of abandoned villages, defunct industries. My trip was beginning to resemble a failed salvage operation: my uncle's boat rentals, Wadhams Cannery, the hospital and residence at Brunswick Bay, and now Namu. My family, too, was in ruins. Two months earlier, I'd spent a week wandering around Orkney, sticking my nose in Pictish burial mounds with graffiti left by marauding Vikings, a crumbling broch, the remains of an underground Neolithic village, a ring of ancient standing stones and a maritime museum full of artifacts from two world wars. I was beginning to feel like the English poet Oliver Goldsmith, ruminating over the slabs and markers of a deserted village, wondering about unfulfilled lives and unsung Miltons, or the American lawyer-poet Edgar Lee Masters, trying to reconstruct a community's complicated network of loves, hates and thwarted ambitions from tombstones in his *Spoon River Anthology*. Was I getting hooked on loss, on love amongst the ruins?

I had on board a copy of Louise Glück's book of essays, *Proofs and Theories*, in which she tries to voice the emotional or aesthetic attraction ruins had for Rilke and other poets: "What wholeness gives up is the dynamic: the mind need not rush in to fill a void. And Rilke loved his voids. In the broken thing, moreover, human agency is oddly implied; breakage, whatever its cause, is the dark complement to the art of making; the one implies the other." Ruins, in other words, are attractive not only because they flirt with danger and destruction, but also because they activate a simultaneous urge to contemplate the act of salvage, restoration. Sailing home was more complicated than I'd imagined. The home-place, it seems, is a state of mind, a series of routines, a reservoir of memories, rather than a unique location in space. Displaced persons all, we are reminded daily of our separation from the mother and from much that we love but cannot keep in our grasp. We cling to old photographs, to stories, to relics, not out of morbidity, but because, as John Berger suggests, "To whisper for that which has been lost. Not out of nostalgia, but because it is on the site of loss that hopes are born."

The fascination with ruins certainly goes hand in hand with a determination to delay the ruin of the body. As I sat talking with Heber in the growing dark, I realized I had forgotten to eat lunch; I was famished. The talk had shifted, appropriately, from hearts to engines, those faithful and intrepid marine equivalents. I did my best imitation of a one-cylinder Easthope engine starting up, a quite unsanitary process that involved a lot of unintentional spit flying around the cabin of the *Groais*. Heber laughed, nodded his approval, and described for me the first Pedder engine to be installed at Hartley Bay reserve in 1929. You had to use a blowtorch to heat it up, he said, before throwing the flywheel of the single-stroke engine. At night the light above the Pedder would blink three times, warning that there were only fifteen minutes left before shutdown.

The gods that watch over the Namu site are compassionate, obviously, as the call for dinner was extended to include me. We sat in the galley-cum-wheelhouse of the *Tiara II*, with Gordie perched on the captain's rotating chair, Heber and I on kitchen stools, and Marie installed on the stairs. A home-cooked meal with ham, rice, mashed yams, cooked carrots, baked potato and coffee—not everything was in ruins. Gordie gave me a quick tour of his high-tech navigational equipment, the whole coast of B.C. on floppy disks, showing every rock and wrinkle. He also had a depth sounder that located fish and enabled you to zoom in so close you could count the scales. It had not yet learned to identify species or predict dietary preferences. We'd come a long way from George Vancouver with his plumb lines and cartographic approximations.

"Nothing is risk-free," Heber warned, lest I abandon my plans to learn more about navigation or forget what little I knew about reading charts. "Sometimes the computer goes haywire and you have to depend on the old methods."

After dinner, the *Tiara II* and *Cheryl-C* left together to anchor in Rock Inlet, where they wouldn't have to pay moorage fees. I watched them hug the north side of the entrance, giving the Loo Rock a wide berth. Namu, digitalis, talk about Jan's dad and Heber's litany of medical concerns in Prince Rupert had stirred up memories of my own father, who had died in Rupert four years earlier and is buried there. He and Marge had left Cumberland to live in a basement suite my brother Lloyd had built for them in his new house in Port Edward. My father was failing, but he rallied for a short time. He managed a trip to the Prairies and one to visit me in Ontario before the end, but nothing pleased him quite so much as his daily drives from Port Ed to watch the ships come and go in Prince Rupert harbour. Occasionally, he and Marge would visit the Legion, but their principal stop was Tim Hortons for doughnut and coffee.

My father had been something of a medical miracle. He'd smoked for thirty years, was a lifelong heavy drinker, and had not exactly been diet conscious, having a typical Scottish aversion to most vegetables. In his sixties he'd had triple bypass surgery and bounced back, though his lungs were weak and he suffered increasingly from emphysema. Between his oxygen hits, puffers and nitro pills, he managed a surprising amount of activity, including several trips to Winnipeg and visits to his Hutterite friends in Alberta. Though he always complained about Quebecers, his favourite trip of all had been a visit to Quebec City. The only bad moment had been my running a yellow light in Montreal, where I just missed being side-swiped by a pickup truck; that little misadventure had necessitated three nitro pills and left him feeling even more vulnerable than usual.

When I arrived in Prince Rupert a few days before Christmas in 1995, my father was no longer in control of himself.

His battery-operated cart, a final offering from the Department of Veterans Affairs, stood unused below the back porch. A hospital bed had been supplied for his comfort, but also for Marge's sake, so she could more easily care for him, cranking him up to a half-sitting position and changing his soiled linen. He was no longer eating and could scarcely speak, but his hand would sometimes seek out the metal frame of the bed below the mattress and flutter there weakly until the dog, Toughie, would notice and lick it or stand close enough to feel the nudge of a finger. I took shifts to spell Marge off; I would sometimes hold his hand and sing to him, songs I knew he'd recognize like "Danny Boy" and "Loch Lomond." In those moments, there'd be a slight flicker of movement around the mouth and eyes as he tried to communicate his awareness of my presence.

I felt wretched for betraying him, advertising his failings in my poetry, which I could already see was a way of deflecting attention away from my own weaknesses. As one of my friends remarked, "You are your father's son." Although my father had never seen the poems in question, I told him I loved him and quietly asked his forgiveness. I left Prince Rupert on the afternoon of December 24, so I could spend Christmas Eve with my troubled family, but the news of his death reached Victoria before I did. I flew north again a few days later for the funeral. My cousin Ed Bates, whom I had not seen for twenty-five years, was on the same plane and had arranged to sit next to me. Ed was a twin—I knew him, as it were, in tandem—but he had fallen out with his brother, and womb-mate, Arthur. He was coming to Prince Rupert for Marge's sake, he said, wanting her to know that Uncle Laurie had been very good to him as a kid. He remembered happy times at the beach and rides to Stanley Park in a variety of trucks and cars. Ed's presence, as it turned out, proved a welcome buffer, allowing us the distraction of talking about other things.

I managed to offend the undertaker by refusing to view my father's body, his latest sepulchral masterpiece. I had no interest in examining the artifice, the cosmetics, eyelids sewn shut, sunken cheeks puffed up with fluid. I preferred to remember the terrible but compelling beauty of my father at the threshold of death, his dehydrated body like an autumn leaf parched and poised on the branch, its brittle stem a grim parody of the original umbilicus we all must shed. I'd been denied access to my mother's funeral five decades earlier, because relatives felt it would be too upsetting for a young boy. Some of that delayed and unresolved grief was with me that afternoon in Prince Rupert as we followed the hearse uphill to the cemetery in the pouring rain.

The archaeology of desire. You try to live in the present with its distractions, its substitutes for a lost unity, but there will always be a word, a face, a snatch of music to break open your heart and let the past flood in. Prince Rupert will always make me think of rain, the kind that fell on Marge, my tender and long-suffering stepmother, where she stood off to one side struggling with an internal deluge of remembered joys, humiliations, grief; rain that pelted down on the ruins of my father lodged in that most intimate of spaces, on my injured brother Lloyd, on my doubly displaced cousin Ed, even on the disgruntled undertaker who fancied himself Van Gogh. And rain—cleansing rain, perhaps even healing rain—that soaked me as I staggered under the knowledge of my altered place in line and under the surprising weight of my father in his box, my feet settling into the boggy soil of the north coast, soil left behind fourteen thousand years earlier by a departing glacier.

Seventeen

"I've reached the turning point"—I was simultaneously shouting into the mouthpiece and using a finger to plug my exposed ear—"so there's a pretty good chance of making it back."

This remark, followed by an brief, if exaggerated, list of my near disasters at sea, was not exactly what I'd intended to say to my soon-to-be-ex-wife, Jan. I'd decided to ask her to fly out to join me for a trip to Ocean Falls via Gunboat Passage. There was a lot of noise and interference around the only pay phone in the Heiltsuk co-op in New Bella Bella, cash registers pinging, the machine-gun rattle of antiquated debit-card printouts, the cacophony of colliding shopping carts, greetings shouted, engines revving outside the door, a ghetto blaster belting out a staticky version of "American Woman," and a child screaming to get out of the large cardboard box her older sister had placed her in.

Sailing to Ocean Falls with Jan was an idea that had taken shape over the previous week or two, doubtless connected with my accumulated feelings of solitude and loss, as I tallied up my dead relatives and witnessed the disappearance of so many familiar landmarks. It was a crazy conciliatory gesture, a last-ditch reaching out for family, for home. I'd made a side trip to Ocean Falls years earlier, during a coastal reading tour, to see where she had spent several formative years. As I barrelled down the runway at Bella Coola in the co-pilot's seat of a Piper

Cub, the pilot was busy rummaging in his briefcase for the list
of flying instructions he attached to the steering apparatus
with a clothespin just as the plane parted company with the
ground. Aloft, en route to Bella Bella, I asked him if we passed
anywhere near Ocean Falls. In response, he banked the plane
abruptly and plummeted a thousand feet, sweeping down over
the lake, the falls, the roof of the abandoned mill, and the
extensive townsite with its maze of boardwalks where Jan had
lived as a child. I was so intrigued by her stories of cougars and
endless rain, as well as this bird's-eye view, that I chartered a
plane to spend a day photographing the ghost town, which had
once been famous for producing Olympic-class swimmers.
Aside from the movies Jan's dad showed regularly, swimming
had been the only pastime. When government grants and
efforts to keep the pulp mill open and employee-operated
failed, people moved out and the papermaking equipment was
sold by auction, some of it going to a newspaper in Guatemala
to crank out nasty propaganda. I was not keen to make a
return visit on my own, but I thought it would be an exciting
excursion to make with Jan.

"Congratulations. Sounds as if you're experiencing a
rather high learning curve," Jan said. I could barely hear her
voice over the noise of the co-op. To my overly sensitive
antennae, her measured tones radiated distance and felt as if
they were directed to a psychiatric patient—which may have
been the way she viewed the situation. Only two months
earlier, she'd proposed getting back together. Twenty-three
tumultuous years of marriage, and three more of separation,
and we were still not through with each other. I made a few
inquiries about our mutual friends in eastern Ontario,
recalled a joke I'd heard along the way and said goodbye. We
seemed doomed by bad timing and unreliable filters.

259

The cardboard box was now empty, its outraged inhabitant rescued by her mother and placated with an orange popsicle. If I'd been a foot shorter, I'd have crawled in there myself.

New Bella Bella, now known as Waglisla, is a thriving if somewhat down-at-the-heels community at the northwestern tip of Lama Passage, one of the tighter spots on the Inside Passage. Cruise ships don't stop there but loom dramatically large as they manoeuvre the narrow and sometimes congested waters between Campbell and Denny islands. The older Heiltsuk settlement across the channel dwindled into insignificance, due in part to sharing Denny Island not only with a B.C. Packers cannery, but also with RCAF Shearwater, a base for seaplanes established during the Second World War. Bella Bella had played a significant role in coastal defence after Japan's bombing of Pearl Harbor and its invasion of Hong Kong, Manila, and various other Pacific islands, including Atu and Kiska in the Aleutians. Shearwater provided regular reconnaissance flights in search of enemy submarines, which, though few in number, were sometimes spotted, having shelled Estevan Point Lighthouse on Vancouver Island on June 15, 1942, torpedoed a number of ships, and sowed a little havoc on what was considered an indefensible coast. These aircrews were assisted by the Fishermen's Reserve Service, cobbled together quickly by conscripting equipment and men from the commercial fishing fleet, including approximately forty seiners and packers. These small wooden vessels and their crews, known as the Gumboot Navy, operated out of Esquimalt, Ucluelet, Nootka, and Prince Rupert, where there were ten thousand Americans stationed, and patrolled the perilous waters off the west coast of Vancouver Island and Hecate Strait, as well as providing escort for shipping that used the Inside Passage. As facilities increased at the new site, including the United Church mission hospital run by George Darby, more elaborate docks, government services, and a large modern school that doubled as a theatre and community centre, the shift in population to New Bella Bella became inevitable.

Shearwater Marina, two miles east in Kliktsoatli Harbour, was now my destination, as it had ample moorage and a large restaurant. As I carried my groceries down the ramp at Waglisla I noticed an odd-looking sailboat tied up at the dock. The mast was stepped far forward, almost to the bow, and had the single-sail rigging of a yawl. There was a net-like apparatus on either side of the boom to catch the mainsail when it dropped, a clear advantage for single-handing in a storm, when bouncing around on the foredeck amongst loose lines and flapping sails can be tricky. Having just met the Darwins in Finn Bay, I was somewhat startled to discover that the owners of this strange boat were the Melvilles. Ed and Irma Melville, who lived on Vancouver Island at Deep Bay, described the *Dunnottar IV*, a Nonsuch 29, as a "gem," which had taken them safely out the St. Lawrence River and down the eastern seaboard of the U.S. They'd named it after a castle in Scotland that had some family or sentimental connection. I wasn't sure what to expect from these distant kinsmen of Herman Melville, a white whale or a white squall. As it happened, when she learned I lived near Victoria, Irma, who was baking bread while Ed changed the oil, had a few queries of her own.

"Then you must know Susan Musgrave and her husband Stephen Reid." She flicked away a mosquito from her face, leaving a small smudge of white flour on her forehead. I explained that Susan was an old friend but that I'd met Stephen only once, at a party for poet Al Purdy's eightieth birthday. When he heard I was heading north, perhaps as far as the Queen Charlotte Islands, Stephen had invited me to visit them at the house they were building.

"Just ask for the bank robber," he'd said, with his winning smile.

I was grateful to learn that Irma was interested in them as writers, not because Stephen had been arrested again for armed robbery. She did wonder, though, why he might have done this. I could offer no explanation. Privately, I wondered if a recalcitrant muse had driven him to drugs. Writing is a difficult, lonely activity, and one which seldom, if ever, delivers the kind of attention or notoriety that is associated with criminal activity, especially crimes directed towards banks, which make too much profit, are loved by no one, but are staffed, nonetheless, by innocent citizens. Ironically, his flight from the ascetic life of the writer was likely to have driven Stephen to a more total, exacting and terrifying form of monasticism.

The first thing I noticed after tying up at the floating concrete docks at Shearwater was the large pizza sign in the restaurant window. I was ready for a gross culinary indulgence. I hadn't endured the hardships and privations of an ocean crossing like Gérard d'Aboville, who rowed across the North Atlantic, then the Pacific, in a not quite watertight capsule that capsized numerous times, smashing him in heavy seas, so that he arrived on the coast of Washington a possibly sadder and wiser man, but certainly bruised and thirty-seven pounds lighter than when he'd left Japan. The photo in his autobiography, *Alone*, shows him exhausted, bleeding, emaciated, but smiling and quietly triumphant. It's all relative, I thought; I'd had my own mini-epic to contend with, and more to come, enough at least to help me rationalize my greeting to the waitress.

"I'll have the biggest pizza you've got, with everything on it."

After lunch, I scrubbed *Groais* down with soap and water to try to remove some of the black marks from the car-tire fenders I'd encountered at marinas and fuel docks on the way up the coast. Across from me, a group of men from three large Bayliners were trying to repair a busted downrigger. An enormous amount of energy and discussion was going into this operation, as if the future of Western civilization depended on it; between them, they must have assembled a hundred tools. The wives were gathered on another boat, sipping martinis. At the far corner of the T-shaped dock, a lively conversation was underway. One man was leaning out of the wheelhouse of a boat that caught my attention. It was a classic wooden yacht, about forty feet in length, and looked quite spiffy, as if it had just come off the ways. Then I noticed the name on the bow: *Wm. H. Pierce.*

"Excuse me, that's not the original Darby boat is it?" The question surprised me, not only because I'd rudely interrupted a conversation that did not concern me, but also because the answer seemed so obvious: no, the original *Pierce* was sold more than thirty years earlier. That it should be sitting at the dock in Shearwater, only two miles from Bella Bella, the day I arrived, was too much of a coincidence. Still, it was a handsome boat. The owner was smiling at me, probably thinking me daft.

"You know, the one that served as a medical mission boat here and in Rivers Inlet," I added, thinking maybe he knew nothing of the history of his boat—or at least of its illustrious name. A boat could pass through a lot of hands in all that time.

"Yes, it's Darby's *Pierce*. What do you know about it?"

"Nothing. I've never seen it before, not even a picture. But a friend of mine, Garry Wickett, skippered the *Pierce* for several summers. He was so full of exciting stories, I envied him his good luck."

"Well, it's the same boat, but completely rebuilt. Come aboard and I'll show you around."

My host, Gordon L. Cox, who lived in Dodge Cove and was superintendent of public works in Prince Rupert, had bought the *Pierce* a few years earlier from an electrician who had kept it in a shed and dreamed of fixing it, but whose wife did not like boats and was afraid of the water. The man wept when he sold the boat and refused to come down to the cove to see it when the restoration was complete. Gordon had installed a head and shower, replaced thirty planks, various knees and at least six ribs. He put two plastic ribs in the stern, where they're hardest to reach and most likely to rot. He'd also lengthened and widened the cabin and changed the windshield. My friend Garry, who'd graduated from line-chucker to skipper, told me the *Pierce* had been built by a Japanese Canadian on the Fraser River. He had put in a sloping windshield to make it look more modern, but the cabin had always leaked. Gordon's extended cabin and new vertical windshield gave the *Pierce* a more classic look.

According to Garry, Dr. Darby had been impervious to both danger and marine aesthetics. He used to insist on taking a short cut from Millbrook Cove to Rivers Inlet, where the current was fast, the depth shallow, and the surface mired with kelp. On orders, Garry would have to plough through swirling kelp beds, feeling the engine slow down as the propeller tried to cut through the tenacious weed. On the return journey, the engine stalled in the middle of the surge in this narrow channel. Garry somehow managed to get the *Pierce* turned around, but it stalled again. When Darby took the helm, Garry dropped through the hatch to find diesel fuel spraying all over the engine room from a broken fuel line.

After an unspoken prayer and a quick calculation of the relative merits of drowning, fire and explosion, he wrapped the fuel line with a rag and held it in place long enough for Darby to fire up the engine and get them back to Millbrook Cove. Another time, when he was caught behind a slow gillnetter in Gunboat Passage on the way back from Ocean Falls, Darby had tried to overtake, holing the *Pierce* on a reef. It sprang a plank and the pump could not discharge the volume of water coming in; besides, the engine's flywheel was throwing so much water around, the electrical system kept shorting out. Darby made it into a small cove where there was a beach. The gillnetter picked up Mrs. Darby and one other passenger and headed back to Bella Bella, where Garry was dispatched in an auxiliary craft after dark to find the doctor. He saw no sign of him or the *Pierce* near Dryad Point and feared the worst, almost grounding on a shelf of rock himself. Apparently, the captain of a passing seiner had recognized the *Pierce* and, realizing its predicament, come alongside, applied its pumps, secured lines so it could not sink, and towed it—*carried* would be more accurate—back to Shearwater, where it was hauled out, patched, and prepared for yet another of mission of mercy. Or, from the boat's beleaguered perspective, a merciless mission.

It was getting late, so I spared Gordon the story of Billy, the Barnum and Bailey trapeze artist who had lived out his life on a tilted float house in Gunboat Passage.

The following morning the *Wm. H. Pierce* was gone, along with Irma and Ed Melville on the *Dunnottar IV*, leaving me to my own devices. I spent a couple of hours with my laptop plugged in at the restaurant, sipping coffee and making a few notes. The place had been hopping the night before while I wolfed down my pizza and played a couple of games of billiards with a man from the reserve. Now it was empty, except for me and a young woman at a nearby table shuffling through a pile of paper. She was joined by a friend, and I over-heard her reading aloud from what appeared to be fragments of a script. While I eavesdropped, I unplugged my computer and pretended to read an outdated edition of the *Vancouver Sun*, which featured news of a Bayliner sinking off Point Atkinson when it tried to pass between a tug and barge and struck the towline, flipping over and drowning several members of a family. One of the bodies, a small child, had not been recovered. Sadly, my grandfather had company.

"It's a script for radio. Slow going." My nosiness had got the better of me.

Sandy was a creative writing student in Victoria, studying with several of my friends. She also turned out to be a tenant of Susan Musgrave and Stephen Reid in Sidney, working for the summer at Shearwater to pay for another year at school. Two references to Susan and Stephen and the world of writ-ing in twenty-four hours made me wonder if something was in the air. I remembered Susan when she was not much older than Sandy. Because of her name and the interest in Native legend evident in her poetry, she was often mistaken for an Indian and invited to participate in tribal events. I suggested she change her name to Susan Muskrat. Her curiosity once got her into trouble in Whitehorse during a literary weekend. She came dashing into the beer parlour and planted herself between Robert Kroetsch and myself, the two largest males she could find. Fortunately, the two Dogribs who followed her into the bar decided the odds were not good.

I seemed unable to escape the subject of writing, even in remote Bella Bella, this ragged enclave in the Inside Passage. Pablo Neruda insisted that literature occurs where the land meets the sea; and this was certainly proving a creative intersection. Whether by the Melvilles, the Musgraves, the Reids, the Darwins or a lone student of creative writing, I was being constantly reminded of how writing is the focus of so many lives, often at the expense of relationships and other responsibilities. I'd spent a lot of time on this trip thinking about place, trying to sail and write my way home, as if home were a region, a patch of shoreline, when perhaps it was something else altogether. It was not so-called wilderness I was looking for, as I found huge expanses of uninhabited forest or ocean as scary and intimidating as they are refreshing. I had no desire to be alone for extended periods in the bush or mountains, thinking about hungry grizzlies or waiting for the next avalanche. I didn't believe untamed nature to be intrinsically hostile, but I knew I'd be easily bushed. On my way up the coast, seeing no one for days at a time, I'd sometimes felt as if I were on a shuttle to outer space. All those vast spaces took my breath away, made my heart beat faster, evoking what Emily Carr describes as "a great lonesomeness smothered in a blur of rain." I'd worked on farms and fishboats, so I was familiar with the difficulties and dangers of living off the land. I'd also known loggers and the injuries and deprivations they suffered to provide the lumber and paper products we carelessly enjoy; and Native people who had been displaced from "virgin" territory to make way for resource capitalism or to keep it pristine and empty for tourism. These were things that weekending urbanites, worshipping at the shrine of nature, seldom considered as they enjoyed their two-day "wilderness experience."

Although I was not inclined to idealize wilderness, I did pay tribute to the idea of wildness, which is the necessary complement to the structures we've inherited and continue to create to make our lives easier, safer, and more predictable. The idea of wilderness reminds us of where we have come from, of essential elements in ourselves that we share with nature, which will not be regulated and which thrive on variety and on the unexpected. Many of the small float camps and coastal communities I knew as a child had disappeared. Most of them were industry-based, contributing to the displacement of indigenous populations, to the near death of the salmon industry, and to the removal of old-growth forests. In the midst of waste and exploitation by large companies, however, there had grown up several generations of people who loved the coast, who stayed on to do sustainable logging by hand, who, when they could no longer make a living as commercial fishermen, set up sport-fishing resorts and ecotourism businesses, and celebrated the resurgence of aboriginal culture and the settlement of land claims. These west coasters might not think of their place as virgin wilderness, something sacred to be worshipped but never used, but they support the setting aside of large pockets of old growth, with its stunning biodiversity; they also support strict controls over who takes fish and lumber and game, and in what quantities.

The trouble with the quasi-religious view of wilderness— according to William Cronon, an American geographer and environmentalist whose collection of essays by different authors, *Uncommon Ground*, I'd been reading in preparation for one of my classes in the fall—is that it "sets humanity and nature at opposite poles. . . . We thereby leave ourselves little hope of discovering what an ethical, sustainable, honorable human place in nature might actually look like." Or worse, he says, we don't take responsibility for the parts of the world we do inhabit—bogs, grasslands, backyards—our real as opposed to our imaginary, or recreational, home. We want to maintain a sense of primitive, ungoverned space, the more so because of the helplessness we feel in a society dominated by large-scale economic and political forces. Rather than challenging those forces, making them more humane, we turn to nature for recreation, as a cure-all.

Cronon and his fellow writers in *Uncommon Ground*, it seemed, were asking whether nature or wilderness can tell us anything useful about home, about how to create a livable world in which we take full responsibility for the Other that exists in trees, parks, gardens, and in those we interact with daily. And, equally, for the marks we choose to leave in our brief passage through this world. Our clear-cuts can be seen from outer space; the pace and extent of the degradation appal us and have galvanized our attention. And yet we live in time as much as we live in space. Art, music, dance, sculpture, film, architecture and poetry are all part of our human heritage, natural human expressions, capable of appealing to the wildness that is in us, wanting nourishment, recognition. Often, I'd found a greater refuge in words than in woods, more comfort in language than in landscape, though I would fight to save both. The books I'd brought on my voyage were as likely to take up my time as wandering the shore, examining rocks, sea life, flora. It seemed clear to me, in retrospect, that all along, like a turtle, I'd carried my home on my back, or in my head—not *Groais*, which had become a comfortable shell, but the words, the books, the literary voices lining its shelves.

Gaston Bachelard, whose thoughts on the role of intimate spaces in our lives had comforted me in my initial confinement on board *Groais*, eloquently positions the power of words, suggesting language as the real home-place:

Words—I often imagine—are little houses, each with its cellar and garret. Common-sense lives on the ground floor, always ready to engage in "foreign" commerce, on the same level as the others, as the passers-by, who are never dreamers. To go upstairs in the word house, is to withdraw, step by step; while to go down to the cellar is to dream, it is losing oneself in the distant corridors of an obscure etymology, looking for treasures that cannot be found in words. To mount and descend in the words themselves—this is a poet's life.

Words had certainly been the key to many places I had visited or inhabited. I had felt quite at home in a strange house, a foreign country or a busy restaurant, even with several conversations, or an aggressive monologue, raging nearby, as long as I had a pen or a good book in hand. I remember precious little of Fiji because of Peter Carey's Australian epic, *Oscar and Lucinda*, which I happened to be reading during my visit; some of the scenes in that novel are indelibly etched in my mind. Words in a book or words taking shape on a page provide not only a place of entry, but also a refuge, a sanctuary. A rigorous but comforting labour, this life in words. Although poetry cannot repair loss, John Berger insists, from his place beside the first-aid kit and spare batteries, poetry "defies the space which separates . . . renders everything intimate. There is nothing more substantial to place against the cruelty of the world than this caring. . . . In this sense one can say of language that it is the only human home, the only dwelling place that cannot be hostile to man."

Thinking I'd solved a problem or two, I thumbed through my copy of John Berger's *And Our Faces, My Heart, Brief as Photos*, and came across an underlined passage that expresses a most unusual variation on the idea of home, or the home-place:

What reconciles me to my own death more than anything else is the image of a place: a place where your bones and mine are buried, thrown, uncovered, together. They are strewn there pell-mell. One of your ribs leans against my skull. A metacarpal of my left hand lies inside your pelvis. (Against my broken ribs your breast like a flower.) The hundred bones of our feet are scattered like gravel. It is strange that this image of our proximity, concerning as it does mere phosphate of calcium, should bestow a sense of peace. Yet it does. With you I can imagine a place where to be phosphate of calcium is enough.

Here, at the turning point, I was confused. Was Berger placing his faith in language or in love? I thought of the years I'd spent with Jan. She had certainly provided a refuge, a safe harbour. Could nature or writing ever replace that? I had my doubts. If, as the poet insists, the grave's a fine and private place, especially when shared with the beloved, perhaps a poem on the subject's even finer; it's certainly more inviting and practical, given the fact that lovers seldom die in tandem. In life, one survives to love again and relocate those precious bones. Only in art is such immortal housekeeping guaranteed.

I planned to leave the following morning, but not before I'd done some shopping and had another look at Waglisla. The water-taxi, free on a trial basis to see if it attracted sufficient business at the Shearwater Marina and restaurant, scooted smoothly and confidently along the ragged shore I'd studied so hesitantly on my chart.

"Case in point. We should be selling fresh water. The whole world needs it and we're letting it spill into the sea."

I was seated next to Andy, whose grandmother was Heiltsuk and grandfather a Scots logger and fisherman. I tried several lines of argument, but he was determined to make so many cases in point that I soon fell silent, watching light play in the water-taxi's wake. Selling water? Everything in B.C. was for sale, it seemed, to the highest bidder. Nationalists, environmentalists and the First Nations Council protested the sale of bulk water, though doubtless for different reasons.

Nationalists feared it would further weaken Canadian sovereignty; environmentalists expressed horror at increased degradation of streams and lakes by greedy entrepreneurs; and First Nations people were divided over issues of sanctity and jurisdiction, that is, whether to side with traditional values and fight against a total rape of the environment or to make a stand for ownership and the right to conduct water sales themselves. Who could blame them for that? With more than a century of clear-cutting and the recent purchase of MacMillan Bloedel by U.S. giant Weyerhaeuser, we seemed on the verge of losing control of the forest industry and making British Columbia as bereft of resources and old growth as Europe and the rest of North America.

The thought of multinational corporations dictating the death rate of our forests, of factory ships with flags of convenience ravaging offshore waters of their fish stocks, much of which is chucked overboard as non-target catch, and of mines, mills and fish farms polluting coastlines and endangering wild stocks—all this ought to have set Andy and me on the warpath, side by side. We'd both witnessed the mesmerizing beauty of Ocean Falls and seen the tremendous volume of water being released into the sea. It was not being wasted. Some of it still provided electrical power for Waglisla and Shearwater. The rest was doing its ancient work of renewal, on the coast and in the ocean.

I wanted to challenge Andy, but he was off on a new tangent. The cannery, apparently, had ripped him off for twenty thousand dollars' worth of fish he had brought in. He hadn't bothered to insist on a written statement. He'd had to sell his fishing licence to pay for repairs on his father's boat, which they hoped to use for beachcombing and eco-charters. The caulking alone had cost him six thousand dollars.

"You can't trust anyone," he said, offering me a cigarette, "not even your own people. Case in point."

On the way back to Shearwater, the driver invited me to sit with him up front. We passed the federal fisheries dock on the north shore of Denny Island and a rough assembly of logs and houses farther along the shore, which he told me proudly was his new home. He'd just moved up to Waglisla from the Lower Mainland with his father, stepmother, and daughter, Raven, who was part Heiltsuk. He loved the place and his job. When not driving water-taxi, he spent his time gathering logs to sell or to use as supports for his float house. I described my own experiences on the coast, gillnetting in Rivers Inlet, teaching and driving a water-taxi on Texada Island, but I couldn't stop thinking of Billy, the injured Barnum and Bailey trapeze artist Garry had told me about, who had lived out his last years on a tilted float house in Gunboat Passage.

Living, writing—it was all a trapeze act, trying desperately to maintain some sort of balance.

# Eighteen

The sea was strangely flat the morning I headed south from Waglisla. I'm referring not to the absence of waves, as they increased in intensity throughout the day, especially where the open Pacific blasts down Hakai Passage into Fitz Hugh Sound, but to the fact there was no perceptible downhill slope. The phrases "up north" and "down south" may be little more than useful fictions, but because the amount of energy required to travel north on a small boat is not unlike that expended in mountain climbing, the terms assume an almost physical reality on the coast. Besides, there were all those Mercator maps I remembered hanging vertically on the walls of public schools to reinforce the notion that north is up. Horizontal though it might be, the trip back seemed miraculously faster and easier; it was the same distance, but I had some idea of what to expect and could relax and enjoy details that had escaped me earlier as I plunged into the unknown, my eyes darting from reef to chart and from chart to cliff face. This may not have been the home stretch, but it definitely felt like the clubhouse turn.

The sky was overcast, getting ready to piss on this disreputable turncoat in his shabby ark, heading back so soon to the comforts and refuge of the south coast. The shoreline on either side of me as I turned into the eastern leg of L-shaped Lama Passage was uninhabited but not uninviting. While the cliffs on Denny Island to my left were imposing, they shared with the more gradual and jagged shoreline of Hunter Island on my right the coloration that characterizes the north coast at mid-tide: the black waterline, which today was picking up no blue from the sky or green from the trees; the caramel-coloured band of exposed rock that is covered with marine vegetation, consisting mostly of barnacles and bladderwrack; above this, the dark grey of still wet rock and a lighter grey fringe where it dries below the treeline, with the occasional bleached white log thrown up ages ago by strong seas; then the dark-green forest that disappears gradually or abruptly into low-lying cloud.

I had my raingear on, including sou'wester and white rubber boots, with a batch of carrots, a container of cranberry juice at the ready, and, in one of my indispensable zip-lock bags, half a dozen "sandwiches" consisting of extravagant applications of peanut butter and jam between almost taste-less square crackers.

Such is life afloat. I couldn't help comparing my stringent shipboard routines and modest fare with what I knew of the social and culinary habits of George Vancouver and Francis Drake. Having alienated most of his crew by his sour behaviour and ill-advised floggings, Vancouver was nonetheless obliged to live in close quarters with them daily and concern himself, if not with their moral and emotional well-being, at least with their physical welfare, forcing men who detested him to drink the dreadful spruce beer that would protect them from scurvy. It was all medicine and no fun aboard the *Discovery*, except for the presence of botanist and medic Archibald Menzies, who remained curious and enthusiastic about the New World and its creatures and did his best to mediate between captain and crew as well as provide un-wanted medical advice.

In contrast to the sour taste aboard the *Discovery*, life aboard the *Pelican*-cum-*Golden Hind* was like stepping from a prison cafeteria into a gourmet French restaurant. Drake always dined in style, with good silverware and musicians; if he'd been skipper of the *Groais*, he'd have installed a proper stereo CD system, a bar, a rack of select wines, a shower and an auto-pilot, just for starters. Drake was ready for all eventualities. He brought with him a preacher, Francis Fletcher, who read Scriptures and offered up prayers until he made the mistake of criticizing his captain and ended up in the brig. Also along for the ride were a tailor, a shoemaker, an apothecary, soldiers, ten "gentlemen," and several musicians who could play the trumpet and viol. Drake wasn't a big reader, but he did carry a copy of Magellan's *Discovery* and two other books on navigation, one in English. Never bored, he apparently sketched and painted varieties of sea life, including birds and fish. In other words, his hobbies and interests extended beyond mere piracy. Charles Darwin would have approved.

This is not to suggest that life below decks, where I would surely have been lodged, was quite so benign or the cuisine so lip-smacking. It was not all smooth sailing aboard the original *Golden Hind*. Drake had a falling-out with one of his junior partners, whom he subsequently hanged for treason. Once into the Pacific, he lost the *Marygold* and all hands and was separated from the *Elizabeth*. After taking as a major prize the Spanish treasure ship *Nuestra Señora de la Concepción*, known affectionately as *Cacafuego*, which translates literally as *Shitfire*, Drake began to think of home. Ice and bad weather had prevented him sailing farther north in search of the fabled Northwest Passage. Instead, once he'd retreated south and repaired ship in northern California, which he took possession of and named New Albion, he concentrated not on counting his losses but on safeguarding his gains—enough gold and silver to make Queen Elizabeth I happy and himself and his backers very rich—and sailed west to the Spice

Islands, planning to head home via the Cape of Good Hope. In the Spice Islands, he picked up six tons of cloves, but shortly after ran aground off Celebes. While the *Golden Hind* hung perilously on a reef and Fletcher prayed aloud, pompously and indiscreetly, Drake was forced to chuck three tons of cloves overboard along with several cannon, though not, it should be noted, any of the treasure. Fortunately, the wind shifted and blew the *Hind* off its perch and Reverend Fletcher off his ecclesiastical high horse.

With my gourmet cuisine beside me in the cockpit, I was set for a long day at the helm. I hadn't decided whether to stop again at Namu or push on to Finn Bay, a good jumping-off point for the dreaded journey past Cape Caution and whatever broth the open Pacific might brew for my benefit. I was still pondering my options, unsure what Fisher Channel and Fitz Hugh Sound might have to offer in terms of wind or fog. I had my eye on two fishboats approaching in the distance and was recalling a pilothouse sloop from Alaska that had passed me a few days earlier in this same spot heading south. I'd had so many sweaters on under my raingear that only my hands and nose were cold from the wind and spray; as the sloop passed me, I'd seen two figures in the teak pilothouse dressed in light turtlenecks and holding cups of hot coffee. They did not return my greeting. It's unlikely that they had not noticed me, the only other boat in Lama Passage, but quite possible they could not make out the gesture from this amorphous blob of orange rubber wedged into the open cockpit. Alaskans, I thought, are used to isolation and probably not so desperate for the illusion of human contact that they must acknowledge complete strangers.

As I plotted a course midway between the two trollers still a mile ahead of me, a boat shot past less than ten feet to star-board with a shrill whine, sending up a fishtail in its wake. I let out a startled shout. It was a flat-bottomed aluminum craft with a high-powered outboard engine, similiar to the one carrying the Owikeno kids to their picnic down Darby Chan-nel, only this one carried a mother and child and a young man at the wheel. I had seen him in Shearwater the day before, roaring into the marina far too fast, setting a dozen pleasure craft thrashing at their lines. One of the boaters, an old-timer who was trying to repair his busted steering gear, cursed, "There goes that goddamn hot-rodding Siwash again," indi-cating a repeat performance. Though *Groais* was being knocked about, I was amused as I'd only seen the anachronism "Siwash" used as a derogatory term in books.

The young helmsman turned with a broad grin and gave me a thumbs-up. Was he out joyriding or did he have a destina-tion in mind? I know that if I'd made a sudden turn to avoid a deadhead, we wouldn't have needed an introduction. This appeared to be the new regulation Indian runabout, with no troop of muscled paddlers, no drummer, and no decorative carving on the bow; it was, with its control column and driver's seat mounted a few feet to the rear of amidships, unquestionably utilitarian and ugly, but with a hundred horsepower to burn—the Colt or Mustang of the Inside Passage. I don't know whether Emily Carr or Hughina Harrold and the other schoolteachers of Village Island would have found it any safer during the storms they encountered in Blackfish Sound and elsewhere on the coast, but the agony would at least have been shorter lived. No life-jackets, of course. The two young Heiltsuk adults must have been amused at the spectacle I presented, with my snail's pace and a life-jacket underneath my raingear, making me a pretty good replica of the Pillsbury Dough Boy. I certainly felt as if I'd been poked in the belly and had the wind knocked out of me.

As the two fishboats passed me on either side, I wondered if Steve Martin in *Ocean Fury*, Gordie Widston in *Tiara II*, and Heber Clifton in *Cheryl-C* had put their lines and nets in the water yet. All that abundance of salmon gone, thanks to human greed, technical efficiency and government ineptitude. What was the point of reducing the number of commercial fishing licences if you didn't control the size of catches and the kind of boats allowed to fish? We'd spent so much time lamenting and sentimentalizing lost ways of life on the coast that we'd failed to halt the ravage made in their wake, huge factory ships scooping up everything in the ocean, high-tech logging that, with only a handful of men, can skin a whole mountainside in a matter of weeks.

I'd talked to enough people about the collapse of the coastal fisheries, but felt I needed more detailed information. My friend Steve Hume, who'd survived my malfunctioning reverse gear, recommended Terry Glavin's *Dead Reckoning*, so I'd picked up a copy in Campbell River. It was an eye-opener. According to Glavin, the problem with West Coast fisheries is the "concentration of catching power—which translates into fish, money and political clout—in a handful of companies. It's about too many boats with too much mobility, too much catching power and not enough accountability." What's happening is that large ships using enormous trawl or driftnets are scooping up unprecedented numbers of fish, many of them non-target catches that are inadvertently killed and chucked overboard. "This is not fishing, in any conventional sense of the term," Glavin says. "This is mining." Canada is not only failing to regulate the industry, but is actually subsidizing it in order to ensure a place at the trough—or the altar of extinction—for its own fleet. The official tally of bycatch discards by foreign boats is horrific. As Glavin notes:

Asian driftnetting soon came to be regarded as the northern-hemi-sphere equivalent of the liquidation of tropical rainforests. A 1989 study completed by a team of scientists from DFO's Pacific Biologi-cal Station that attempted to calculate the mid-Pacific fishery's annual bycatch mortality came up with these estimates: 50,718 northern right-whale dolphins, 14,825 Pacific white-sided dolphins, 14,045 northern fur seals, 6,245 Dall's porpoises, 780 striped dolphins, a 'guess' of 331 tons of Canadian salmon and an estimate of 750,000 seabirds.

In addition to the overfishing of juvenile stock, and a lack of discrimination between safe and endangered runs of wild salmon, there seems to be no informed and effective manage-ment. The cost of running DFO is greater than the value of the annual yield of all species taken by Canadian fishermen. The assessment offered in 1991 by Peter Larkin, a respected fisheries scientist, was uncompromisingly bleak: "Manage-ment of fisheries in most parts of the world today is a morally bankrupt, unmitigated disaster. . . . largely an exercise in documenting errors of judgment." The common view of dragnet fishermen, including inshore shrimpers, is that they are maritime loggers, clear-cutting the ocean floor, stripping it of flora, the subaquatic forests that are as essential to sustaining sea life as old growth and mature forests are to sustaining certain forms of wildlife.

Five miles ahead, I'd seen the daredevil in the aluminum boat make an unexpected turn towards shore, then swing abruptly in the direction of mid-channel, a manoeuvre that seemed completely foolhardy until I approached the same spot myself. Since Lama Passage is open to the Pacific at one end and Fisher Channel at the other, the volume of incoming and outgoing water has difficulty deciding whether to take the short and narrow or the broad and leisurely route; so it tries to do both. And these conflicting forces contend towards the eastern end, cheered on by a large reef extending from the south shore. I was fighting with the tiller to keep *Groais* on course and heading, quite unintentionally, towards mid-channel. My hot-rodding friend obviously knew the local waters so well he could dance with the currents, however complicated the steps. And, of course, the advantage of a flat-bottomed boat, at least in relatively calm water, is that it planes across the surface and is far less susceptible to the direction or speed of the current.

Once in Fisher Channel, I hugged the eastern shore of Hunter Island for two hours before crossing over to the mainland side just below Fog Rocks. By the time I'd reached the open trough where the winds have a pretty straight run up Hakai Passage and Burke Channel, it was getting sloppy. *Groais* was showing no signs of pain, but I had to brace myself with one foot on the opposing cockpit seat and drape an arm over the stainless-steel tubing behind me to stay in place. I couldn't tell what the current was doing, though the GPS confirmed I was still making 4.5 knots, and I felt as indecisive as a small child at a dangerous intersection. Although Fitz Hugh Sound, which stretched out ahead, showed a lot of whitecaps, I figured that the conditions of rain and mist did not suggest worsening seas; besides, I'd soon be in the relatively protected leeward side of Calvert Island. Since it was early afternoon, I decided to skip Namu and take my chances on making it to Finn Bay, another four hours away. I could always duck into Kwakume Inlet, rated highly by both cruising guides.

By then visibility was below one mile, as it had been on my way up, so I hugged the mainland shore, watching again for

those familiar names: Ontario, Uganda, Koeye, Widbey,
Kwakume, Addenbroke. They sounded like the roll call at a
Commonwealth conference. As I hunkered down in my
raingear and finished the last of the unpeeled carrots, I
thought again of pre-Columbian visitors to the coast. As the
Bering land-bridge hypothesis for early immigration now
seems inadequate to explain bones, ruins and artifacts found in
North and South America, more attention has been paid to the
possibility—some would say the certainty—of Polynesians,
the Innu of Japan and others reaching the Americas by sea
thousands of years earlier than had previously been thought.
I'd talked to First Nations people on the coast who, though
appalled by the suggestion that they might have Chinese,
Japanese or Mongolian ancestors, were quite content to identify themselves with the Polynesians, who, over a period of
four thousand years, colonized Hawaii, Easter Island and New
Zealand. They were brilliant navigators, using the night skies
to guide them, keeping in memory or on crude bark charts the
position of stars at each stage of their daunting journey so
they could find their way back home again.

No one knows exactly what prompted those epic Polynesian
voyages—perhaps a combination of curiosity and necessity.
Wars, natural disasters, overpopulation of resource-sensitive
areas. Whatever it was, they learned to travel long distances at
sea in canoes fifty to a hundred feet long and twenty to fifty
feet wide, sometimes with outriggers for balance. They developed the triangular sprit sail, which looked like an inverted
pyramid and enabled them to navigate to windward. In addition to masts, anchors and primitive navigational aids, they
even kept pigs on board, not just for food or later farming
purposes but because pigs have a keen olfactory sense that
enables them to detect land long before it is sighted. The
shape, colour and movement of clouds, wave action, the flight

of birds, flotsam, ocean currents—all of these provided information for the intrepid Polynesian navigators.

"Balls," Paul had said as we climbed the stairs of the Western Washington University library, passing in front of a small Coast Salish pole depicting bear, wolf and salmon. I thought he was speaking of the totem.

"Where? Aren't these figures supposed to be sexless, or at least androgynous?" We'd been talking about a conference Paul attended in Hawaii on the subject of pre-Columbian voyages. He was telling me about one of the papers presented on methods of navigation used by early Micronesian mariners.

"The Yaps," he said, ignoring my distracted look, "used to gauge the direction and speed of ocean currents by lying in the bottom of the boat with their testicles against the wood."

"You sure it wasn't just to cool their ardour?" Paul stopped in front of the circulation desk. He smiled. He suggested I keep that bit of information in mind for my trip.

"You never know when it might come in handy. For either purpose."

Not much ardour had survived to need cooling during the nervous rigours of this trip. As for navigation, I'd have to be a contortionist, or dismantle the boat, ribs and all, to be able to perform such a delicate operation on *Groais*. I wondered if the job of testicular mapping was considered a fine art, a cut or two above that of paddling. Was it performed by captain or by crew? Could the nude lying prostrate in the bilge with an ecstatic look on his face as he gauged the vibrations in his seed pouch be ranked alongside the shaman, that other semiologist (or semenologist), as a genuine reader of signs? As I pondered these weighty issues, the aluminum skiff I'd had my close encounter with earlier shot out of the mouth and across the bar of the Koeye River and turned north, presumably back to Waglisla. This time, without an audience, the driver had neither antics nor interest in acknowledging my snail-like progress. Perhaps he'd been on a mission of mercy, delivering the mother and child to waiting relatives; either that or he was running a simple water-taxi business. He made a beeline for Lama Passage, surfing the north-running waves. Another advantage of the flat-bottomed aluminum boat, it suddenly occurred to me, is that it would be even more likely to permit, metal being a better conductor than wood and with fewer interfering ribs, the testicular testing of ocean currents. Perhaps, after all, I had stumbled upon the proof Paul wanted for the Polynesian origin of the Heiltsuk and Kwakwaka'wakw.

The one thing I'd forgotten was that the protection provided by Calvert Island disappears the closer you get to Rivers Inlet. By the time I'd reached Kwakume Point and was some distance past the mouth of the inlet, I was punching my way into a stiff southwester. I was also getting hungry and thirsty. Thanks to the spray coming over the bow, I had to keep removing my glasses to wipe them with dry tissue. If I turned back, I'd sacrifice the opportunity for a shorter run to Hardy the next day and would have to take a chance on being stranded in uninhabited Kwakume Inlet with electrical problems. The situation was far from dangerous yet, but it bore thinking about. Hunger proved the deciding factor. I did not fancy my regular dreary cook-up in a cramped cabin in the rain in a remote inlet, however idyllic. I had in mind building a huge fire in the ocean-buoy barbecue on Pete Darwin's floating gazebo, even if it had to be a tofu stir-fry.

By the time I bucked my way past Addenbroke Island Light

and a glorified rock called Bald Islet and turned into the still and reflecting waters of Finn Bay, I was salivating so much I almost needed to switch on the bilge pump. Not only was there room at Pete and Rene Darwin's new dock, but a huge shrimp dragger was tied up stern-first, disgorging its steel cable the length of the float in order to mend a break. I secured the lines, put up my plastic awning, and started hauling out supplies for the cook-up. Potatoes, broccoli, more carrots, a limp piece of celery, onion, red pepper, and garlic. I looked without enthusiasm at the unopened package of tofu I'd kept alive with ice and neglect for three weeks. Then I saw one of the guys go past me with what turned out to be a twenty-pound package of fresh shrimp, which he was giving to Pete in gratitude for the use of the float, but also, I learned later, because Pete had rescued one of them a few years earlier when his boat was adrift in bad weather.

Setting aside my reservations about clear-cutting the ocean floor, I marched over to the shrimper and purchased two pounds for five dollars, uttering a prayer to the gods for rescuing me yet again from the dreaded tofu. Over a sputtering fire in Pete's gazebo, I began to sauté the veggies and garlic in olive oil. I looked at the shrimps. In my panic to eat, I'd forgotten the number of times I'd been served cooked shrimps in their transparent shells and how easily they'd come off. So I began the laborious task of removing the uncooked shells by hand. The first half-dozen looked as if they'd been put through a shredder. The veggies were close to being done; at this rate, they'd be mush by the time the shrimps were shelled.

"It's easier if you cook them fully clothed." Pete was lifting my wok and throwing several logs on the fire. "But just for a few moments until they turn pink."

He stirred the ashes and inserted a few pieces of kindling.

"So, you made it. You look like the last rose of summer."

"Hey, thanks. I should have stayed in Kwakume Inlet. The bears may have bad breath, but at least they're polite."

Pete, wearing plaid shirt, work pants and suspenders, was carrying the rust-coloured and mentally challenged Fur Ball in his arms. He picked up a large chunk of fallen red pepper from the floor, took it over to the sink for washing, then chucked it into the wok. Fur Ball, whom Rene insisted—judging from his colour and limited intelligence—must be related to William of Orange, seemed oblivious to the elements of fire and water. Natural mediocrity and royal inbreeding had not dulled all his senses, though, as his nose was twitching at the smell of fresh seafood.

"Hang on, I'll bring some dry wood. You won't get a decent fire out of that stuff."

As he rounded the corner of the house, Pete's shoulder brushed the pot of geraniums hanging from the eaves. It swung back and forth, its bright red flowers catching the last of the daylight. I could never stand the smell of geraniums—or is it gerania?—but they looked quite magical in the half-light of Finn Bay. The German shepherd, prostrate beside the float house, opened an eye as Pete passed with an armload of wood.

I was practically dancing with anticipation and joy at my good luck to have shrimps for dinner. I directed a couple of squirts of soy sauce into the wok and scooped out my first helping, which I ate while circumnavigating the fire that was roaring in Pete's salvaged ocean buoy. I hadn't cut the carrots small enough to cook properly and the broccoli had been in the icebox so long its complexion had altered from green to khaki brown, but the meal was exquisite. I regaled Pete with my Namu and Bella Bella adventures and asked about Rene.

She was resting, he said, after a long day of cooking for the fly-ins at Buck's Trophy Lodge.

"Tell her she deserves a trophy for helping you keep this paradise afloat." I hadn't shaved for two days. My jeans were spattered with a precious mixture of olive oil, soy sauce and the juice of cooked shrimp. If I'd been able to wring them out and drink that precious nectar, I would have done it. With my index finger, I extracted the last residue of sauce from the wok. "I may never leave."

"If you want to see the rest of Eden, come up back in the morning and I'll show you what I have in mind."

Pete pointed up the incline to the half-cleared no man's land of broken stumps, piles of rock and dirt, several fuel drums and a small caterpillar. I tried not to look skeptical; hell, I thought, if he's created a floating garden, why can't he do the same on land. Besides, hadn't his illustrious forebear, Charles Darwin, nursed precious specimens on board ship during three and a half years at sea and, braving all weathers, brought them safely home for the edification, and eventual mortification, of a sleeping and morally complacent Europe? While I pondered the wonders of evolution and coastal gardening, Fur Ball had leapt onto the rough-hewn picnic table and was pawing through the discarded shrimp husks.

I went back to the boat and poured myself a glass of wine. I wished I'd brought along something elegant and classical for the occasion, such as my I Solisti Veneti recording of Vivaldi, but Stan Rogers' "Northwest Passage" seemed as if it might do the trick, a songwriter's lament for Sir John Franklin and other explorers searching for something they did not quite understand:

287

Ah, for just one time, I would take the Northwest Passage
To find the hand of Franklin reaching for the Beaufort Sea
Tracing one warm line through a land so wide and savage
And make a Northwest Passage to the sea . . .

The narrator, behind the wheel of a car and heading west, imagines Kelsey, Mackenzie, and David Thompson, explorers all, racing towards the western sea and wonders if he's that different from these men:

Like them I left a settled life, I threw it all away
To seek a Northwest Passage at the call of many men
To find there but the road back home again.

I loved this song—it had just the right mix of sentimentality and schmaltz for my last evening on the north coast. I'd not arrive home in two or three weeks smelling of roses—not even of cloves; I had taken no prisoners, won no cargo of precious metals, not even a freezer full of salmon, yet a booty of sorts I had in abundance. *Groais* was a couple of hundred pounds lighter from all the food and fuel consumed, but my spirit was riding low and secure in the water from the rich cargo of images, experiences and stories I'd gleaned along the way.

A blue heron stood guard as the sun disappeared behind the sawtoothed ridge of pines in Finn Bay, a study in dignity and concentration, exuding wisdom when there may have been nothing happening in his small brain but the imperceptible sigh of time winding down. Perched on one stick leg—the other pulled up to approximate the number four—he weighed the odds, judgement for the moment suspended, listening to arguments from both sides, the Crown's case burdened with fact and innuendo, objections sustained, the defence casting reasonable doubt and working, as always, on the heart. Your

Worship, I addressed him from the cockpit, raising my glass of Pinot Grigio. I wouldn't have been surprised to see him draw from under his dark wing the Book of Knowledge, in which all is written. Instead, less than amused by my trite antics and emotional slither, he lifted off and glided deeper into the shadows.

Nineteen

When I pulled into Mitchell Bay at the south end of Malcolm Island, the few spaces at the government dock were occupied by visiting American powerboats, so I tied up at a string of private floats extending out in a long line from the beach, rafting alongside a boat owned by my friend Mel Dagg. I'd predicted my arrival time fairly accurately from Port Hardy, but there was no sign of Mel and Lynn, who'd warned me they had tasks to do in Sointula. This time the run past Cape Caution had been easy. As I passed Egg Island, whose light-house had once been swept into the sea during a raging storm—the keeper and his family saved by retreating to higher ground—I thought of Malcolm Lowry's conundrum: the lighthouse invites the storm. On this occasion, it had invited only a warm day and a placid sea. Apart from warnings of fog that never materialized, the trip was deliciously uneventful except for two cruise ships in the distance, a small naval vessel passing close astern then steaming up the centre of Rivers Inlet, and a pod of transient killer whales crossing my bow just north of Pine Island. *Ocean Fury* was nowhere to be seen this time in Port Hardy, and I assumed Steve Martin had given up on salmon and gone to fish halibut off the west coast of Vancouver Island. To my surprise, the Alaskan pilothouse sloop that had snubbed me in Lama Passage a week earlier was up on the ways.

"Problems?" The guy could hardly ignore me this time, as I stood at the foot of his ladder. Like the *Penguin*, this fibreglass sloop was moulded to look as if made of planks. There appeared to be nothing amiss, no damage to the hull. Perhaps they'd wrecked the propeller or bent the driveshaft on a dead-head. Was I subconsciously hoping for something like that, as revenge for their fancy boat and superior ways?

"No, why do you ask?"

"I saw you near Bella Bella recently and just assumed you were heading farther south."

"We come down to Hardy every summer to paint ship. It's a great trip and I like the facilities here. Besides, there are no icebergs." He stopped painting, came down the ladder, and wiped the excess paint from his roller. He seemed quite willing to answer all my questions about sailing in northern waters. In fact, his volubility took me by surprise. "You're not on the Golden Hind that just came into the marina, are you?"

"Yes."

"Great sea boat. And a helluva track record."

"I'm surprised you know the design."

"I've read half a dozen articles on Golden Hinds over the years, but never seen one in the flesh."

"Like me, it's a bit the worse for wear. If I had time, I'd pull up here as well."

Sointula, only a few hours south of Port Hardy by boat and a short ferry hop from Port McNeill, is located on Malcolm Island, which serves as a natural barrier between Queen Charlotte Sound and Johnstone Strait. The closest community is Alert Bay on nearby Cormorant Island, the largest Kwakwaka'wakw settlement on the central coast. These three towns, in such close proximity, give the area a unique flavour. Port McNeill, on Vancouver Island and now linked by highway to the south, has eclipsed its neighbours in development

and ugliness. Sointula, on the other hand, still retains something—if only a touch—of its ethnic origins and exotic history
as one of British Columbia's most colourful communal experi-
ments. In *The Invention of the World*, where Jack Hodgins
examines the utopian mentality as it unfolded on the coast,
one of his characters complains about the pointlessness of
trying to write history here. Julius Champney, resident
grump and cynic, is making fun of Strabo Becker, a displaced
academic turned B.C. ferry worker and local historian:

I expect he is looking for an ancient crab with a memory. So he can
ask for an interview, with his tape recorder, and discover even
darker secrets about the past. . . . I can't imagine what he thinks he
will find. You can't pretend there is any history on this island, this
is still the frontier. . . . The best he can dig up will be little more than
gossip. You can't turn that into history, no matter how hard you
try. Not in a place like this. You are the inheritors of a failed
paradise. This island is littered with failed utopias.

It had been a summer of refugees. As the century drew to a
close, rusted hulks were slipping into remote inlets and bays
on the coast to discharge illegal Chinese immigrants destined
for the sweatshops and underworld of Toronto, New York
and Chicago, where they'd exist in virtual bondage to the
thugs known as "snake eyes" who arranged their passage. It
was not a new story for the Chinese, who had been recruited
to do the dirty work building the Canadian Pacific Railway,
and were then denied citizenship and kept under strict
control through a head tax of five hundred dollars. At the
beginning of the twentieth century, a group of Finns fled
Russian persecution for the well-advertised sanctity and
opportunities of British Columbia, only to find themselves
working in hellish conditions in the coal mines of James

Dunsmuir in Nanaimo and Wellington. Tyranny, whether czarist or capitalist, was not what these proud people were looking for and they wasted no time exploring alternatives. First, they wrote to Matti Kurrika, in self-imposed exile in Australia, and invited him to be their spiritual leader, saying that here was a land big enough and rich enough in resources to support a self-sufficient colony, where church and state would not interfere and where the precepts of socialism might be freely practiced.

As soon as Kurrika arrived, they founded the Kalevan Kansa Colonization Company and set about looking for an appropriate spot to build their first settlement. They chose remote Malcolm Island, which had a bounty of timber and seafood, and the first half-dozen set out by sailboat from Nanaimo on December 6, 1901. Rough Bay, where they would build Sointula, the Place of Harmony, was treed to the waterline, with no space for grazing cattle or planting gardens. The task of clearing was Herculean and slow, the more so because many of the shareholders were professionals—doctors, lawyers, poets, intellectuals, not a useful trade amongst them—who knew nothing about felling timber, milling lumber, and building houses or boats. There was no paid employment, no base industry to support the community. Kurrika was a dreamer, a visionary; he had enough good sense to send to Finland for Austin Makela—his old friend who had a more practical bent—but not always enough sense to entrust him with major economic decisions.

A sawmill was built, a series of cabins, then a three-storey communal structure to house the families and single people who were arriving each week from Europe, the Prairies, and parts of the U.S., including North Dakota. Rough structures were built from timber milled on the spot, but the green boards shrank as they dried during the first winter and, while they may have impeded, they certainly did not keep out the damp, cold wind. A Finnish newspaper called *Aika* (*Time*) was published, providing Kurrika a forum for his ideas and a vehicle for promoting—with no shortage of hyperbole—the new colony. By midsummer 1902, more than 125 shareholders and their families had arrived and still there were no sources of income to be tapped, other than the banks. When the Finns weren't signing on at logging camps, they tried fishing in Rivers Inlet—thus the name of Finn Bay, where I'd spent two nights—but they could not make a go of it because of cannery monopolies and low prices for salmon, sometimes as little as five cents a fish, regardless of size. Although they were granted the right to start a cannery in Knight Inlet, they could never afford the capital expenditure; the purchase of a donkey engine, a seine boat, and two tugs had already put them sufficiently in debt that they had to take out a mortgage on the land with Dominion Trust. They were determined and rich in resources, but could not afford to get them to market. The irony was not lost on the Kalevan Kansa's managers, as Vancouver writer and journalist Scott Lawrance has pointed out; even the practical Makela had to admit that "though we turned away from the world of capitalism, we were completely dependent upon it."

Although many of their ideals were lofty and widely accepted—socialism, equal rights for men and women, harmonizing human progress with the laws of nature—the community was divided on the issue of free love. Kurrika argued against the feudal habit of treating women as chattel, but he also questioned institutions such as marriage: "Let us aid woman into a position of unconditional freedom and responsibility. Let us build marriages on foundations of ideal love. Let us dissolve those unstructured marriages that, as vestigial parts of the church, still haunt us. Let us not acknowledge a marriage in which the relationship is not centred on love, goodness and tenderness." While there is no evidence to suggest that this overworked, idealistic community was ever troubled by divorce or sexual freelancing, even those who could not argue with Kurrika's logic were uneasy about the effect such ideas might have on outside perceptions of the colony.

Two events loom large in the destiny of the fledgling utopia: fire and financial fiasco. On January 29, 1903, the three-storey communal structure caught fire, the same night that a public auditor arrived to study the colony's books. No one knows what caused the fire, wind tipping over a lamp or overheated ducts, some of which were made of wood. From the instant the tailor shouted the alarm, only priceless seconds remained to escape the inferno that was to engulf and destroy the building. Some fled screaming; others left by way of orderly evacuation. The less fortunate dropped children out of second- and third-storey windows and then, clothes and hair aflame, leapt after them. Of the eleven lost, at least six were children. A story is told of Maria Hantula, recently arrived from Dakota with six children, who carried her two sons to safety, then ran back into the building to rescue her four remaining daughters, one of them a baby, trapped in another room. She didn't make it, this angel of mercy, and was found only feet from the door where she'd been overcome by smoke and heat, using her body as a shield as the flames licked higher, gathering the small girls and infant into the protection of her enveloping arms, which had become wings of fire. In the cold drizzle of morning, all that was left of this bakery, tailor shop, dormitory and meeting place—where bright futures had been dreamed, where lectures, debates and concerts had been held—was a smouldering heap. Here and there, a skeletal stove, a ghostly sewing machine, or a metal bed frame, upended and askew, protruded from the sopping mess of charred rubble.

This tragic conflagration—which injured many more, including Makela, who burned his face and suffered temporary blindness—was also a severe moral and financial setback for the colony, further fracturing its solidarity. Some blamed the spiritual leader, hinting darkly that the fire might have been deliberately set to avoid the exposure of irregularities in the books. While he appears to have been beyond reproach in terms of both sexual behaviour and accounting procedures, Kurrika was definitely a bad manager, authoring the colony's demise two years later by tendering too low a bid for the construction of bridges across the Capilano and Seymour rivers in North Vancouver. Not only did Kalevan Kansa lose thousands of dollars in unpaid wages, but he also lost most of the lumber for the project, 150,000 board feet, all of it cut and milled on Malcolm Island, when it was confiscated by creditors. By May 1905 Kurrika had left with half the colony and Makela had arranged with Dominion Trust to cover the colony's debts in exchange for the surrender of all its holdings.

Under adverse conditions, idealism shrinks as readily as green lumber. Of course, it was heady stuff at first, all that talk of shared values, seeking out the rhythms in nature, finding God in trees, in hard work, in one another; but four years of rain, fog, back-breaking labour and subsistence living put that into perspective. After Kurrika had returned to Finland to carry on his struggle against the czarist oppression that had driven so many of his people abroad, a number of families stayed on in Sointula, conducting most of their business privately, though they did try to start a fishermen's cooperative. Their efforts were defeated by the big companies. The island experienced a slow growth, but there was a brief surge in numbers during the sixties, when a new wave of hippies, draft dodgers and utopian back-to-the-landers began to arrive.

Into this milieu my friends Mel and Lynn leapt when they were looking for property on which to build. I'd been to Malcolm Island twenty-five years earlier, also looking for property. I went with Jan and our friends Ron and Pat Smith to check out a farm and a hundred acres. We found the island remote and desolate. The listed farm was in ruins; some of the fruit trees were still bearing, but the apples were stunted. I remember fighting my way through the wet undergrowth, almost deaf from the frequent blasts of the foghorn at Pulteney Point half a mile away. If we'd had any doubts about living there, they were all dispelled when we took the road to Mitchell Bay and saw the entire top of the island clear-cut, completely denuded of trees, with no evidence of clean-up and reforestation. Whatever magic and promise of harmony the island had held for Kurrika and his followers had perished; not only were the dreams and ideals that had filled so many fine heads gone, but the scalp had been removed with them.

Mel had inherited a house at Wall Beach near Parksville that would make most dreamers relax and thank their lucky stars. He might have done that, too, but he had no pension and no regular income. He owned a valuable property, but had no way to support himself. In a previous incarnation, he'd left a tenured academic post in Montreal to move west and build a house on the San Juan Islands. The dream had collapsed around his ears. He had a doctorate, had published a collection of stories, and was a gifted teacher, so he started again from scratch, teaching part-time at several institutions in Calgary, developing technical writing courses, and working as a writer-consultant for one of the pipeline companies. When his father died, he moved to the coast, thinking he'd find similar work at Malaspina College or the University of Victoria. After several years of commuting to Victoria, he realized he could not count on permanent employment, not even the part-time literature courses he loved to teach.

"It's Disneyland," he shouted across the noise of his diesel engine, "all the way from Victoria to Campbell River. Nothing but campers, condos, marinas, strip malls, and tasteless architecture. From the air, you can't distinguish it from Florida or southern California, a solid line of Socreds in minivans."

I had to agree with him about the Disneyfication of Vancouver Island, but I thought moving so far north was not the answer. Mel had decided to sell his valuable Wall Beach home and "buy down," in order to live on the interest and whatever he could earn from his writing and occasional forays as a teacher, consultant and technical writer. He and Lynn, recently married, had bought ten acres at Mitchell Bay and planned to build there.

Always the enthusiast, I'd said, "Don't forget what happened after your last house-building project."

"This will be different. Lynn's different."

"And you?" I extracted the mangled, waterlogged herring strip from my hook and chucked it overboard. I tried to assume an apologetic expression as I ploughed relentlessly on. "You're going to find things there you can't stand, too. Bigoted neighbours, developers, clear-cutters, realtors, they're all moving north as surely as you are."

There was no arguing with Mel. He and Lynn had met Ridge and Rosemary in the café at Sointula and struck up a conversation. Ridge, who had been a tugboat captain and knew the coast well, owned a piece of property at Cape Scott which the government wanted to expropriate, so he'd talked them into exchanging it for fifty acres at Mitchell Bay, where the cedar had been logged off almost a hundred years earlier, but where there was still old-growth hemlock and fir. Ridge was selling the occasional ten-acre lot, with strict covenants determining what could and could not be done with it. This suited Mel and Lynn, who wanted only to build their own house, get on with their writing and pottery, and keep Disneyland North at a safe distance. It seemed ideal to me, too, but also a recipe for disaster.

I'd visited them the previous summer. They were living in a small camper while building their pole-frame house. They'd been working at it more or less non-stop for several months, clearing trees, digging trenches for water, plumbing and electricity, pouring cement, even cutting boards from their own timber with a small portable mill Mel had purchased that consisted of a chainsaw on a sliding track. Like Chris Law, the original owner of *Groais*, he'd already surrendered a piece of thumb to the dream. Before that, they'd been up on weekends, bringing in supplies, looking for contractors who might give them help and advice, milling a few more boards. It seemed endless and they were showing the strain. I offered to help cut shakes from the old cedar nurse-logs that littered the ten acres. They'd already done thirty bundles, but needed another hundred. After a few hours a dispute erupted between Mel and Lynn over the thickness of the shakes. I'd been cutting them on Lynn's specs, but Mel insisted they were all too thin and could not be used. It was a small matter; there was no shortage of cedar, only a few hours of time had been wasted and, hell, not even that, since I needed the exercise and was glad to be learning something about building.

What I learned, though, was that building your own house while trying to live in it, or near it in a tent or camper, can fry the nerves and strain even the best relationship. I did not stay long on that visit, but I did manage to get Mel away from the job for several hours of fishing in the bay. We talked about his novel, which was languishing in a mildewed box in the camper. And we drank a few beers while the fish checked out our gear.

"You need to hire some professional help on the place. You can afford to contract out some of the work. Consider it an emotional investment."

"Lynn's great." Mel smiled and the clouds parted. He was in love again, building a dream house with his dream woman. "I couldn't have done this with anyone but her."

"It seems a long way off."

I had no right to be lecturing Mel on relationships or on conjugal choreography. My own track record was not good. Travelling to foreign countries with a partner had been enough to throw me completely off kilter. I couldn't imagine surviving such hard work and unrelenting proximity. I was obviously not good settler material, however utopian I might pretend to be. I wouldn't have lasted two weeks in Sointula in 1902. I would have celebrated the project, even espoused the ideals, but I would have caught the first boat back to Nanaimo.

We were drifting across the mouth of the bay, casting from opposite sides of Mel's boat. Behind us, the old-growth forest had a luscious depth of green. I could imagine Lynn sitting in the camper reading, light filtering through the branches high overhead and falling in parallel lines across the pole-frame house, the mounds of cut shakes, all their mutual efforts.

"Hey, you've got one!" Mel had seen the five-pound pink hit the surface even before my reel started to sing.

The small group of Americans I'd seen earlier at the government wharf were hunkering down for some serious cocktails and computer games on the afterdeck of a sixty-foot power-boat. As I was tidying the cabin—stray laundry, unshelved books, various papers in need of filing, unwashed dishes, a mess of extension cords, and computer link-ups for the cell-phone that was once again operative—Mel appeared in *Groais*'s companionway, looking more like a logger than a writer and academic. In fact, he could, with his not-quite-blond hair, have been one of those original Finns, Swedes or Norwegians so famous on the coast for their prowess in the bush. He sized up the boat quickly, nodded his approval, and explained that he and Lynn had been slower than usual gathering supplies for the house because several other house guests were arriving the next day—his sister and brother and their families, planning to camp out on the property and do some fishing. He hadn't mentioned this on the phone, not wanting to discourage me from stopping on the way south. Mel grabbed my bag and the two bottles of wine I'd picked up in Port Hardy and set off ahead of me, perfectly balanced, up the wobbly line of floats.

The pole-frame house they'd built, nestled in amidst the old-growth fir and hemlock, was enough to make a colonist weep. It was spacious, cleverly designed, full of light, with a large open central area for living, dining and cooking, and various more secluded nooks in which to locate the bathroom, study, laundry and pottery studio. Upstairs, the huge bedroom area had its own balcony, a ledge for peering down into the kitchen, and a stunning array of windows, mostly seconds or "mistakes" that Mel had bought at fire-sale prices from dealers and retail outlets in Nanaimo and Vancouver. While some tiles had been laid and a few slabs of gyproc and plaster were in place, the house was far from finished; in fact, the framing and rough work of last year seemed rather minor and straightforward compared to the number of small tasks that remained to be done, especially when nothing, not even a kitchen cabinet, would be store-bought. It would all be done by hand—Mel's hand, Lynn's hand. I was as much in awe of the half-finished place this time around as I had been of its skeletal presence the summer before.

After a supper of poached salmon, Lynn gathered the dishes in a large basin and took them into the yard, which still resembled an assault course or series of bomb craters. Then she made a couple of trips inside for hot water. I offered to help, but she insisted she had the routine down pat and would feel better doing it herself. I asked how long she'd been doing dishes outside.

"Would you believe three years?" She said this with a grim resignation I hadn't noticed before.

"But you've got water inside. The toilet and bathroom sink are working, why not the kitchen?"

"Well, you'll have to ask Mel that. He's been trying to get a plumber-electrician over here for six weeks to hook up the dishwasher, but the guy's too busy. Or too stoned."

"You could be using the kitchen sink, even if there's not a proper rock pit for drainage."

I realized I was treading on dangerous ground. They'd had too much company recently, including a German couple who had sat around waiting to be served. Today me, tomorrow Mel's relatives, next week some friends they'd met on holiday the previous Christmas. I obviously didn't understand the priorities operating here. A working kitchen sink seemed more important to me than tiles or gyproc. However, there were so many jobs to be done that any one of them could turn into a Berlin Wall—inconvenient, maddening, and implacably there. And then, if you survived in the interim period— poof, it was gone. I decided to leave Lynn to her fate, to the romance of building your own home: rinsing, if not dancing, in the dark.

I loaded up an armful of milling scraps for the wood stove in the kitchen. The door opened and the music of Miles Davis spilled into the yard, the trees, the uninhabited space awhirl with stars. Mel was doing a slow dance by himself across the half-finished floor, his eyes closed, moving to the beat.

"Listen to that. Crazy."

Mel was a complex character, in many ways a typical West Coast academic—the product of a culture that has only recently begun to respect the mind—highly educated and well read, but uncomfortable about the fact and scornful of pretension. He knew how to fix anything—cars, boats, houses—with the possible exception of a dishwasher. He was also an expert on jazz and a specialist on aboriginal history and culture. Although he did not suffer fools gladly, Mel credited me with having saved his life years ago by getting medical help in time for an undiagnosed bowel obstruction. This undeserved status gave me the latitude to be nosy and intrusive to a degree he would not otherwise have tolerated. Even then I was pushing it, beginning to sound like a damaged CD.

"How do you feel about the project at this stage?" I addressed this comment to Mel as we wrestled with a new airtight stove on the porch, trying to jockey it through the front door. The top-heavy firebox swung precariously towards the frame, pinning his left hand.

"On second thought, I withdraw the question."

I'd just come back from the boat, where I discovered I'd left the depth sounder on by mistake. I'd gone down to pick up a toothbrush and half-finished bottle of scotch—giddy as a kid at having my first big night off in two months from the boat and its cramped quarters. The spinning light of the depth sounder, as it sent little electronic signals bouncing off the bottom of Mitchell Bay and reflected crazily off the walls and bulkhead of the shadowy cabin, seemed to be trying to tell me something, beyond the fact that there were only two fathoms of water under the boat at half-tide. I was clearly out of my depth, even if *Groais* wasn't.

I sat for a moment on the top step of the companionway, which also served as engine cover and as extra counterspace for cooking. I'd arrived in Sointula with my own emotional life in a shambles and Oscar Wilde's words about the desire for perfection, and the impossibility of achieving it, still turning in my mind: "A map of the world that does not include Utopias is not worth even glancing at, for it leaves out the one country at which Humanity is always landing. And when Humanity lands there, it looks out, and, seeing a better country, sets sail. Progress is the realization of Utopias." Intellectually, I had to admit that utopias must fail. But emotionally, I had thrown in my lot with Mel and Lynn, with their new marriage, their determination to build a house, to follow a dream. I was concerned for their happiness, of course, but I also, at some deep level, needed their success. That's what was driving my impertinent questions.

I switched off the depth sounder, with its disorienting light show, and thought of Maria Hantula, lost with her children in the Sointula fire so soon after responding to Matti Kurrika's appeal to join him at the Place of Harmony, that remote dot on the coast of yet another foreign country. The first wrinkled issue of *Aika*, a pamphlet really, passed from household to household, had been smoothed out on the table in North Dakota by the same strong hands that, amidst a swirling requiem of flame, would draw four small children back into the cooling protection of her body. Rough hands, but capable of the utmost tenderness. I imagined her dream of a better life—the intense soul searching, the arduous journey over-land—and a deep sadness came over me. Emotional slash and burn, dreams of connubial bliss twice shattered, not by poverty, exile or fire, but by internal flaws, a jury-built conscience, insecurities too easily ignited by the spark in a stranger's eye. Against the obscene clear-cut that was my life, nothing stood but the possibility of second growth.

"Shit." Mel extracted his hand from between stove and door frame and shook it vigorously, as if a rapid infusion of new blood would help to ease the pain. When we had the stove more or less in place over the ventilation hole I'd chipped out of the newly tiled floor, Mel returned to my question.

"Hell, you know I never learn anything except from hind-sight. And then not very much. But let's not get into that. Don't worry, we'll make it through the rough spots."

The stovepipe running twenty feet to the roof sagged badly, so I braced it with a couple of metal straps while Mel arranged the heat-resistant bricks inside the stove. Within an hour the three of us were lounging like basking sharks, our insides warm from the small amount of Glenmorangie single-malt scotch I'd retrieved from the boat, our outsides tingling from the heat being given off by the newly installed airtight. Mel looked at Lynn, his lovely partner in crime and madness, with her frizzy hair and dishpan hands, and produced a smile as wide as Mitchell Bay.

"There now, ain't this just heaven?"

Twenty

As I set out across Blackfish Sound, I spotted four porpoises fifty yards to starboard, surfacing with their familiar rolling motion. If I'd shut the engine off or been under sail, I'd have picked up their noticeable huffing noises as they came up for air, the black, streamlined bodies and small rectangular dorsal fins glinting for a moment in sunlight. They're such graceful creatures, one of the faster mammals in the sea, somewhere behind dolphins in terms of speed and cost efficiency in water. Unlike dolphins, who are professional show-offs and hitch-hikers, surfing the bow waves of whales and boats—not just for fun, but as a means of expending less energy, getting a cheap ride—harbour porpoises are less sociable and certainly less theatrical, avoiding boats whenever possible. Since they had readapted from land to sea, theirs was a great success story. I'd been thinking about my own adaptability not only to the sea, but also to the new life and the dislocations facing me: aging, early retirement, divorce, moving back to the coast. Living alone, like living on the water, requires adjust-ments, the first of which is that you have no one else to blame for your moods or problems, a missing sock or a missed opportunity, a burnt lasagna, an empty gas tank or an empty bed. You have to make your own decisions, organize your own social life rather than coasting along on someone else's energy and initiative. When the porpoises, who'd grown legs and lungs in order to survive outside of water, returned to the sea, their vestigial limbs—ghosts within the body—persisted as skeletal reminders of another way of life, another mode of coping. I'd spent so much time in the care of women, from the inland waters of the womb to the sea of matrimony, it was going to take me a while to develop land legs, to learn the skills needed to survive on my own. Meanwhile, I floundered, I hyperventilated, I lay gasping and self-pitying on the shale, thinking of the millennia that would have to pass before I could stand upright on my own and walk.

"Who are you kidding? Your thoughts are more mixed than your metaphors."

The voice of my ex-wife Jan was so clear, I almost took my eyes off the disappearing porpoises to glance into the cabin. She was always ready to point out that much of my married life had been spent writing or dreaming in isolation, from which I would emerge in body, my mind still lost to its own imaginings. To be out of your element, I could hear her arguing, you have to have been, at least once, fully immersed in it. I was an uneasy amphibian, at home in neither element, yearning for company but quickly eschewing it for solitude, much as the porpoises were now doing.

On the assumption that I could see it later, travelling by bus or car, I passed up the opportunity to explore the U'Mista Museum at nearby Alert Bay, which contains many of the ceremonial items that were confiscated and improperly sold after the Village Island potlatch. I wished I could visit Tom Sewid and his bears on Village Island again and chat with him, one on one this time, about his artistic dreams and his illustrious family. I also recalled, guiltily, my half-promise to drop in on Bob Stewart at his hermitage in Lower Potts Lagoon. I'd had enough talk for now; and a hermit, I reasoned, as I swept in the strong current past the entrance to Clio Channel, ought to be grateful for such oversights.

Besides, I had a date to keep with a beauty in Kelsey Bay.

I'd spent most of the trip north avoiding Johnstone Strait and its funnel tip, Seymour Narrows, which serves as a sort of hourglass waistline between Georgia Strait and the central coast. All the stories I'd heard from my father, from fishermen, and from a lifetime of news reports had convinced me that Johnstone Strait was a nasty piece of work to be avoided at all costs, a vast trough seeded end to end with the ribs of men and boats. However, having braved a tiny stretch of open Pacific and parts of the north coast, I had decided I was ready for it, come hell or high water. Well, perhaps only medium water. I swung out of Blackney Passage and began the part of my voyage south that would, predictably, take me mostly east. A light wind was in my face, as usual, so I motored on, giving *Groais* her head. The sky was low, obscuring the mountains of Vancouver Island on my right. I'd avoided checking either the weather channel or the tide book, only to find the wind and tide both against me. What looked, in the morning, like a westerly that might be avoided by hugging the west side of Johnstone Strait had somehow wrapped itself around the land masses and insinuated itself along remote valleys and inlets to meet me head-on as a southeaster. Rather than subsiding, the waves doubled as I neared Vancouver Island, lifting the bow at an alarming angle and sending it crashing down the slopes like a suicidal snowboarder. Before I had the sense to grab my raingear, I was drenched. When the tide turned to flood, things would get worse, the waves steepening with shorter intervals. The two other sailboats I'd observed earlier had both trimmed sails and were heading for Havannah Channel, where I'd made my first cowardly exit from Johnstone Strait on the way up the coast, a performance I did not wish to repeat.

On the chart, Robson Bight is a slight indentation into which the Tsitka River empties that looked as if it might provide temporary respite from my trials. Unfortunately, the cruising guide listed it as a recently designated ecological reserve, given over exclusively to resident killer whales, an official scratching pad for itchy and barnacle-encrusted bellies. I'd have been happy to exchange my current discomforts for a quiet evening amongst the spouting blackfish, mafia of the Inside Passage, although I knew that the whale-watch volunteers across the strait would quickly descend on me like Valkyries in their high-powered inflatables. Adam River looked even less promising and it was mentioned nowhere in my small index of nautical sanctuaries.

Although I'd left Mitchell Bay around noon and been underway for five hours, I couldn't have travelled more than fifteen miles. Badly stowed items were crashing around inside the boat. The strait was white, huge waves snarling, flashing their teeth. With its severe pitching motion, rising up and slamming down into the oncoming waves, I felt as if *Groais* and I were being pummelled by a gargantuan bully who showed no signs of tiring of his malevolence. In fact, the smell of fear and the spectacle of me trying to hang on and steer the boat seemed to inspire him to even greater abuse. Now he was doing it with his eyes closed. Havannah Channel was only four miles off, but back on the mainland side of Johnstone Strait. If I delayed much longer, I'd end up having to make a dash for it with the full force of the waves hitting me broadside. The dinghy, which I was inclined to forget as it trailed leisurely behind at the end of a forty-foot piece of yellow quarter-inch polypropylene line, was jerking spasmodically at the end of its stretched umbilicus, stalling at the crest of a wave that had had its way with me and thundered astern. For an agonizing second, it looked as if the rope might break and I'd lose the dinghy or have a hell of a time trying to retrieve it. Then, with a heave, it would plunge headlong towards the stern, as if it intended to take refuge in the cabin or on my lap, always stopping just short of the rudder or veering off to port thanks to my uneven stowing of the oars, the only benefit of nautical incompetence I'd observed so far on the trip.

I'd originally hoped to get as far as Port Neville, where there was a public float and postal drop, run for years by the late Ole Hansen and now by his family, located on one of the ragged extensions of the mainland that borders Johnstone Strait, but the sight of the tea kettle in mid-air inside the cabin settled the matter. I swung the bow to port. Better a sinking heart than a sinking ship. With water coming over the starboard side and the boat taking a pounding, I made a zigzagging second retreat towards Havannah Channel at the southwest corner of West Cracroft Island, where I knew I'd find good anchorage in Port Harvey.

Once a lively community called Cracroft, with a hotel and beer parlour that had a regular clientele of thirsty fishermen and rowdy handloggers, Port Harvey plays a minor role in M. Allerdale Grainger's classic memoir, *Woodsmen of the West*, as a scene of "high" energy and hijinks, where no evening was complete without fiddlers and fights. According to poet-publisher Howie White of Pender Harbour, these lonely loggers climbed the walls in more ways than one. You could see the spike marks from their caulk boots, where they'd tried to outperform each other by running full tilt the length of the beer parlour and then letting their horizontal momentum propel them upwards for a gravity-defying second before they landed in an intoxicated heap on the floor. Fire destroyed the settlement in the 1920s and it was never rebuilt. When I arrived, the narrow, protected anchorage was silent and virtu-ally empty, except for a float house and a couple of summer residences, the larger of which had the ancient tug *Texada*, retired and put to pasture, anchored just offshore.

I dropped the hook in several fathoms of water, relieved at last to be out of the maelstrom, and set about preparing a meal and replacing items that had been catapulted together onto the cabin floor: flashlight, tea kettle, travel clock, Kleenex, a jar of jam that had, miraculously, not broken, Hughina Harrold's *Totem Poles and Tea*, and a zip-lock shaving kit containing a package of condoms. They wouldn't be needed in Port Harvey except, perhaps, for sending up heat-filled balloons, a last-ditch effort at intercourse with stars and passing aircraft. When I stepped into the cockpit two hours later, the light had all but surrendered and a platoon of shadows was conducting its final mop-up operation. Everywhere I looked, the surface of the bay, though dark and passive, seemed to throb with an as-yet-indefinable life force. I leaned over the gunwale for a closer look. There, in the cabin's reflected glow, I saw them. Countless jellyfish pulsed past the boat at anchor, their pale white parachute bodies expanding to kiss the surface of the water, so it looked as if a small rain had begun to fall.

These sublimely prolific, disk-shaped moon jellyfish, with four sets of sexual organs in the form of a cross, were appetite personified. Untroubled by history or by fine discriminations of conscience, they prided themselves on their transparency, on being colourless, except, of course, for the sexual organs, which came in three shades—brown, yellow and orange—and were paraded in full view. Their principal task was not public service, not even the provision of food for other species, but self-replication, which they did with enthusiasm, abandon and absolute precision, as G. C. Carl's *Guide to Marine Life* confirms:

Eggs are discharged into the water, where they are fertilized by sperms from another individual. The fertilized egg becomes a swimming organism which soon settles on some solid support, where it develops into a tubular individual with a central mouth surrounded by a series of tentacles. In time the tubular stalk becomes divided into a stack of saucer-shaped disks; the outer one, bearing the tentacles, separates from those below to swim away as a tiny jellyfish, and the rest follow as they in turn acquire a mouth and tentacles. Each of these is either male or female, which in time attain adult size and begin to reproduce sexually.

It wasn't exactly *Playboy*, but Carl's book certainly had the recipe for success in politics or showbiz, which seemed to involve little more than the acquisition of mouth and tentacles.

In the morning I was back on Johnstone Strait, heading south towards Kelsey Bay, lathered with sunscreen and wearing shades. The strait stretched out ahead, not the despair-reflecting mirror of Baudelaire's poem "Man and the Sea," but a giant and dazzling sheet of reused aluminum foil, the wrinkles ironed flat, their creases permanently registered. The cruising guides all warned: *Never go to Kelsey Bay on an ebb tide in any westerly wind.* In addition to the heavy tide rips off nearby Earl Ledge, the consensus was that the local waters could be brutal. And the logging communities of Kelsey Bay and Sayward, wanting to fuse form and substance, had done their damnedest to earn a matching reputation for brutality. The isolation and single-mindedness of their commercial pursuit—to remove every last tree on Vancouver Island—played havoc with all the finer instincts. My uncle Gerald, who was no saint, had worked there for years as a cook; he loved the banter and camaraderie, but said it was like living beside a stockpile of

dynamite. He couldn't wait to get back home to the amenities and relative sanity of Campbell River. However, the one
piece of information—the siren song—that was drawing me
irresistibly towards Kelsey Bay was a brief note in the
Waggoner guide about the ships that had been used there to
construct a breakwater.

Waggoner describes the breakwater at Kelsey Bay as made
up of the hulks of five ships: three Second World War
frigates—Her Majesty's Canadian Ships *Runnymede*,
Longueil and *Lasalle*—an unknown hulk, and the SS
Cardena, the Union Steamships that had transported my
stepmother, two brothers and me from Vancouver to Rivers
Inlet in 1952. I could not resist a final glimpse of this charmer
that had figured so romantically in my distant past but had
come to so inglorious an end. In the three computer-gener-
ated photos of her I'd found in the provincial archives in
Victoria, *Cardena*, with its single stack, was 226 feet long and
35 feet wide, graced with an elegant, perfectly rounded
cutaway stern. As she edges into the dock at Englewood, a
Vancouver Island logging community with train tracks
running to pier's end, there's a turbulence of white froth at
the stern, the huge propeller responding to a command from
the bridge. A few passengers watch from the upper prome-
nade deck and a small viewing area outside the lower smoking
lounge, but most are clustered in the bow near the gangway.
A matching cluster waits for them on the pier.

The second photo consists of an interior shot of the dining
room which shows off *Cardena*'s varnished pillars, dark
captain's chairs, and a dozen tables with white linen cloths and
white napkins folded to stand erect like bishops' hats or engaged
spinnakers. The tables are set for six and eight with white soup
plates, each framed by an elaborate array of glistening flatware,

small and large forks on the right, and an even more impressive lineup on the left, consisting of a knife and three spoons, a small one in the middle of two larger ones, like a child standing between parents or a prisoner being escorted by burly guards.

"Look, Mom. I've got an extra fork." Before I could replace the two forks and comment on the surfeit of spoons, my shin recoiled from a sharp kick administered in the shadowy nether regions of the table, another of the unforeseen perils of intimate space.

I turned to my brother, ready to reciprocate, but my step-mother's brows furrowed in disapproval. A quick, barely perceptible nod of her head commanded silence and corrected any impression I might have had about the origin of the assault. Marge picked up the large spoon farthest from her plate and began, without looking up, to eat her soup. I followed suit. My two-year-old brother Lloyd was seated beside her, mounted like a miniature Buddha on a hard cushion provided by the steward, and gnawing on a piece of bread, bits of which surrounded his plate and were dropping onto his lap. Jim, beside me, was trying to hide his smile behind a facade of disapproval and superiority that is the unique talent and prerogative of older brothers.

The two men sharing our table were headed up the coast to work: Pierre to the cannery in Namu, Axel to a small gyppo logging camp in Knight Inlet. Pierre, whose accent struck me as quaint, was wearing an army tunic over a blue turtleneck sweater; Axel, whose name and permanent bucked-toothed grin made me laugh, was wearing a plaid shirt and red-and-white-striped suspenders. Pierre had warned him about the formal dress expected at suppertime, so he'd borrowed a yellow wool tie that bulged like a lemon at his throat and protruded here and there from under the plaid collar. I'd met them in the smoking lounge the first day out from Vancouver while they were playing cribbage at one of the round wicker tables. When I saw them enter the dining room later, I called out a greeting and was thrilled at their decision to join us, though dismayed to find they directed their full attention to my stepmother, commenting that she looked far too young to have such grown-up sons. I beamed at the compliment, but my brother Jim, seventeen at the time, stared crossly at his soup. Lloyd chucked a piece of half-chewed bread across the table. Pierre picked it up and popped it into his mouth. We all laughed, but Marge's hand went out to Lloyd to forestall a repeat performance.

The *Cardena* was launched on the River Clyde near Glasgow in March 1923 and assumed its duties in the Union Steamships fleet on the west coast of Canada in November. It had a long and productive career moving passengers and cargo, and experienced some exciting moments, one of which took place in Seymour Narrows, the spot featured in my third archival photograph. In that shot, the *Cardena* is seen from a bird's-eye perspective heading south through the narrow gap between Maud Island and a cauldron of whirlpools, rips and white water all emanating from the infamous Ripple Rock, where it rises in mid-channel, like a deadly punch or scoring tool. The rock sank countless large and small vessels before a long tunnel was blasted to its core in 1958 from Maud Island and it was blown up with dynamite. When I was a boy, the *Cardena* seemed gargantuan, with endless parts to explore, a small town afloat, but this picture conveys more accurately its modest size and finite shape in the face of a vast, unforgiving panorama of turbulent waters and a still largely uninhabited coast. One flick of the cosmic switch—with fog, say, as the *deus ex machina*—and a passing vessel would have been about as safe as a spider in a toilet bowl, mid-flush.

I could find no photographic record of the two incidents that most intrigued me. In the first instance, the *Cardena* was proceeding cautiously towards the Narrows, where it would hug the shore of Maud Island, when Captain Andy Johnson received a distress signal from the Canadian National ship *Prince Rupert*—it had grounded on Ripple Rock with 137 passengers aboard, damaging its rudder in the process. When he saw the helpless ship, an involuntary shiver ran through Johnson's body. He edged in close enough to remove the passengers, then towed the *Prince Rupert* off the reef and to a safe harbour nearby. By broadcasting the rescue but refusing to bill its rival for services rendered, Union Steamships scored a public relations victory in the competitive arena of coastal trade and passenger service.

In a lesser known incident of daring, Captain Johnson ran the *Cardena* without mishap through Gunboat Passage in order to beat one of his rivals to a huge consignment of canned salmon in Bella Bella that was waiting to be shipped to Vancouver. The *Cardena*'s rival had a head start out of Ocean Falls and was already steaming down Fisher Channel towards Lama Passage, the principal route to Bella Bella around the south end of Denny Island. Johnson knew his only hope was to take the short cut, which was used with great caution by small boats but never by larger vessels. This involved navigating a tricky, reef-littered stretch between Denny and Cunningham islands. I had contemplated taking this route myself and studied the chart fastidiously, especially the inset, which offered a detailed enlargement of the more dangerous and precarious spots in the passage. In the end, I'd decided against it. Johnson was familiar with the passage and he knew that there were two main spots where a large ship was most likely to come to grief. He took no chances. Posting two lookouts in the bow, he alerted the engine room to stand by. The two-mile run from Georgie Point to Flirt Island was easy enough, but as soon as he'd passed Leila Island he reduced speed to dead slow, so as not to be swept by the following current onto the reef extending, almost unbroken, from Denny Point to Maria Island. Two hundred yards east of Maria, he rang for half-astern to resist the force of the current and to position the *Cardena* for the narrow opening in the reef. With Algerine Island dead ahead, he set the bows into the breach and inched through at a crawl, with short thrusts of speed at several intervals, the lookouts holding their breath as fast-moving water broke over the rocks on either side. Once Denny Point was cleared amidships, a quick turn to port gave the mid-channel rock a wide berth and allowed for easy passage to Draney Point and Picture Island, where things got tricky again.

Charged with these stories and conscious of my own fragile position in an eggshell craft sailing down Johnstone Strait, I seemed to be afloat in both space and time. I was not in flight from history; in fact, the entire trip thus far had been a descent into history, dredging up my personal and tribal past, trying to lay claim, to give some permanent shape to those evanescent shapes. *Groais* was bursting at the seams with spirits of the dead and the living, speaking to me from books, from passing vessels, from every rock and promontory. These memories, and the subterranean emotions they elicited, were not recollected in tranquillity, but took me by the throat, broke out in my heart like a plague or insurrection. I wanted to give them their due, but they would not sit still; like light playing on the water, they sometimes held back, obscured by fleeting clouds, sometimes flashed bright enough to blind me.

There could be no full portrait; I had to settle for ruins, for an art of fragments.

I was prepared for this piecemeal process of recovery, with Walter Benjamin's words in mind: "To articulate the past historically does not mean to recognize it 'the way it really was' . . . . It means to seize hold of a meaning as it flashes up at a moment of danger." I knew, in my bones, that the dangers and challenges of this trip would either kill me or jolt me into a new space, although what this new space might be I could not imagine. I had made contact with my drowned grandfather through the good offices of an orphaned killer whale and an anecdote about false teeth; my mother, who died before life could smudge or complicate her portrait, spoke to me through a stretch of water, a small box of relics and a few words of handwriting on the back of a photograph; Uncle Tom, whose airborne spirit inhabited so much of the coast, alighted more than once in the form of an eagle on the boughs of snags and arbutus; and my father, not quite at rest in his grave in Prince Rupert, had come to me through the physical landscape of Rivers Inlet and the medical complaints of a Tsimshian elder.

Was there any point to this salvage work, these sightings or reconnections with people and moments in the past? It was something I wanted to know as I gunkholed my way home down the middle of this colossal trench and ancient waterway. Life seemed more meaningful and more bearable when I knew there were hands reaching out to me from the past, as mine would reach into the future. While I tied the tiller in place and rummaged briefly in the cabin for something to eat, the echo of lines from Paul Ricoeur's *History and Truth* came back to me: "I learn of the necessity of my death empirically by witnessing the death of others, one after another. Thus every death, even the least expected, intervenes in life as a severance. My own death floats outside of me, I know not where, pointed against me by I know not what or whom."

The run from Adam River to Kelsey Bay proved shorter than I expected, the current being with me. The GPS now had me ticking along at a ground speed of seven knots. I was taking it on the flood, but fast current and accompanying mild weather seemed less likely to bring me fortune than a few miles closer to home, with a brief stop for tea in Kelsey Bay to sweeten the prospect. I stayed as close to the Vancouver Island shore as I could, passing a few small boats whose occupants were jigging or casting for salmon while the current carried them past their favourite spots. Then they would motor back a mile or so to drift the same way again. For all its reputation as an important marine thoroughfare, the Inside Passage seemed largely deserted.

As I putted in a southeasterly direction down Johnstone Strait, I was thinking again about history and the meaning of home. Clichés about the home-place abounded and were chucked overboard, one by one; then I'd fish them out again for a second look. Where the heart is? The heart, in my experience, can be several places at once, subdividable little organ that it is. I loved my children, scattered in three cities; I loved two ex-wives in separate countries; I loved relatives, a few friends. None, exclusively, represented home for me, though they all provided a brick, an iota of what home really is—little oases of peace and security where I could relax and let down my guard. I knew I was more comfortable, physically, here on the coast, though it often frightened and exasperated me. I told myself I felt more at home in my body than I had for years. I was alone, but not lonely; I lived on a remote beach on the southernmost tip of Vancouver Island, well below the forty-ninth parallel, where I was more likely to see life on board a passing ship through binoculars than on either side of me or on the road out back. Yet I was content to watch the constant changes in the weather, the seasonal gradations, and, finally, to let the city check its own pulse rate, worry about its polluted air, count its riches.

Although I'd occupied myself with these self-congratulatory musings on Ararat as the flood tide rose, I knew most of what I'd been thinking was only half true. I needed people around me; I loved the buzz of the classroom, the city, if only for brief periods. I didn't fancy living alone, although I required plenty of solitude. I was a compulsive worker, inclined to confuse being productive with being at peace. All-encompassing nature, whether on land or sea, inspired but silenced me. While I might wax lyrical about herons, seaweed or jellyfish, it was obvious that, if it weren't for the moorage fee, I'd most often choose a busy marina over a secluded inlet to spend the night. Although I was a joiner of words, rather than a joiner of groups, and found refuge in language, I was no hermit. I could no more isolate myself in books, or in my own writing, than I could ignore the cries of my children.

I'd been warned about the fierce current around Kelsey Bay, but did not expect to find it behaving like a dervish in the harbour. I brought *Groais* in slowly, remembering just in time to shorten the line to the dinghy. As soon as I was inside the basin, a back eddy grabbed the boat and swung it hard over towards the pilings of a decrepit pier no longer in use, threatening to drag it under, where the mast would break or the boat flip. There were no vacant spots to tie up at the floats, though several faces watched my erratic performance with some amusement. One moment I'd be gunning the boat in reverse; the next, giving it a blast to straighten it out. If engine or reverse gear failed, *Groais* would be a goner; me, too. I'd never get out from the tangle of logs and jagged boards of the abandoned pier. So much for my brief romp ashore and midday cup of tea, never mind my long-awaited reunion with SS *Cardena*, whose round cutaway stern I could see protruding from the huge makeshift breakwater. Her superstructure had been stripped for scrap and to make it easier to truck on board the hundreds of tons of rock and gravel needed to keep it in place. I thought of Vancouver's *Discovery*, ending its brilliant career as a convict hulk in Deptford, and Drake's *Golden Hind*, an untended monument eventually rotting away on the Thames. SS *Cardena* had come to an ignominious end, but she was more elegant, even in disgrace, than her four rusting companions.

Nature was in charge here, so history would have to wait. The current was so strong and the boat's movements so unpredictable, I didn't dare leave the helm even to search for my camera. From a distance, the white rocks resembled propeller turbulence under the stern of the *Cardena*. I'd have to settle for the illusion of Vancouver Island being towed inextricably away by the *Cardena*'s titanic thrust. I had the binoculars at hand. Maybe, if I looked hard enough, I'd see Axel and Pierre on the afterdeck, leaning against the rail in their fancy duds, enjoying a smoke and talking about the attractive young mother and her strange assortment of kids.

Axel and Pierre, neither of whom would have noticed that during the entire voyage the flatware was out of place, that the settings should have been reversed, with the knife and bevy of spoons on the right, the extra fork and its mate on the left.

Twenty-one

The run from Kelsey Bay to Small Inlet at the north end of Quadra Island was uneventful and put me in an excellent position to catch the change of tide at Seymour Narrows the following morning. Rather than wait for low slack, which would provide a following current to assist me in the short run to Campbell River, I passed through the Narrows half an hour ahead of the high slack, judging that I could make the distance before the full force of the ebb tide hit Discovery Passage. It was a measure of the confidence I'd gained in the boat and in my ability to read the charts and tide tables accurately. At the southern tip of Maud Island, I made almost no headway for several minutes, as the current was reduced to a slow boil, but finally caught a lull that permitted me to cross over and hug the shore on the Campbell River side, following contours and skirting sandbars in order to avoid the increasing speed of the water in mid-channel and to take advantage of the contrary back eddies.

I retrieved my bicycle from storage at the Port Authority offices, stocked up on groceries, and made a few calls. Neither Steve Martin nor the *Ocean Fury* were to be found. Trevor McMonagle came down to the boat for coffee, bringing a photograph to show me of the new Earl of Orkney, the friend of his who taught university in Winnipeg. The jovial man in the photograph looked somewhat bemused as he stood in front of a maple tree on his front lawn in the heartland of Canada, holding up his elegant sword of office for the camera.

Trevor had spent most of the last month in pursuit of an early model Mercedes, a veritable *Groais*-on-land—beamy, comfort written all over it—for knocking about the island and taking longer trips.

I phoned my daughter Sarcy in Victoria. Now that her two kids, Hannah and Jeremy, were in school, she was gearing up for a full-time course in graphics and interior design. She'd always hated competitive situations, including sports and formal education, but was determined to find a niche where she could indulge her creativity and get paid for it. I told her I was proud of her determination, though my heart ached at the thought of the disappointments and stress such a decision might bring. She was only three when I'd first met her and Jan in Ottawa. She used to ride in the child's seat on the back of my bicycle, her blonde hair streaming in the wind a foot or so below my brown ponytail. When I took her skating on the canal that first winter, she'd sat down on the ice and cried. I asked her what was wrong, why she didn't want to skate.

"I don't want to skate because I don't know how."

Sarcy, whose earliest pronunciation of the name Charlotte had become a permanent fixture, was an extremely sociable child, organizing games and inventing scripts on the front porch at Wilmot Place in Victoria for her little troupe of friends, one of whom went on to become a professional actor. But she did not like school and had developed a phobia for certain subjects, especially arithmetic. We did not discover until she was in grade two that she'd been struggling with poor eyesight and could barely make out the blackboard, never mind sorting out the mysteries of multiplication and division tables scratched like so many chicken tracks over the graphite surface. After all that negative reinforcement, she'd opted for early motherhood and the subculture, getting herself arrested at Clayoquot Sound for protesting the clear-cutting of old-growth timber. My grandchildren sat in the police station colouring while the charges were being read.

"The student loan came through. I start in ten days. How are you? I'd hoped we could spend a few days with you on the boat."

"I'm okay, a bit waterlogged." I could hear in the background the piping voice of my seven-year-old granddaughter, Hannah, berating her brother Jeremy for some fraternal infraction, most likely a lightning assault by one of his Transformers on her entourage of bathing Barbies. At nine, Jeremy was, not surprisingly, addicted to shape-changers, creatures who could turn legs into wings, hands into laser-equipped talons, and spinal columns into rocket launchers, all those items you need to protect yourself against the injustices of being a child in a world organized around adult stupidity. I'd performed the same escape routine more laboriously as a child, climbing the spike ladder on my favourite poplar tree and pretending to be a pirate, looking out over the billowing wheat fields, spotting the occasional gopher, crow, or coyote through my makeshift cardboard spyglass.

"Maybe we can still manage a day or two on the boat."

Jeremy and Hannah, quite unfazed by the technology, offered their obligatory telephone greetings to Bumpa, my honorary title, then Sarcy rang off with the ritual "Love you," which she knew always caught me off guard, touched by the sentiment it didn't quite transmit but feeling guilty for the unconvincing and awkward slowness of my response.

My initial destination for the day was Hornby Island, where Keith and JoAnn Harrison had invited me for dinner. When I set out from Campbell River, it was one of those glorious days when everything radiated sunlight. Off Cape Lazo, with jets from the airbase doing training exercises overhead, I saw swimming off my port bow a brown pelican. It was moving slowly, even philosophically, like a good Isaac Walton angler, and did not seem either disturbed by or interested in my presence. However, when I came within twenty yards it lifted ponderously into the air and with a few flaps and a long glide removed itself to a safer distance. Pelicans are not common this far north, preferring to hang out in California or Oregon. Occasionally, they're sighted in Washington. To find one in Georgia Strait was evidence of either climatic warming, poor navigational skills, or simply a youthful spirit of adventure. I came to this subtle conclusion, of course, not from any first-hand knowledge of birds, but from having a Peterson guide next to me in the cockpit. According to Roger, only immature pelicans have a brown neck and head, the adults sporting more white, depending on the season and whom they're trying to impress. Being an immature navigator, and having no one around to impress, I too was sporting a brown neck and head, though frequent applications of sunscreen had brought on this condition slowly, like cooking a pot roast at a ridiculously low heat. Fortunately, my advanced stage of decrepitude had not yet produced an equivalent throat pouch. This sighting of a brown pelican was reported shortly afterward to a group of birders in Bellingham, who declared it a first, but my name was not mentioned and fame once again eluded me.

I considered calling Keith on the cellphone to meet me at the dock in Ford Cove at the south end of Hornby, as it occurred to me that I might need help docking. Also, I thought it would be fun to show off my navigational skills. Thinking better of it, and not wanting to keep him waiting, I proceeded down Lambert Channel where a small ferry was crossing from Denman Island to Hornby full of tourists and summer residents, many of them from the States. Although

Ford Cove has a government wharf and is mentioned in the cruising guides, it is not marked or named on official charts, an oversight or a deliberate ploy to discourage the horde of boaters who ply the coast every summer. It obviously hadn't worked, as the marina was packed. Giving the reef a wide berth, I crept into the cove and manoeuvred so I could raft alongside a bright red sloop. As I approached, a middle-aged woman started jumping up and down in the cockpit, warning me off, directing me to the other side of the float, which I'd been trying to avoid because of a light southeasterly in the making. My only choice was rafting beside a nondescript fibreglass sloop, so short and beamy it offered only the smallest arc of contact for fenders. My erstwhile traffic director was on hand to grab a bowline as I stepped aboard the sloop, sternline in hand. The problem was that, unlike *Groais* with her immovable seven and a half tons, the receiving boat was light with a rounded deck and tipped under my weight, throwing me off balance and causing my foot to surrender its inadequate purchase.

So it was that the conquering hero, having braved the demons of the coast—fog, tempest, whirlpools, rapids, grizzlies, sirens and a hundred thousand deadly asterisks—and having survived surprise encounters with both denizens of the deep and two-legged creatures of the shore, found himself descending, inch by inch, into the saltchuck at the very apex of his glory. I had time to observe, before my feet entered the water, the slovenly condition of the vessel responsible for my ignominy, its ugly contours, slack lifelines, unwashed cabin, even its badly marked and weed-encrusted hull. Before gravity had its way with me and water lapped my belly button, I noticed the bemused expression of a nearby boater who was holding a paintbrush that inscribed a bright red arc in the air, as if to underline my folly. Although the information was totally useless to me in my deteriorating situation, it now became clear that I had been shunted around to this side of the float to avoid the red sloop, which was receiving a fresh coat of paint.

It also occurred to me, in the midst of this descent, this fall from grace, that my wallet, thanks to the various transactions I'd conducted in Campbell River, was no longer safely stowed in the chart table, but was in my back pocket, and that it was already several inches underwater. This crass material consideration, stronger than mere vanity, brought me quickly to my senses and I hauled myself along the lifelines and onto the float, soaked to the nipples.

By the time Keith arrived, I'd changed clothes and was spreading out my receipts, currency, and sundry credit cards to dry in the cockpit. He and JoAnn laughed at my embarrassing confession and treated me to a splendid dinner, fit for the prodigal son, with plenty of music, wine and good talk in their cedar-and-glass retreat overlooking Tribune Bay, where several boats were already weighing anchor to run from the gathering southeaster. We talked about his forthcoming non-fiction novel, *Furry Creek*, on the life and tragic death of Pat Lowther, who'd been murdered by her husband Roy at the peak of her fame.

"How do Pat's daughters feel about what you're doing?"

"Quite supportive. I think they trust me."

Keith's eyebrows formed a solid black line across his forehead, giving everything he said the authority of permanent italics. He raised his hand to fend off a pesky wasp that had been dive-bombing our glasses, intent on wine tasting. I could see how Pat's daughters might trust him. I'd published his first novel, *Dead Ends*, in the early eighties and watched him develop as a writer, moral sympathy and verbal precision two of his chief attributes. His second novel, *Eyemouth*, had been a foray amongst the riptides of Scottish history; a recent book of stories, *Crossing the Gulf*, had established his imaginative claim to the West Coast. Now he was diving into the whirlpool of literary theory and feminist politics.

"You must have a suicidal streak, taking on such a sensitive subject. Literary ethics, appropriation, sensationalism, ghoulishness—and that's just the first barrage of critical arrows they'll let fly. You'll make St. Sebastian look like a prematurely bald porcupine."

If Keith had knitted his brow, I couldn't tell because of that continuous ridge of black hair. He was trying to finish his wine in advance of the kamikaze wasp. He smiled. Dinner was ready. He brought a folded copy of the *New York Times Book Review* down on the wingèd boozer and signalled a cautionary retreat.

"O Death, where is thy sting?"

I don't know if Keith and JoAnn noticed me the next morning as I bucked my way past Tribune Bay and St. John's Point en route to Lasqueti Island. The southeaster had quickened overnight in the gulf to something between a small craft warning and modest gale-force winds. *Groais* was taking another pounding, but not as much as I was, a reminder, like my dunking of the day before, that I was not out of harm's way yet, that there was still plenty of time to make a complete botch of it. I managed a brief reprieve for lunch at False Bay on Lasqueti, just long enough to try phoning Pete Darwin's father and to meet a boater named Gus Lund. Gus, whose wife ran a restaurant on Gabriola Island, recognized *Groais* as a Golden Hind and told me he'd emigrated from Africa to Canada by sailing a small boat across the Atlantic Ocean to a landfall in Florida. I said I was sure I'd be terrified to lose sight of land.

"That's when I start to relax," Gus said. "No rocks, fast currents or other boats to worry about."

"Sure, just typhoons, tsunamis and sharks."

"The biggest threat comes from the half-submerged containers blown off freighters."

After a night at Jedediah Island Marine Park, I picked up Bronwen and James at Secret Cove. They'd left my car at Horseshoe Bay and come up by bus for a two-day outing that took us down the Sunshine Coast to Plumper Cove on Keats Island, then to Snug Cove on Bowen Island, where my mother had spent at least one summer as a young girl at Mrs. Gordon's camp. I was reminded again of Bronwen's resemblance to her maternal grandmother. When she'd decided to spend a year abroad studying at East Anglia University, I told her I'd support that decision as long as she didn't fall in love with an Englishman. Of course she'd done just that, but had the good sense to bring him home. The two of them were living together in a flat on West Fourth Avenue in Kitsilano, Bronwen pursuing an M.A. in environmental studies at the University of British Columbia and working part-time for the campus waste-management program, and James with a three-year post-doctoral fellowship to work on the Georgia Basin project, a think tank charged with making proposals for future development and environmental protection. With two modest incomes, they were already quite snug.

"Well, Dad." Bronwen was knocking back a pint of dark lager at the Jolly Roger Restaurant, high above the harbour at Secret Cove. "Did you find what you were looking for?"

"More or less, but I've forgotten what it was." She had a habit of manipulating the skin around her mouth, pulling it all to one side, during moments of interrogation. If I thought I could get away with a flippant reply, I was wrong.

"Male menopause," she announced. "You had to prove to

yourself you could do this trip and, look, here you are, all in one piece."

"Is that conclusion subject to a body search?" I'd finished my drink and was using one finger to make the impression of an anchor in the sweat on the beer glass. "And what about you—concocting a thesis topic that will shake up academia?"

"You mean, other than trying to distribute recycling bins to self-important and uncooperative professors? I'll need another beer before I answer that."

I left *Groais* at the Vancouver Rowing Club and cycled along English Bay to False Creek. My first stop was the Plaza of Nations Marina, to look for my benefactor, Hank of Holland. His dilapidated station wagon, which sorely tested the confidence of his Japanese customers, was parked in its reserved spot. I found Hank bent over the engine in his cruise boat, *Strike Force*, parts strewn everywhere. A cracked cylinder head was costing him a week's business, during the high season. I wanted to thank him for the loan of the survival suit, flares, and smoke bomb and say I'd return them in a couple of weeks. I flung my arms out theatrically.

"I made it."

We were both born in the summer of 1940, I on June 9 in Vancouver and Hank on July 3, in the midst of the Nazi invasion of Holland. Since I'd been gone he'd dyed his hair blond and started wearing a single earring. He looked ten years, not four weeks, younger than I was and could have passed for one of Van Diemen's swashbucklers.

"Ya, ya, I knew you would."

"So why the survival suit? With all that collateral invested, you never even mentioned your last name."

"You don't want to know," he said, wiping oil from his hands with a striped tea towel. When I insisted, he told me his ancestors settled in Amsterdam during the eighty-year

Spanish occupation of Holland in the sixteenth century and had never left. After the Second World War, his father wanted to find another port as far from Europe as possible.

"It's de Questroo."

I had to laugh. George Vancouver was an Englishman of Dutch descent who'd been bested by the Spanish on this very coast. And I'd just spent two months myself under the benevolent eye of a Canadian Dutchman who turned out to be a Spaniard. I knew Hank was too busy to waste time nattering, so I promised to take him out to lunch when I returned his gear. As I went out the door, I turned around and patted the aluminum bulkhead appreciatively.

"Ah, nice boat. Good, good, Ha!"

"You're crazy," he said, rolling up the striped towel and chucking it at my head.

Porlier Passage, the narrow, turbulent reef-strewn channel that separates Galiano and Valdez islands, had claimed a variety of boats, including the large steam-tug *Point Grey*, which was towing a barge of CPR railway cars to Victoria on February 26, 1949, when it ran aground in fog. The crash of the heavy barge from astern was like a fatal hammer blow, driving the tug more firmly onto the jagged Virgo Rock, where it hung precariously until a winter storm swept the remaining hulk into deeper waters in 1963. Its appetite sated for the time being, Porlier Passage seemed content to let me off lightly with a bit of a bounce and a few grabs at the rudder. Once through, I struck the mainsail and putted alongside the cliffs that line the western shore of Galiano. The Gulf Islands, remote but well serviced and close enough to Vancouver and Victoria for comfort, have served as a magnet for writers: Audrey Thomas, Brian Brett, Jane Rule,

Joan Skogan, Terry Glavin, Phyllis Webb—the list seemed endless. I'd planned to stay overnight at Ganges and see if Phyllis was available for dinner, but she was either not home or not answering her phone. Never having been to Galiano, I made a quick decision to anchor in Montague Harbour, one of those seemingly random choices that prove to be so meaningful.

The shadows were lengthening as I came around the point. There must have been a hundred pleasure craft at anchor. I drifted past a huge, friendly scow of a boat that looked vaguely familiar, with a superstructure that was far too high for stability. Twice the length of *Groais,* it might have been a tugboat in one of its previous incarnations and was sporting a large sign advertising fresh bread for sale. As I jockeyed into position and dropped the hook, the bow came into view and I could read the name quite clearly: *ATREVIDA*. I was stunned. Not because *Atrevida* was the name of one of the Spanish ships of discovery sent north to study the flora and fauna of the coast under the command of José de Bustamente, but because this floating bakery had once served as a car and passenger ferry between Westview and Blubber Bay and had transported me to my first teaching job on Texada Island in 1962. I untied the dinghy and rowed over to inspect this unlikely relic from my past. As I came alongside, I was besieged by the smell of fresh bread and cinnamon rolls.

"We moor the old girl in Maple Bay and bring her over here on the weekends."

Lee was giving me a tour of the *Atrevida*'s refurbished quarters. He and Judy had bought the business and the old ferry a few months earlier from a friend who'd grown too old to manage it. On the bulkhead, they had a 1965 Blubber Bay-Westview ferry schedule and a one-way ticket, both mounted and framed, along with photographs of *Atrevida* in various roles and time periods on the coast. I could hardly believe it had been possible for a vessel this small to handle five cars and sixty passengers.

"It was cozy." Lee was delighted to elaborate on the routines that were so familiar to me. "The cars used to drive in from the side and had to do quite a bit of jockeying."

"I remember that. It was slow, too."

I told Lee the staff at Vananda Elementary-Secondary School had depended on *Atrevida*'s turtle-like pace to give us time to prepare for certain important visitors. We had a mole on the other side who let us know by phone when the superintendent was coming over to inspect the school. Since the ferry was so slow, we knew we had at least forty minutes before he'd step ashore in Blubber Bay, even more in rough weather, and another twenty before he could reach us in Vananda by car. By the time he arrived, everyone would be ready, including me, standing in front of my class, guitar in hand, singing along with the students the folk songs I'd translated so crudely into French.

"*Où sont allées toutes les fleurs?*" Pete Seeger would never have recognized it as his signature piece, "Where Have All the Flowers Gone?"

"We like the slow pace, too." Lee smiled and replenished my coffee as we sat between flowerpots on the stern, watching cabin and masthead lights come on around the bay. While life on a floating bakery may be relaxed, there is plenty of scurrying amongst the boaters to buy the fresh items. Later, I saw a lad of ten rowing frantically towards *Atrevida* in pursuit of cinnamon rolls. On his return journey, I inquired how he'd made out.

"Too late for the buns. I got a dozen cookies instead." He

lifted his oars out of the water as he drifted past in an inflatable dinghy, holding up the bag of cookies as proof positive.
"I'll be the first one there in the morning."

I rowed back from *Atrevida* with a loaf of whole wheat
bread, two cinnamon rolls, and an apple pie I thought I'd share
with Bruce and Karen Bourquin and their kids back in Sidney.
Before pushing off, I mentioned to Lee that one side of my
family had run a bakery in Calgary shortly after immigrating
in the first decade of the century. I hadn't thought of it before,
but it seemed, given the principal trades of my maternal and
paternal grandparents, that we'd pretty well cornered the
market, not only for boats, but also for loaves and fishes. I gave
Lee and Judy one of my floating writer-in-residence
brochures, commenting as I did on how people and boats
evolve, the various transformations they undergo. Lee glanced
through the brochure as I pushed off, then shouted after me,
"Books, boats and bread—good ways to stay afloat!"

No one was waiting to greet me when I pulled up to the repair
dock at Westport Marina, which is located between the
Swartz Bay ferry terminal and Sidney on Vancouver Island,
the spot where I'd purchased *Groais* from Karen and Bruce.
No pipe band, not even a familiar face. I went up to the
marina store and bought a Fudgsicle and two ropes of black
licorice from Elaine. She asked if I'd been away. Bruce's friend
Jerry was mending his boat on the ways, a smart little fibreglass sloop with a red hull, which he'd holed on a reef.

"What's that piece of shit you're working on?"

Jerry squinted, then wiped his face with a paint rag. When
he recognized me, he smiled. "I knew you were coming back.
I figured you'd be interested in a real boat this time, something with class."

Groais had become as comfortable as an old slipper. I hadn't sailed as much as I'd expected, the wind either in my face or too strong, but I'd come to appreciate its stability. With its own history and list of exotic ports of call, my Golden Hind sloop had introduced me to Plymouth, England, and sent me into libraries to pore over accounts of the Pacific voyages of Drake, Vancouver, Darwin. Chris Law, its first owner, was still out there in Cape Breton and full of stories about the boat, if I were inclined to learn more about its origins. In fact, I'd just received another e-mail account of his adventures on *Groais*, which included running afoul of salvage pirates off Madeira, being bombed by the Venezuelan Air Force and delivering mail from Panama to Pitcairn Island, a run of fifty-three days. *Groais* was eccentric, practical, stripped to the essentials, and slightly dumpy—but it was me.

I'd had time to consider Bronwen's question about finding what I was looking for. I wasn't sure what I'd been looking for, but I'd found adventure, or at least misadventure, the trip assuming at times the aspect of a comedy of errors. I'd located my watery roots, including some waterlogged members of my family, moving through time like a swimmer underwater. I'd peered into a deep-sea diver's mask and seen my father's face and stubbly beard, heard the sound of oxygen in his hoses, which resembled the slow release from the small tank by his deathbed. Like Captain Nemo in his *Nautilus*, I'd felt strangely at home down there, everything slow, bent, oddly distorted by the refracted light. My salvage work was hardly complete. I'd dived into the wreck and was coming up again for air. I wasn't there yet, but I'd found a portal, a way back.

Bruce and Karen had gone to Sidney for parts and groceries. I polished off the second piece of licorice. So that was it—no glamour, no welcome party, no fanfare. I thought of Conrad's description of his first command in the *Otago*, beautifully fictionalized in *The Shadow-Line*. After contending with a ship becalmed, a crew decimated by malaria, and his own personal failings, the young captain brings his ship into port in Singapore almost single-handedly. Although he has had a nearly sleepless run of twenty-one days from Bangkok, he announces his intention of setting out with a new crew first thing the next morning. His mentor and guardian angel, Captain Giles, nods approvingly and says, "Precious little rest in life for anyone. Better not think of it."

Jerry, glad for an excuse to stop working, consented to have a coffee with me as I waited for Bruce and Karen. He wanted to know if I planned to celebrate. Six pelagic cormorants were perched on the pilings that supported the boat hoist. The two females, in breeding mode, had double crests and white patches on the sides. The four males, johnnies-on-the-spot who served as a silent cheering section, were not big talkers; instead of the usual mating song and dance, they bided their time, simply flexing their wings, replenishing the oxygen they'd need for the next dive. The tops of the creosoted pilings were whitewashed from their droppings. These creatures were still wild, not like the ones I'd seen on the Li River in Guilin, China, which were as domesticated as chickens, wooden rings around their necks so they could not swallow the fish they so cleverly caught.

Having spent several months in a space smaller than a walk-in closet, I was unprepared for solid ground. Floors heaved, walls swayed, as if to confirm the assertion of modern physics that solids are merely dense clusters of energy in motion: terra not-so-firma. When I arrived home, I knew I would stagger through my house, lost, ill at ease, and slightly bewildered at the size and number of the rooms. Public places would be even more problematic. I'd be caught more than once using my *Groais*-induced collapse-and-jump routine for exiting a cramped, closet-sized toilet, the restaurant patrons wondering if they should call a psychiatric hotline or Alcoholics Anonymous. It occurred to me, too, that the stereotype of the drunken sailor might have more to do with a delay in getting land legs back than with the consumption of alcohol. And drinking itself, just the cheapest means of replicating and prolonging that familiar but comforting state of permanent imbalance associated with long periods at sea.

I could see Bruce's blue live-in van, with the spare tire and propane tank mounted on the outside, turn into the marina parking lot. This was what they'd lived in since selling *Groais* to me. Karen and the kids, Tasha and Bjorn, would be with him. Tasha would hop on her bike and go looking for friends; Bjorn would show me the new model boats he'd made out of scraps and driftwood. Karen and Bruce would look at me the way you might look at a friend who has just married or had sex for the first time, to see if you can detect the difference. What I had not expected was that Karen would stand on the float and watch me make a perfect reverse manoeuvre from the work dock to my permanent berth, with less surprise on her face than I had on mine; in fact, she'd be thinking mainly of the safety of the kids, both of whom would have hopped on board their erstwhile floating home for the ride but also to help me tie up. I would buy them all dinner later in Sidney, I decided, or at least treat them to a dessert of *Atrevida* apple pie.

No, I said to Jerry, as I stood up to greet my friends. I have work to do. I've made the journey, I'm halfway home. Now I must write the book.

Acknowledgements

Before the ink dries (nothing else on board will), I want to thank my friend and editor Phyllis Bruce for her confidence and wisdom; she is the GPS, the global positioning system, every writer needs, but so few ever find. I also want to thank Bruce and Karen Bourquin (along with Tasha and Bjorn), Chris and Anni Law, Don Alper, Len Clay, Keith and JoAnn Harrison, Garry Wickett, Hank de Questroo, Pete and Rene Darwin, Richard Dobell, Lewis Poteet, Geri Walker, Steve Martin on *Ocean Fury*, Ron and Pat Smith, Larry Sinitsin, Marty Hitchcock, Ed Bates, Mel and Lynn Dagg, Mary Hagey, Maurice Tremblay, Ron Marston, Doreen, Bill, Mel and Mike Turner and the host of coastal relatives and friends who rescued and reclaimed me.

Most of the books I consulted have been mentioned in the text, but I would like to acknowledge Derek Hayes' *Historical Atlas of British Columbia and the Pacific Northwest*, A. M. Twigg's *Union Steamships Remembered 1920–1958*, and work by Howard White and other writers in *Raincoast Chronicles*.